A Pictorial History of the

GREAT LAKES

A Pictorial History of

Bonanza Books • New York

The
GREAT LAKES

by Harlan Hatcher and Erich A. Walter

Assisted by Orin W. Kaye, Jr.

This edition published by Bonanza Books,
a division of Crown Publishers, Inc.
K   L   M   N   O   P   Q   R

Contents

A Pictorial History of the

GREAT LAKES

Chapter I

A View of the Heartland of America

From Duluth to the Gaspé

The Great Lakes—Superior, Michigan, Huron, Erie, and Ontario—make up the largest body of fresh water in the world. Their sparkling 67 trillion gallons cover 95,000 square miles. No large rivers drain into them. They exist as the visible part of a vast water table fed by springs and rains, and in time of prolonged drought their level may drop a menacing two and a half feet. Then they fill up again.

With their connecting waterways, they form by far the world's largest inland-water transportation system. From Duluth, Minnesota, the westernmost port, a ship goes 1,160 miles to the St. Lawrence River and 2,342 miles to the open ocean. Two other long, inland routes carry vital shipping via canals and rivers to New Orleans and the port of New York.

Let us now imagine—man's conquests being limitless—that we have put an astronaut into suborbital space. From this vantage point, our astronaut looks down upon the Great Lakes, shimmering jewels of blue shadowed by their green setting of timber and vegetation. He is high above the lakes with an unobstructed view from Lake Superior to the mouth of the St. Lawrence River where it rolls past the peninsula of Gaspé.

**A VIEW OF
THE HEARTLAND
OF AMERICA**

An aerial view of the western end of the Great Lakes at Duluth shows the beginning of the long, thin tongue of land that breaks the force of lake storms and gives Duluth and Superior a natural harbor. Along the harbor front extend high grain elevators and ore docks which load an endless procession of ships. Over two thousand miles away, by water, is the sea.

Duluth Herald and News-Tribune

Across this long natural waterway, he would find a stream of floating commerce headed toward the sea: iron ore, iron, steel, copper, automotive products, wheat—the riches of the great heartland of America. That heartland itself would offer its glowing panorama: to the north, the province of Ontario running the length of all the lakes and, to the south, eight of the United States pressing to locate at least a part of their boundaries on the water.

Right under the astronaut, the deep reddish-brown of Duluth, Two Harbors, and Silver Bay hints the mineral abundance of the Mesabi Range still farther west. Along Superior's northern shore, the mighty grain elevators of Fort William and Port Arthur thrust up, and along the south shore, the reddish cargo of ore continues past Superior and Ashland. Beyond the Apostle Islands, the Keweenaw Peninsula juts out into the bold blue water. Farther east beyond Marquette are the engineering marvels, the locks and the canals at the Sault—"the miracle mile"—linking Lake Superior and Lake Huron.

Another view of the same harbor with a group of ships lying safely behind the strip of protecting land. Duluth's Aerial Lift Bridge rises over the ship canal to the left, sharply outlined against the water. Volcanic bluffs rise steeply six and eight hundred feet up to the Skyline Drive, shown in the foreground.

Duluth Chamber of Commerce

A closer view of the grain elevators of Duluth, with the Aerial Lift Bridge beyond.

Basgen-Photography, Duluth

Lake Superior is the largest of the lakes, so large that when the first explorers entered it, they were amazed to find it wasn't salt. In Longfellow's poem, *Hiawatha*, it bears the Indian name, "Gitche Gumee," the "shining Big Sea Water." The French called it *"lac supérieur"* or "upper lake." It is the largest single body of fresh water in the world—350 miles long and 160 miles wide at its widest point and with a maximum depth of 1,333 feet. Astonishingly, it has a tide, though only about three inches. The other lakes too have their minuscule tides.

Assume our astronaut's gaze for the moment goes by the end of Lake Huron and past Mackinac City, St. Ignace, and the imposing Straits Bridge into Lake Michigan. Lake Michigan is the only one of the Great Lakes located entirely within the United States. The U.S.-Canadian boundary runs roughly through the middle of the other lakes. Lake Michi-

At Isle Royale in Lake Superior may be seen a shoreline, untouched and unchanging, which may be the same as that viewed by the first explorers. Dense spruce, balsam, and birch grow to the water's edge, and beaver, mink and antlered moose are probably as abundant as in the early years of the seventeenth century when Etienne Brulé gave the first reports about the island.

National Park Service

A new port at Silver Bay, Minnesota, on Lake Superior, has been developed for the shipment of taconite, pellets of iron made from residual ore in the Mesabi and Vermilion ranges after the high-grade ore has been mined. Escaping steam marks the pelletizing building. In the foreground an ore carrier moves into loading position near the stockpiles and storage bins. The community of Silver Bay can be seen in the background.

Basgen-Photography, Duluth

gan is a little over three hundred miles long and is 118 miles wide at its widest point. Its greatest depth is 925 feet. Through the Illinois Waterway (which includes the Chicago Sanitary and Ship Canal and the Des Plaines and Illinois rivers) and the Mississippi, it connects with the Gulf of Mexico.

But now let's look at it as our astronaut would. Down its western shore he would see Escanaba and Menominee and the harbors of Wisconsin—Marinette and Green Bay, Manitowoc with its Pilot Island Light, Sheboygan, and bustling Milwaukee, Racine, and Kenosha.

Waukegan and Evanston introduce the southern beaches where the impressive skyline of Chicago provides dramatic backdrop. Calumet City and the blast furnaces of Gary present the fiery potential of steel, for military as well as peaceful purposes.

North along Michigan's eastern shoreline stretch beaches of shining sand dotted with such neat harbors as South Haven, Grand Haven, Holland, Muskegon, and Ludington. There is Grand Traverse Bay on the shores of which grow some of the world's finest cherries.

The great docking facilities at Port Arthur, Ontario, handle seven million tons of shipping a year. The monolithic grain elevators, which gather in the wheat of many Canadian summers, dwarf even a large ship.   *Ontario Dept. of Travel and Publicity*

An ore freighter in loading position next to an ore bin at Marquette, Michigan. For eight months of the year (while the lakes are open), Marquette hears the steady rumble of ore cars coming in from the iron mines and the crash of ore into the waiting ships. Michigan Tourist Council

Another view of the Marquette ore docks. Munson Collection

*When launched in 1950, the **Wilfred Sykes** was the largest ship ever built on fresh water and the lakes' fastest ore carrier. It still remains one of the great freighters, 678 feet long, with a cargo capacity of 21,500 tons. Flagship of the Inland Steel fleet, it was named for the company's president from 1941 to 1949. It quarters two crewmen to a room, each with private bath. It has a top speed of 17 miles an hour, and when put into service it made 44 round trips during a shipping season compared with 34 for the fastest lakes carrier up to that time.* Great Lakes Marine Museum

St. Marys River and the four great locks at Sault Ste. Marie—MacArthur, Poe (which has been completely torn out to make way for a new $37,000,000 lock), Davis, and Sabin—which raise ships approximately nineteen feet from Lake Huron to Lake Superior. In the background can be seen the American span of the great new International Bridge. To the right of the locks are the powerhouse and the St. Marys Falls, through which the higher waters of Lake Superior flow into the lower lakes. These rapids still have a wild beauty though reduced by the increasing amount of water needed to lock ships through the canals. Whitefish Bay and the Canadian shoreline can be seen in the far background.

An aerial view of Green Bay, Wisconsin, and the Fox River. Massive piles of wood occupy the right foreground, adjacent to the paper mills. In the left foreground, the East River enters the Fox. In the background, along the shores of the bay, grow wild rice and swamp grass.

Lefebvre-Luebke, Green Bay

Now our astronaut's gaze returns to the upper end of Lake Huron. Joined by the Straits of Mackinac, Lake Huron and Lake Michigan are the only lakes with the same water level. Huron is the second largest of the lakes, 206 miles long and 183 miles wide at its widest point. It is 750 feet at its greatest depth. Two large bays indent its shores, Saginaw Bay on the Michigan shore and Georgian Bay on the Ontario shore, where the busy shipping communities of Owen Sound, Collingwood, and Midland have come a long way since the canoes of early days.

A near view of the bascule bridge at Green Bay, Wisconsin, opened for passage . of a freighter. Lefebvre-Luebke, Green Bay

A windy morning on the lakefront of Chicago.
Courtesy of the American Museum of Natural History

At Navy Pier in Chicago, against the city skyline, three ships load and unload cargo. In the foreground is the Bilbao *from Hamburg, Germany. Next to it is the Finnish ship* Peter, *and at the far end is the* Maria Teresa *of Palermo, Italy. This diversity is typical of the worldwide commerce of the Great Lakes.* Chicago Port Authority

8

A VIEW OF
THE HEARTLAND
OF AMERICA

A long line of ships at the Chicago Regional Port District development at Lake Calumet.
Chicago Association of Commerce and Industry

Our spaceman now sees Alpena and Rogers City, home ports for many "lakers." In Saginaw Bay is Bay City and up the river from it Saginaw itself, surrounded by coal beds and oil wells. Lower down, he finds Port Huron on the American side and Sarnia on the Canadian, joined by the Blue Water Bridge at the point where Lake Huron flows into the St. Clair River.

At Gary, Indiana, unloaders are removing iron ore from the hold of an ore freighter. The operators of these unloaders ride in a cab right above the grab bucket and descend into the hold. The lifted ore is deposited either in ore cars or in a stock pile further back on the dock.
Carnegie-Illinois Steel Corp.

A near view of Canadian and overseas vessels loading grain at the twin elevators at Lake Calumet Harbor. *Calumet Studio*

At Ludington, Michigan, a narrow strip of dune land protects the harbor. At the railroad yard in the foreground, a car ferry is loading, preparatory to crossing Lake Michigan to Wisconsin. In 1675, Father Jacques Marquette, the famous missionary-explorer, died nearby. *Munson Collection*

Then it is south through Lake St. Clair into the Detroit River, which flows between Detroit and Windsor at a point where, strangely enough, Canada lies south of the United States border. The Ambassador Bridge, under which ships and vessels of all sizes and shapes pass twenty-four hours a day, joins Detroit and Windsor. The Detroit River is one of the busiest waterways in the world, and connects Lake St. Clair and Lake Erie.

Lake Erie is the shallowest and next to the smallest of the lakes. It is only 210 feet at its greatest depth and is 241 miles long and 57 miles wide at its widest point. It is linked to the Atlantic Ocean by the New York State Barge Canal and the Hudson River. Looking along its islands, beaches, and harbors, our spaceman sees Toledo at the mouth of the Maumee River, then Sandusky, then his glance catches the gleaming Perry monument in Put-in-Bay. Beyond lie the orchards, wheat fields, and vineyards marking the shoreline before the heavy industry of Lorain comes into view, and the breathtaking spread that is Cleveland, Ashtabula, Conneaut, and Erie.

Monument marking the site of Father Marquette's death.
West Michigan Tourist Association

Limestone, quarried in large quantities near Rogers City, Michigan, is loaded on freighters like this one. Millions of tons of limestone go from Michigan quarries to the great steel-mill cities.

Michigan Tourist Council

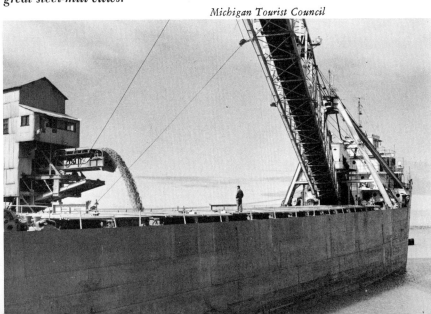

The customs port of Midland, Ontario, has grain elevators and modern harbor installations. Besides grain, it ships lumber, textiles, and foundry wares, produced locally.

Ontario Dept. of Travel and Publicity

A VIEW OF
THE HEARTLAND
OF AMERICA

Modern sails dot the Great Lakes in the annual Mackinac Race near Port Huron. Lakes racing began near here, in the Detroit River, when in 1839 two racing boats, one a famous Crolins boat brought west on the Erie Canal, were matched against each other on a course going from the Detroit bank to Belle Isle (then Hog Island). This was the "first event of its kind in Western Waters."

Great Lakes Marine Museum

The Blue Water Bridge over the St. Clair River connects Port Huron with Sarnia, Ontario. The two port cities are also connected by a fleet of ferries and an underwater railway tunnel. Through the St. Clair River, ships from Lake Huron sail down on their way to Detroit and Lake Erie.

Port Huron Chamber of Commerce

Sarnia, Ontario, port of call in 1962 for 2,085 ships (some from as far away as Asia and Australia), is the site of Canada's greatest petro-chemical industries, including the country's largest ore refinery and fiberglass, synthetic-rubber, glycol, and carbon-black plants.   Sarnia Chamber of Commerce

At the eastern end of Lake Erie is another great city, Buffalo, and from there it is only a short distance to that small ribbon of water—the Welland Ship Canal—which takes shipping from Lake Erie to Lake Ontario, avoiding the mighty falls of Niagara, one of nature's greatest wonders.

Lake Ontario is the baby of the lakes, only 193 miles long and 53 miles wide at its widest point. It is 804 feet at its greatest depth. Our astronaut's gaze here passes the dynamic cities of Hamilton and Toronto on the Canadian shoreline which then becomes dotted with factories and farms up past Cobourg and on to Kingston. On the lake's eastern end, above Oswego, the water flows into the St. Lawrence River among the Thousand Islands. Foaming rapids once barred shipping here, but with the completion in 1958 of the series of locks and canals that is the St. Lawrence Seaway—a great monument of engineering genius—the last obstacles barring ocean-going ships from the Great Lakes were eliminated.

Outlined against an early morning sky is the great Polymer synthetic-rubber plant of Sarnia. The harbor front beginning at Sarnia runs 30 miles, along the entire east shore of the St. Clair River.   Polymer Corp. Ltd.

A VIEW OF
THE HEARTLAND
OF AMERICA

The Ambassador Bridge over the Detroit River, joining Detroit and Windsor, Ontario, is almost two miles long and, at its highest point, 152 feet above the water. Under the river goes the Detroit and Windsor Fleetway Tunnel, the world's only vehicular underwater tunnel between two countries. Detroit Edison Co.

Modern skyscrapers dominate the Detroit skyline along the St. Clair River waterfront.
Detroit Edison Co.

Ashtabula, Ohio, is an important shipping center for coal and iron ore here shown in large stockpiles on the wharves. Loaded freight cars are ferried from here across Lake Erie to the facing ports of Ontario.
Richard E. Stoner, Ashtabula

Large ore carriers loading at Conneaut, Ohio. Like Ashtabula, it is a great transshipment point for coal to the upper Great Lakes and ore to the steel mills of eastern Ohio and Pennsylvania.

The Perry's Victory and International Peace Memorial at Put-in-Bay, Ohio. Built in 1913 to celebrate the centennial of the Battle of Lake Erie and the enduring peace that followed, it is 352 feet high and has a promenade at the top that can accommodate 50 people. In 1938, Secretary of the Interior Harold Ickes dedicated it and the fourteen acres surrounding it as a National Monument.   Ohio Development and Publicity Commission

As a terminus of the Erie Canal, Buffalo was catapulted into prominence as one of the great American cities, and it is today the largest grain-milling city in the world. A mighty panorama of grain elevators borders the Buffalo River where it flows into the upper end of Lake Erie.

Buffalo Chamber of Commerce

A closer view of the grain elevators of Buffalo.   *New York State Dept. of Commerce*

A close view of the foaming American Falls from Prospect Point lookout.

Power Authority of the State of New York

A ship passing under the lift bridge on the Welland Canal near Port Colborne, Ontario. Starting from Lake Ontario, such a ship goes through three locks which raise it 140 feet to the Niagara Escarpment. The ship then climbs the escarpment through 4 locks, an abrupt rise of 186 feet. Two more locks take it to Lake Erie. Lock 8, a guard lock of 1,380 feet, is the longest in the world.
Ontario Dept. of Travel and Publicity

Piers 12 to 15 at Hamilton harbor, Ontario. Producing primary iron and steel, smoky Hamilton has been called the "Pittsburgh of Canada." Its triangular-shaped harbor, guarded by a sandbar known as Hamilton Beach, ranks third among Canadian ports in tonnage handled.
Photo by the Hamilton Harbour Commissioners

16

A VIEW OF
THE HEARTLAND
OF AMERICA

Toronto harbor looking toward the city skyline. Metropolitan Toronto has well over a million population and the port, protected by Toronto Island (with its lighthouse dating back to 1798), is one of the best in all the Great Lakes region. Ontario Dept. of Travel and Publicity

The outer harbor breakwaters of Oswego, New York, date back to 1869. The first English ships on the Great Lakes were built here in Colonial times. Visible in the foreground, the New York State grain elevator with a capacity of 1,000,000 bushels, and the adjoining freight warehouse with a floor space of 12,000 feet, give Oswego outstanding port facilities. In the inner harbor is the northern terminus of the Barge Canal system, which links Lake Ontario with the Hudson River. Henry Dewolf, Rochester

A few of the innumerable and lovely Thousand Islands which make the St. Lawrence River one of the world's most beautiful as well as most important waterways. Library of Congress

A nearer view of the Oswego grain elevator and freight warehouse. Henry Dewolf, Rochester

An aerial view of Montreal. Montreal stores and ships more grain than any other port on earth. Although 1,000 miles from the sea, it is nearer Liverpool than is New York. It has 10 miles of berthing accommodation, with 105 berths. It is, incidentally, second only to Paris in French-speaking population. Canadian Government Travel Bureau

It is now down the river (as the eye travels north and east) to Montreal, the great bilingual city that has been a center of trade and commerce on this continent since the coming of the first white man.

Quebec, strong and graceful around its rock, is next. There is the renowned Chateau Frontenac, built on the site of the Chateau St. Louis which once was the seat of government for all of North America. From there the city can view the river stretching out below.

The river widens and flows past the Gaspé Peninsula, into the Gulf of St. Lawrence.

**A VIEW OF
THE HEARTLAND
OF AMERICA**

Elevator No. 4 at Montreal harbor is 1,200 feet long and 240 feet high at its highest point. It can store 5,500,000 bushels. A laker can be unloaded at the rate of 100,000 bushels per hour. Two or three ships may be loading simultaneously at the rate of 216,000 bushels per hour. The potential handling capacity of this one facility is over 100 million bushels per year, one third of Canada's yearly grain export volume.

C. D. Howe Co., Ltd.

An aerial view of Quebec. To the left may be seen the Chateau Frontenac. In the foreground are the extensive harbor installations. Quebec is a terminus of Atlantic passenger lines using the St. Lawrence route.   Canadian Government Travel Bureau

A skyline view of Quebec from the St. Lawrence River.   Canadian Government Travel Bureau

The famous Percé Rock off the Gaspé Peninsula at the mouth of the St. Lawrence River. To the right is Bonaventure Island, largest bird sanctuary in the world, which protects gannets, cormorants, and other sea birds of the Gulf of St. Lawrence. It was near here (just beyond Cape Gaspé) that Jacques Cartier landed in 1534, erected a 30-foot cross, and claimed the territory for the King of France.
Office Provincial de Publicité, Québec

And now to the east is the open sea.

This is what our astronaut has looked down upon—an incomparable farming and industrial heartland on a highway of water that links mid-continent America with the oceans and with all the parts of our planet.

This is the Great Lakes region.

Chapter 2

Geology of the Great Lakes

The Great Lakes as we know them today are relative newcomers to the map, mere Johnny-come-latelys when measured against the panorama of the earth's long and slow evolution. Their present formation dates from the late stages of the glacial period, or somewhere between 7,000 and 32,000 years ago.

Long before, at the start of "modern" geological time—roughly 500 million years ago—this whole area was covered with molten lava bubbling up from within the core of the earth. This subsided to become the base of the present lakes region and is responsible for much of its mineral wealth.

Then the great basin was covered with water, the shallow seas of the Cambrian period. Emerging as a pattern of land and marsh, the area had alternate periods of flooding and draining. Roughly a million years ago, glaciers started slowly but relentlessly sweeping southward. Freezing cold prevailed the year around in the region that is present-day Labrador and Canada.

The snow piled higher and higher, reaching a peak at one point in Labrador of more than six miles. This caused massive pressure on the ice field below, pressure that pushed outward and started the whole field on its sluggish but irresistible way south.

A dozen feet a day the ice flow traveled, south over the St. Lawrence, across modern New York, Ohio, Michigan, Indiana, and Illinois, and as far as Kansas and Nebraska.

This powerful mass of ice smashed and ground everything in its path. The huge weight of the flow scooped deep paths in the earth over which it passed.

**GEOLOGY
OF THE
GREAT LAKES**

The Scarborough Bluffs rise 200 feet from Lake Ontario in palisades of extraordinary grandeur. One hundred million years of Great Lakes geology, including the procession of the ice ages, may be read in their strata of stone, sand, and soil.

Sand, eroded with infinite slowness by water and wind, accumulates along Lake Michigan in mountainous dunes, printed with bird tracks across the washboard ripples. Michigan Tourist Council

The Yoho Glacier in British Columbia, photographed in 1902, pours its heavy front over ground and mountain. The figure of a man (in the second picture of the glacier) climbing up the base gives some idea of the enormous mass and of the appearance of the ice ages.   Library of Congress

**GEOLOGY
OF THE
GREAT LAKES**

*A panoramic view of the Illecillewaet Glacier shows how ice could inundate even mountain peaks.
In the closer view, such a peak barely protrudes from the frozen flow.*   *Library of Congress*

**GEOLOGY
OF THE
GREAT LAKES**

The teeth of glaciers chewed this rock on Kelleys Island, in Lake Erie near Sandusky, Ohio. The bite and power of glacial action have seldom been better illustrated. Ohio Dept. of Industrial and Economic Development

Eventually the glacier reached southern points where the sun's rays were bright. The southward march would end, and, melting and crumbling, the mass of ice would retreat northward until it reached a point of equilibrium between sun and cold. Melting would stop, the pressure of snow on ice would begin again, and once more the flow would start moving southward on another invasion.

Geologists have uncovered evidence of five of these major ice invasions.

As the glacial age retreated, animal and plant life returned to the area. Fossilized remains of elephant-like mammoths and mastodons have been found, prehistoric monsters that inhabited the Great Lakes region almost certainly as late as ten thousand years ago, and perhaps later.

Fossilized remains of whales have been discovered as far removed from present oceans as the region around Lake Huron. Once a great arm of the sea came in through the St. Lawrence valley and created marine terraces which are now as high as 600 feet above sea level.

In the geological timetable, the mammoths and the mastodons, wild hogs and musk-oxen disappeared from the area about the time the first human, a forerunner of the modern Indian, came to the area. The date of man's arrival in the region has been set at approximately 6,000 B.C.

Geologists first leaned toward the theory that the Great Lakes were hollowed out by a series of earthquakes and other shifts of the earth's crust. Then it was believed that major credit should go to the pressures of these massive ice sheets that surged back and forth across the northern mid-continent. Now there is a different theory. Holes drilled during the summer of 1961 in the floor of Lake Superior yielded evidence that the Great Lakes were chiefly

In 1799, in a morass near Newburgh, New York, a few fragments of a mastodon skeleton were found. In 1801, Charles Willson Peale, famous portraitist of Washington, got on the track of this find and dug up the world's first relatively complete skeleton of a mastodon. His son, Rembrandt, painted the work in progress, showing the ingenious chain belt of buckets to raise water and drain it off by a conduit and the men still half immersed in mud but eagerly digging, one of them brandishing a just-found bone. The digging, like a public festival, had onlookers all around the edge of the pit.

The skeleton was the first fossil of any kind to be mounted in America and among the first in the world.

The Peales also dug up a second specimen in another New York location and, having two, were able to reconstruct the missing parts of one from the other. The result was stunning. The mastodon was established as an authentic animal and Thomas Jefferson rebuked the French naturalist Buffon for saying that "nature is less active, less energetic on one side of the globe than she is on the other." In his salute to the new discovery, on exhibition at Independence Hall, Philadelphia, Jefferson patriotically referred to the mastodon as "the largest of all terrestrial beings." (Note: he also sent Buffon a bull moose.)

carved out by an ancient river system pre-dating the ice ages. According to this view, put forward by Professor James H. Zumberge of the University of Michigan, the area was drained by a mighty river that either emptied into Hudson Bay or flowed down the St. Lawrence River Valley. The ice sheets then plowed up the terrain and bulldozed dams and dikes of hills that obstructed this drainage and produced the lakes.

The present soundings reveal deep valleys on the lake floor that have been filled with till, the name for rock and gravel that is pushed and carried by an ice sheet. These original valleys owed their existence not to glacier action, but to the relative susceptibility of their rocks to water erosion.

The drill soundings have gone down 144 feet below the lake floor at deep-water points between Keweenaw Peninsula and Isle Royal. At the bottom, the drill hit sandstone bedrock believed to date back to the Cambrian or pre-Cambrian period some 500 million years ago.

All of this speculation is about the early origin. About the recent formation and history, we can be more accurate. It seems reasonable to date the Great Lakes by the age of the Niagara River gorge, cut out over a long period by the tremendous power of the water rushing over the falls. The gorge was almost certainly cut since the last sheet of ice receded from the area. Taking the length of the gorge (from the falls to the river's outlet in Lake Ontario—roughly six and a half miles) and dividing by the average annual amount of recession (about five feet), we reach a figure of about seven thousand years.

Many geologists refuse to accept this figure as an accurate age for the Great Lakes or for the Niagara River gorge. They point out that the gorge has not been the only route taken by

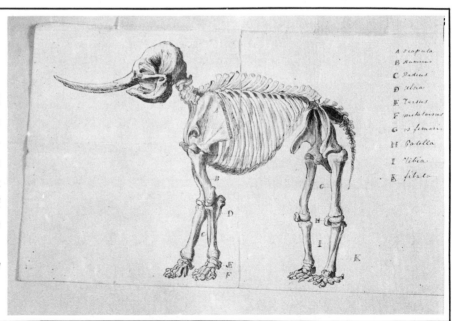

Rembrandt, Raphaelle, and Titian Peale, Charles Willson Peale's three sons (all painters), took a great interest in the mastodon, and Rembrandt Peale drew a careful sketch of the great skeleton, labeling the main bones of the body.

American Philosophical Society

**GEOLOGY
OF THE
GREAT LAKES**

The Warren Mastodon, the most complete skeleton of its kind in existence, was discovered in the summer of 1845 in the same mastodon-prolific area near Newburgh, New York, exploited by the Peales. It was named the Warren Mastodon because it was at first kept in the museum of Dr. John C. Warren of Boston. It was bought in 1909 by the Museum of Natural History in New York through the help of J. P. Morgan and is now one of their most notable display pieces. Its total length is one inch short of fifteen feet.

Courtesy of the American Museum of Natural History

The marshes left by melting ice-age glaciers promoted the lush vegetation on which mastodons fed and reached their great size, nine or ten feet high at the shoulders, heavier than the present-day elephant. They had a coat of heavy reddish-brown hair and tusks that curved upward and out. There is some artifact evidence that they may have survived until four or five thousand years ago, and that they were known to man. This reconstructive painting of the American mastodon by Charles R. Knight suggests the pine-and-marsh period when the mastodons roamed the area of the Great Lakes as the ice retreated north.

Courtesy of the American Museum of Natural History

discharge from the Upper Great Lakes. Thus, they contend, today's annual recession rate of five feet may have been less in the past.

These experts give estimates of the age of the Niagara River gorge that range as high as 32,000 years, with an average falling between 18,000 and 20,000.

One thing is certain. The Niagara Falls that we know today will not exist forever. At the present rate of recession, the falls will continue another five thousand years, but will steadily decline in grandeur. Five thousand years from now only a boiling rapids may mark the spot where today the mighty falls pour down.

The last of the ice ages has been assigned the name "Wisconsin" by geologists, because the southern extent of that ice flow coincides nearly with the state's southern border. When that last sheet began to melt, two small lakes were formed between the glacier and the moraine. One lake, which occupied approximately the present position of the southern tip of Lake Michigan, has been dubbed by geologists "Early Lake Chicago." The other lake covered a small portion of southwestern Lake Erie and also extended into northeastern Indiana. This is known as "Highest Lake Maumee." The two lakes drained down the Chicago and Maumee rivers into the Mississippi, the reverse of today's natural flow.

The glacier then proceeded to melt back towards the north. Saginaw Bay, today the southwest arm of Lake Huron, was uncovered. The water that had been draining through the Maumee now began to flow into the Grand River, which runs crescent-wise across Michigan.

The Great Lakes had begun to form.

These early beginnings of the lakes were virtually obliterated by the next glacial advance. But, with the glacial retreat that followed, these comparatively small lakes expanded. In the case of Lake Maumee there was a contraction from the south and west, and expansion to the north and east.

These forerunners of Lakes Michigan and Erie are estimated to have been between three and five thousand years old before the glaciers relaxed their grip on the territory to the north and the first traces of Lakes Huron, Ontario, and Superior began to appear.

There are differences of opinion on the actual timetable, but in general it may be said that Lake Erie reached approximately its present stage about ten thousand years ago. The age of Lake Ontario is set at six thousand years. The other three lakes—Michigan, Superior, and Huron—reached their present development only two or three thousand years ago.

Nor has all change ceased on the Great Lakes. Shorelines are moving steadily, perhaps only inches or a few feet each year. But the pattern of change is constant and irresistible.

All of the lakes except Erie are of depths that go well below sea level: Lake Superior is lower by 732 feet, Lake Ontario by 559 feet, Lake Michigan by 346 feet, and Lake Huron by 173 feet. Only Lake Erie, being shallow, is 358 feet *above* sea level at its deepest point.

These then are the Great Lakes, mighty basins that have been formed over the billion or more years of geological history, but owing their present-day shape to the shoveling action of glaciers and to the staying power of rock.

**GEOLOGY
OF THE
GREAT LAKES**

This view of rock strata, called Miner's Castle because of its unusual formation, is typical of the geologic contours along Lake Superior caused by the variation in rates of erosion. Similar views can be seen throughout the Pictured Rocks area near Munising, Michigan. Such differences in erosion rates are now believed to be the original shapers of the lakes themselves. Munson Collection

This is a waterfall in the Pictured Rocks area. *Munson Collection*

An even more spectacular rock formation was photographed in 1898 in the Apostle Islands in Lake Superior—Temple Gate, just off of Sand Island.   Library of Congress

Another view of **Temple Gate.**   Library of Congress

The Niagara River

Niagara Falls, called by the Indians the "Thunderer of Waters," is one of the great natural spectacles of all time, though known only to a few Hurons and Iroquois until about three hundred years ago when the French explorer, Father Louis Hennepin, discovered them. They are actually two falls, divided in the middle by a craggy triangle of land called Goat Island. The Canadian fall, called the Horseshoe Fall from the shape, are farther upstream and measure 2,500 feet around their rim. Over ninety per cent of the river pours over them at the rate of about 40 million gallons of water a second. The drop in these falls is 160 feet. The drop in the American Fall is 167 feet and these falls, fairly straight across, measure about 1,300 feet. The total length of the falls is therefore close to four thousand feet.

Niagara Frontier State Park Commission

The falls are part of the Niagara River, which is not a true river but a channel linking Lake Erie to Lake Ontario. This channel is 34 miles long with a total drop of 326 feet.

Of main geologic interest is the recession of the falls. The water passes over the hard rock of the crest and as its enormous mass plunges downward, gaining force as it falls, it cuts back the softer under-rock and the unsupported upper rock breaks off in great fragments and drops into the gorge below. The close-up picture shows the Horseshoe Fall veiled in its own mist.

National Film Board of Canada

**GEOLOGY
OF THE
GREAT LAKES**

This corrosive action over thousands of years has produced the nearly seven-mile length of gorge that now exists. In this picture, the strata of earth, rock, gravel, and sand in the walls of the gorge may be clearly seen.

National Film Board of Canada

The Tahquamenon Falls are on the Tahquamenon River, which empties into Whitefish Bay at the lower end of Lake Superior. The falls are deep in the wilderness where the river goes at times between stone cliffs a hundred feet high. Two hundred feet wide in their sweeping arc, they drop forty feet in pounding spray and are second only to Niagara in the Great Lakes region.

A young Indian agent named Henry Rowe Schoolcraft lived in Sault Ste. Marie a century and a half or so ago and gathered together the legends and folklore of the Chippewas, telling about Gitche Gumee and the West Wind, the nearby Tahquamenon River and Lake Superior's islands and Pictured Rocks.

Longfellow's Hiawatha *made a world-famous poetic version of these stories and so the Tahquamenon River entered into American poetry as the place where Hiawatha built his birchbark canoe and lost his friend Kwasind. He and Kwasind, in fact, cleared the river:*

> *Then he called aloud to Kwasind,*   *Saying, "Help me clear this river*
> *To his friend, the strong man, Kwasind,*   *Of its sunken logs and sandbars."*

And they went to work together and cleared the whole river, from its springs in the mountains to the bay of Tahquamenon.

— Munson Collection

GEOLOGY
OF THE
GREAT LAKES

A closer view of the Tahquame-
non Falls.

—*Sault Ste Marie, Michigan*
Chamber of Commerce

The surviving power of rock: these "castle rocks," photographed near Camp Douglas, Wisconsin,
in 1889, are a dramatic example of the rock formations left from the glacial age.

—*Library of Congress*

Chapter 3

The Early History from Cartier to Cadillac

THE STORIES OF Viking exploration of North America, including Leif Ericson's trip to Vinland around 1000 A.D., described in the Icelandic sagas, have long been accepted as more than literature, but what is still a subject of controversy is the possibility that Norsemen came down from Hudson Bay into the Great Lakes region. Curious swords and shield bosses have appeared inland, and a rune stone was dug up in Minnesota. The Viking story is probably, like much early history, due for revision.

Five centuries after Leif's voyage, in 1535, French exploration started. From this time the story is dramatic, highly human, and surprisingly well documented. It begins with three toy ships with pretty names: *Great Hermine, Little Hermine,* and *L'Emérillon* which sailed from St. Malo to the New World under the command of Jacques Cartier to make the first exploration up the St. Lawrence River, which Cartier had discovered on a previous voyage. By mid-September, they had anchored near the rock of Quebec. Indians had been friendly, generally speaking, but they wanted to keep Cartier from going farther; so they blackened their faces and in black-and-white dog skins went yelling past his ships in their canoes, trying to scare him away from the upper river.

He was not frightened. He made the fateful 160-mile trip up to the site of Montreal. And he liked what he saw.

When he landed there, a thousand assembled Indians listened in wonder as he read them the first chapter of the Gospel according to St. John. Later he climbed the mountain rising above the river and named it Mont Royal.

A stone called the Kensington Rune Stone found in southwestern Minnesota, if genuine (and there seems strong likelihood that it is), was carved by warriors sent by the Swedish king Magnus Eriksson in 1354 to find a Greenland colony of his which, driven off by the Eskimos, had presumably moved west to the main continent of America. The translation of the stone reads:

"[We are] 8 Goths and 22 Norwegians on [an] exploration journey from Vinland through the west. We had camp [by a lake with] 2 skerries one day's-journey north from this stone. We were [out] and fished one day. After we came home [we] found 10 men red with blood and dead. A V M Save [us] from evil!" On the edge of the stone was this added message: [We] have 10 men by the sea to look after our ships 14 days journey from this island. [In the] year [of our Lord] 1362."

The warriors from Sweden and Norway were presumably killed by American Indians.

VIKING EXPLORATION

There seems to be not much dispute about Leif Ericson's early voyage to America. He sailed in a boat that had previously skirted the coast of the new continent without making a landing, a boat belonging to Bjarni Herjulfson which he bought. A replica of the boat, 42 feet long, sailed from Bergen, Norway, and arrived in the "New World" June 15, 1927 with Captain Gerhard Folgevo and a crew of three. It was sold at Duluth for a museum.

The original boat visited several places along the Atlantic Coast, and spent the winter at "Vinland," perhaps in the Cape Cod region. Munson Collection

On May 24, 1930, the famous "Beardmore relics" were found. A prospector from Port Arthur, Mr. James Edward Dodd, working near Beardmore, about seven miles from Lake Nipigon in northern Ontario, blasted a clump of birch trees from a vein of quartz he was investigating and uncovered a large rock about three and a half feet below the earth's surface. On the rock lay a number of fragments of iron, the main ones being here illustrated. They were later brought to the attention of C. T. Curelly of the Royal Ontario Museum, who identified them as a Viking sword broken in two, an axe, and a shield boss for covering the hand. Several local people authenticated the finding of the relics, which match illustrations of Viking weapons published by Dr. Matthias Thordarson, director of the National Museum of Iceland. But the conservative Royal Ontario Museum says the evidence for them is not "unimpeachable."

Nevertheless there is an increasing amount of artifact and other evidence to suggest the Viking presence in the Great Lakes area.

Documents in Scandinavia support the authenticity of this expedition, which evidently came down via Hudson Bay and Lake Superior. Along the line of its possible journey exists a series of mooring stones, boulders with holes drilled in them for ring bolts.

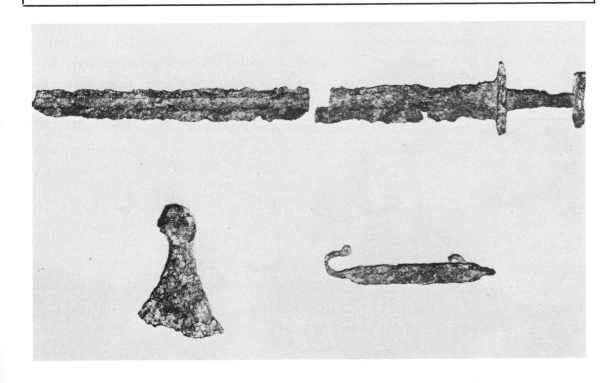

Cartier. A sixteenth-century French painting in the collection of the Marquis de Villefranche, Paris. Cleveland Public Library

Jacques Cartier

Jacques Cartier was born in St. Malo, France, on the last day of 1499. There had been a rumor of a French ship blown off course, reaching America before Columbus, and about a sailor on that boat, Pinzon, going to Spain and telling the discovery to Columbus. Frenchmen began fishing off Newfoundland as early as 1504; and then, in 1522, Giovanni da Verrazano captured two of Cortez's ships loaded with gold coming back from Mexico, and Francis I of France began to be seriously interested in the New World. He sent Verrazano there in 1524, and Verrazano explored much of the Atlantic Coast, including the site of New York.

In his early thirties, Cartier was a skilled Breton navigator with something more than skill. He had command and judgment. Verrazano dropped out of sight (he may have been hanged) and Francis I chose Cartier to go on a new expedition, in 1534. He came first to Newfoundland and then was blown into the gulf and made his way to the Gaspé, where he planted a cross (a mere stop, he thought, on the way to India), and discovered the St. Lawrence River. But he went only as far as the island of Anticosti. Winter threatened and France looked good. He took two Indian children on the home trip with him (maybe stolen, maybe persuaded), but by bringing them back from France the next spring, he encouraged the Indians to trust him. His second trip was that brilliant tour of the Indian villages of Stadacona and Hochelaga which later became Quebec and Montreal. This time he and his men spent the winter and scurvy hit them. Weak, bloated, staggering, with twenty-five of their party dead, they learned from an Indian that a certain evergreen, called *ameda,* was good for their sickness. They made a kind of beverage from it and drank down a whole tree in six days, and began to get better.

Cartier's ships.
New York Public Library

Now they prepared to go back to France, and this time kidnapped all the important local Indian chiefs and hauled them off to France, where they all died. When Cartier returned on a third trip in 1541, to prepare the way for a French colony, the Indians seemed unwilling to believe that their chiefs had married and stayed in France, "living like lords" (whatever that meant). The winter was hard, the country raw and frightening. On his return next spring, Cartier met the French leader Roberval sailing in with two hundred colonists. He defied Roberval's orders to remain and took his own ships back to France. The next year he had to come and rescue Roberval, and this was the end of his American career. He lived the rest of his life in St. Malo, his birthplace, giving technical advice to other expeditions, and died a natural death.

Perhaps one reason for his loss of interest in America had been that some diamonds he brought back from his last trip there turned out to be quartz, and a few grains of gold he scraped out of slate ledges proved to be sham gold. This was no second Mexico.

In 1641, two intrepid Jesuit priests, Fathers Jogues and Rambault, established a mission at the mouth of the Fox River where Nicolet had been, and started three other missions at Sault Ste. Marie, at the tip of St. Ignace, and at the site of today's Ashland, Wisconsin.

In 1673, famed Father Marquette and Louis Jolliet carried through what Nicolet had been so close to doing. They discovered the Mississippi and went down it by birchbark canoe as far as the mouth of the Arkansas.

Later, but not much later, a degree of peace with the Iroquois made it possible to explore directly west through Lake Ontario and the still almost unknown Lake Erie. The Sieur de la Salle, one of the greatest men of his age, took this venture in hand, with three first-rate assistants, Tonti, La Motte, and Father Louis Hennepin. La Salle's design was to build a ship at the head of Lake Erie and with it to voyage west. By now, 1678, he had three small ten-ton ships on Lake Ontario, and he loaded them with the materials to build a large, sixty-foot boat and sent them across to the Niagara River with La Motte and Father Hennepin. There the good priest sang a *Te Deum* to the Senecas and walked through the woods to Niagara Falls.

He was the first European to see the falls, and they were even more soul-shattering then than they are today. There they were in the clear sunlight, thundering through their mist. Table Rock was still there and the Horseshoe Falls were wider than they are today and there was another small cataract to the west. Father Hennepin even originated a now-famous tourist tradition by looking under the American Fall.

The St. Lawrence above Montreal was Iroquois territory. Unfortunately, when the French first settled Quebec in 1608, they made friends with the Hurons and helped them fight the Iroquois (a natural enough thing since the Hurons were their immediate neighbors), but trouble with the Iroquois cut them off from the upper St. Lawrence for a good while to come, and as a result the Great Lakes were discovered by the back-door route of the Ottawa River.

The discoverer was Samuel de Champlain, who in 1615, coming down the French River escorted by a small fleet of Indian canoes, paddled out into the wide expanse of Georgian Bay and found Lake Huron beyond. There is a possibility that the lake had previously been seen by a young French scout, Etienne Brulé, whom Champlain had asked to live with the Indians to get information for him. Brulé went practically native, but did assist the French and eventually was the first white man to reach Lake Superior, in 1622.

Champlain was a great administrator, and the solid development of French interests owes much to him. It was he who in 1634 sent the gifted, youthful Jean Nicolet to the west to find a body of water the Indians had talked about—Mer Douce (gentle sea) and beyond it, surely, Cathay. Nicolet was so positive he would find Cathay that he packed in his canoe robes appropriate for meeting the Chinese emperor—lovely damask decorated with birds and flowers. But

Champlain

Samuel de Champlain was born in Brouage, France, in 1567. He was the son of a sea captain and was carefully educated to be a mariner. But first he had a stint in the army as a billeting officer, from 1594 to 1598. Then he went to sea, to the West Indies and Mexico in command of a Spanish vessel. He wrote an account of this trip, the first of many excellent books. Back from the New World, he was appointed royal geographer, and map-making became one of his main interests. He pleased Henry IV and was asked to go to New France to prepare for a colony there. He sailed across in the *Bonne Renommée* and reconnoitered as far up the St. Lawrence as the Lachine Rapids. The Indians at Stadacona were wary, remembering Cartier. In 1604, he went again and stayed until 1607, founding settlements and mapping the coast as far down as Cape Cod.

He did many local maps with careful shadings to differentiate land from water and with attractive sketches of trees, hills, and Indian villages, and with notations like: "Island where there is a copper mine" (for the Indians mined copper and used coal).

In 1608, he was sent to start a fur-trading post at Quebec (Stadacona), and the rest of his long life he strengthened the colony there. Almost every year he returned to France. In 1610, he married a girl of twelve, Hélène Boullé, who later went to the still wild New World to live with him. Meantime, he had discovered Lake Champlain and named it for himself and had fought the Iroquois and with his allies, the Hurons, had filed out in a procession of canoes onto the lake later named Huron. He founded Montreal.

He was not one to pass up this chance for ceremony. He took out his robes, dressed, and, firing off a pistol in each hand, walked directly to meet the panic-stricken Indians. When they got over their fright, they feasted him.

He went up the Fox River to that celebrated mile of portage which divides the Great Lakes basin from the Mississippi watershed, but did not go on. Missing the Mississippi, he headed straight back home to Montreal, having discovered Lake Michigan.

along the way he heard of the Winnebagos (men of the sea), and turned aside into Lake Michigan to find them. He went all the way down Green Bay to the mouth of the Fox River, and there several thousand Winnebagos gathered to meet him.

In 1627 (Hélène was now back in France), the British blockaded Quebec and captured convoys and supplies coming from France, and finally forced Champlain to surrender to them. He was held prisoner in England for five years. When peace was made, he was returned to Canada as governor under an appointment from Louis XIII. When he died in Quebec on Christmas Day, 1635, he left an enduring and important record of the times he lived in. He had promoted emigration as against just exploiting the fur trade, had mapped much of Canada and New England, and had won the deserved title: The Father of New France.

**FROM
CARTIER
TO CADILLAC**

One of Champlain's own maps.   *Munson Collection*

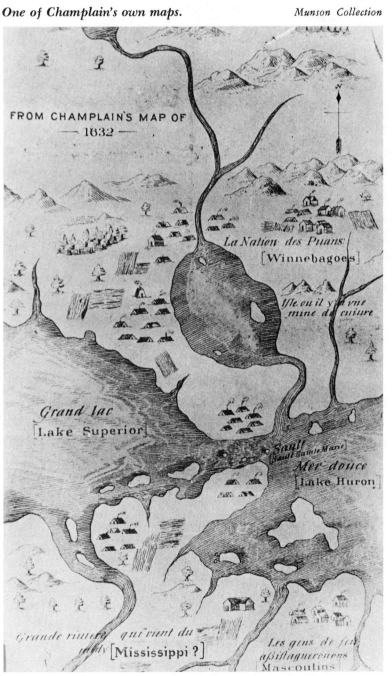

The statue of Champlain at Orillia, Ontario.
Canadian Government Travel Bureau

Isaac Jogues was the first Jesuit martyr in New France. In France he was ordained in the Society of Jesus at twenty-nine and came immediately to Quebec to begin work with the Hurons. In 1642, a year after he and Father Rambault had established the first missions in the west, he was captured by the Iroquois—he had had a chance to escape but stayed to comfort his companions and "neophytes." He was brutally tortured. "Our hands and fingers being all in pieces, they had to feed us like children. Patience was our physician." After the torture, he was taken forcibly into the tribe as a servant, doing "woman's work." His life was in constant danger until he was rescued by the Dutch and sent back to France by way of Holland. He rested and recovered and the next spring insisted on returning to his Indians. He went to the heart of the Iroquois country and worked there successfully for two years. Then the Indians, for some unexplained reason, decided to kill him. A Dutch correspondent (the Dutch were the allies of the Iroquois) wrote in October, 1646: "Know then that on the 18th, in the evening, when they came to call Isaac to supper, he got up and went away with that Barbarian to the lodge of the bear. There was a traitor with his hatchet" who, as Jogues came, split open his head. It was the "nation of the bear" that killed him. The nations of the wolf and turtle tried to save his life.

An engraving done in 1664 by G. Huret depicts the death of Father Jogues and his fellow missionaries at the hands of the Iroquois. The likeness of Father Jogues is considered authentic.

Province of Quebec Film Bureau

There is a touching aftermath to the Father Jogues story. In 1686, his mission on the Fox River still existed, though tiny. The governor of the area at that time was Nicolas Perrot and he gave the mission what was, for those times, a magnificent gift, a silver monstrance or "soleil" to be used in the church service. Probably made in France, it was hand-wrought and stood 18 inches high. Around the base of a salver that went with it is written "Ce soleil a esté donné par Mr Nicolas Perrot á la Mission de St. Francois Xavier en la Baye des Puants, 1686."

The Indians turned hostile and attacked the mission and settlement only a year or two after the gift was made, so the monstrance was buried in the ground and lost. It was dug up by accident in 1802, was used for a while, sent east to Detroit and there was lost. Father Bonduel accidentally found it in Detroit and redeemed it for its weight in silver, and returned it to Green Bay, where it is now on display at the Neville Public Museum. It has been called "the earliest memorial of civilized man in the region which became Wisconsin" and even "the earliest and most valued relic of French occupation and of Jesuit missionary labors throughout the Great Lakes region and the Mississippi Valley."

Neville Public Museum, Green Bay

New York Public Library

Ontario Dept. of Travel and Publicity

Brébeuf

One of the most engaging and incomparable of the Jesuit missionaries in the early years of New France was Jean de Brébeuf. He first came in 1625 and went up the Ottawa to proselytize among the Indians around Georgian Bay. The English invasion of 1629 interrupted his work, but in 1634 he was back among the Hurons, who loved him. In the *Jesuit Relations* for 1637 he wrote some "instructions for the fathers of our society who shall be sent to the Hurons":

"You must have sincere affection for the savages,—looking upon them as ransomed by the blood of the son of God, and as our Brethren with whom we are to pass the rest of our lives.

"To conciliate the Savages, you must be careful never to make them wait for you in embarking.

"You must provide yourself with a tinder box or with a burning mirror, or with both, to furnish them fire in the daytime to light their pipes, and in the evening when they have to encamp; these little services win their hearts."

These were only part of a full and psychologically sound prescription for getting along with the Indians. The portrait of Brébeuf here reproduced is considered authentic. *New York Public Library.*

As the Iroquois began ruthlessly advancing north, Father Lalemant, Brébeuf's superior, gathered the missionaries together in an isolated spot near the present community of Midland, Ontario, and built a stone fort called Ste. Marie, hoping to save them. But Lalemant and Brébeuf were off at the mission village of St. Louis when the Iroquois attacked. They refused to flee and were captured, and Brébeuf was horribly tortured. Because of his unflinching and compassionate courage, after he died a chief seized and ate his heart.

Fort Ste. Marie has been restored and in the distance is the much visited Martyrs' Shrine at Midland.

The Gooseberry River and its falls are a permanent reminder of two early French explorers, Radisson and Groseilliers, who set out from Quebec in 1658 and made a two-thousand-mile canoe trip winding up on the unmapped western shores of Lake Superior. When they got back to the St. Lawrence, it was at the head of 360 canoes laden with furs, the first of the fantastic water caravans that were to tap the wealth of the Northwest. Since the English couldn't hope to pronounce Groseilliers, the Groseilliers River became the Gooseberry.

**THE
EARLY
HISTORY**

Father Jacques Marquette came to Canada from the north of France, Laon. He came after the way had been opened to Lake Superior and worked on the shores of the lake as a missionary to the Indians there, the Ottawas and Hurons, who "often relapse into the sins in which they were nurtured." He was there at St. Ignace when Louis Jolliet came, in 1673, ordered to explore west to some great river or sea reputed to be out there. Father Marquette went with him, over Nicolet's route to the Fox River. They went across the watershed at which Nicolet had stopped and on down to that great river, the Mississippi, floating like Indians in a birchbark canoe along the Father of Waters.

Library of Congress

This portrait of Father Marquette was discovered in the winter of 1896-97 by Donald Guthrie McNab who believed it to be authentic. He had previously painted portraits of Fathers Brébeuf and Jogues (the portraits in this book), using engravings of them done in their own lifetime to get a living likeness.

New York Public Library

At the place on the shore of Green Bay, at Red Banks, Wisconsin, where Jean Nicolet stepped so dramatically ashore, wearing his oriental robe over his voyageur's costume, to greet the Indians and incidentally to discover Wisconsin, that state has erected a handsome monument. It shows a man with some glint of humor, whom the Indians might have liked (as they did).

Neville Public Museum, Green Bay

The famous Champlain Monument on Dufferin Terrace looks out over Quebec which he founded. It was unveiled by Lord Aberdeen, governor-general of Canada, September 21, 1898. The monument is the work of the sculptor Paul Chevre and of the architect Paul le Cardonnel, both of Paris, and the pedestal uses the same stone as the Arc de Triomphe in Paris.

On this early map of the Great Lakes, the name of Lake Michigan is still Lake Illinois and Green Bay is called Baye des Puans—"Bay of the Stinkers," that being the early French name for the Winnebago Indians. The Illinois River is correctly designated as flowing into the Mississippi.

Library of Congress

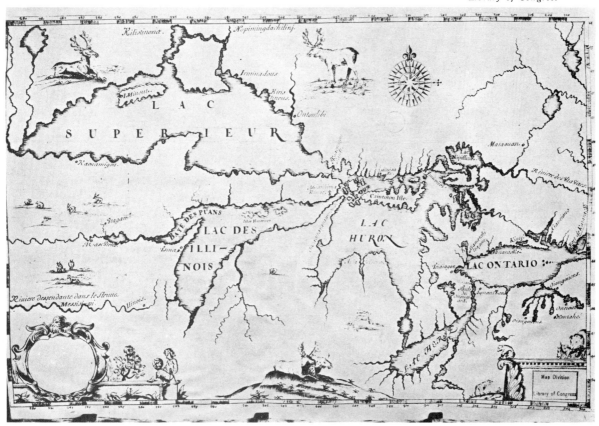

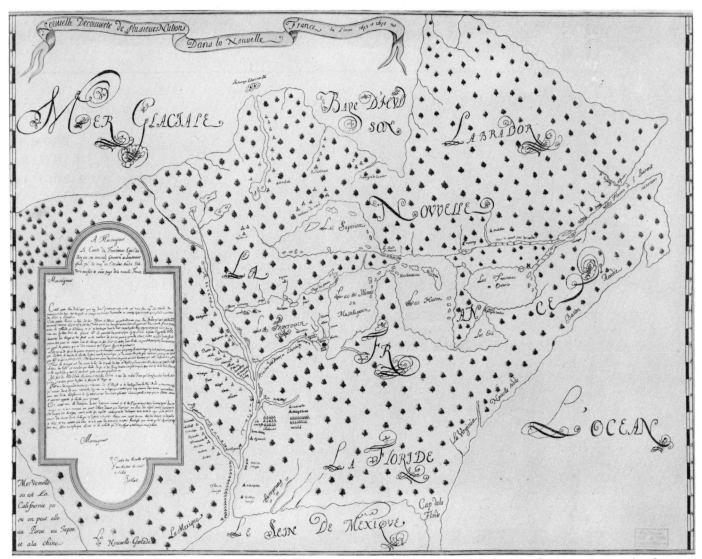

This is a map of Louis Jolliet's "New Discovery of Several Nations in New France in the year 1673 and 1674." Notice that North America consists mainly of the Great Lakes and Florida with a small allowance for Virginia and "New Sweden" in between. "Mer Glacial"—Glacial Sea or Cold Sea—is to the north along with Hudson Bay.

It might be thought that the building of La Salle's great ship *Griffin*[1] was an anticlimax, but it was not. The workmen made an encampment of wigwams and set to work. Just as the Hurons had tried, by their fantastic warnings, to discourage Champlain from going up to Montreal, now the Senecas set themselves against the building of this unheard-of monster which, they sensed, would not be a good thing for them. They pretended they were going to attack. They wouldn't sell corn to the workmen. But the work went on and the magnificent fifty- or sixty-ton ship was built, two-masted and many-sailed, with a griffin on its prow and an eagle on its high stern.

1 *Original French spelling was* Griffon, *meaning a fabulous animal.*

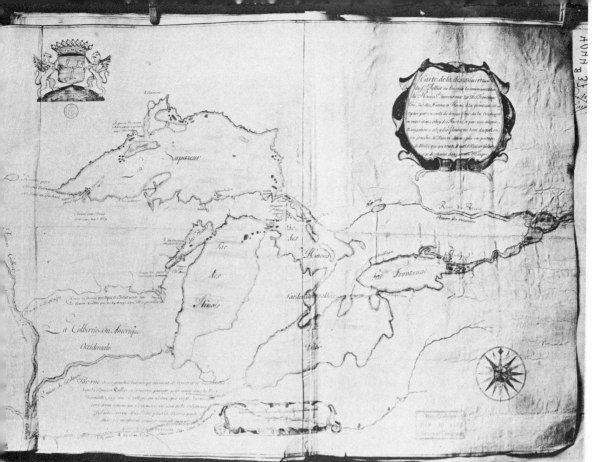

*This is a 1679 map of "Jolliet's Discovery" of a route across the Great Lakes to the Mississippi,
here called the Colbert River after Louis XIV's minister. The Mississippi area is called "Colbertie
or Western America." At the left bottom is "La Salle's route going to Mexico." Lake Michigan is
here called by its early name of Lake Illinois and Lake Ontario is called Lake Frontenac.*

Library of Congress

*This is La Salle's Griffin, drawn by Judge Campbell in Hubbard's Memorials of a Half Century.
With griffin on the front and eagle on the back and with all sails blowing, she heads for the West.*

Burton Historical Collection

52

THE
EARLY
HISTORY

This is the home of Louis Jolliet on Sous-le-Fort Street in Quebec. Jolliet was a native of the city, born there in 1645 and educated in the Jesuit college. His home is now used as the depot of an elevator (ascenseur) which goes up to Dufferin Terrace, to the Champlain monument.
Office du Film de la Province de Québec

Robert Cavalier, Sieur de la Salle was twenty-three when he arrived in New France in 1667 with the grant of a seigneury. He built a house and got a few settlers into his holding, but soon his eyes turned west. The Huron wars were over. Perhaps there was a chance to spread out and work something up for trade and empire. He had dreams. It took ten years of hard maneuvering to put himself into the position of building the Griffin, then that turned into disaster and he staggered back east on foot, by raft, and in a canoe of elmbark that he made himself. But he had visited much of the country opened up by Marquette, Jolliet, and their fellow explorers and adventurers, and that far river at first named for Colbert called him. He traveled to the mouth of the river, claiming the whole valley, which he called "Louisiana" for the French. At forty he returned from France with a party to establish a colony at the mouth of the Mississippi, but went ashore by mistake in what is now Texas. On the banks of the Trinity River, after many hardships, his own men shot him and threw his naked body into the underbrush. Cleveland Public Library

On the morning of August 7, 1679, the *Griffin* set sail. La Salle stood on the quarter-deck, firm, arrogant even, with five cannon and a thirty-two-man crew. He carried a load of trinkets for barter.

He crossed Lake Erie in three calm days, but when he edged up into Lake Huron, the weather changed suddenly, as it does on the lakes, and the boat was gripped helplessly by a violent storm. At the last moment, the winds veered away and they were able to cross safely the full expanse of Lake Huron and take shelter at St. Ignace. From there they sailed to Green Bay, where La Salle did a lively trade and put on board enough furs to make his fortune. Trade, war—guns and furs. It was to be the symbol of the lakes for many years to come. Heavily laden and with a small crew, the *Griffin* started back east, La Salle staying behind to explore the wilderness.

The *Griffin* was never heard of again.

But by now the main pathways of the Great Lakes had been opened.

In 1701, Antoine de la Mothe Cadillac, with fifty soldiers and fifty settlers, built a fort at the site of Detroit. Detroit is the French word for "strait" and Cadillac reasoned that the strait connecting Lake Huron and Lake Erie was the key to Great Lakes power. Here he built Fort Pontchartrain, and Detroit long remained the largest community in the northwest.

Today Cadillac Square and the name of one of the continent's great automobiles perpetuate his memory.

For the next half century, canoes and small boats proceeding along the shelter of the shore carried forward the maritime history of the Great Lakes. Then there was a change.

This unrestored blockhouse, photographed in 1903 in Bois Blanc Park, Michigan, is of particular interest because it shows without change how the old blockhouses looked and how, probably, the corners of Cadillac's fort looked. Library of Congress

Cadillac and Detroit

Antoine de la Mothe Cadillac was born in a small house in a village of Gascony, in southwest France, March 5, 1658. (As is the way in France, people still live in his house.) He was educated in the Jesuit college at Montauban. In his late thirties he was in Canada, serving as commandant of Fort de Buade at St. Ignace, the key to the Upper Country. Then he was recalled in a general pull-back from the interior posts, and went to France with a strong idea in his head. The Straits of Lake Erie—the site of Detroit—were the one place on the Great Lakes where the central power should have a colony and fort. It was essential. He went straight to Colonial Minister Pontchartrain and excited his interest and was allowed to go ahead.

In 1701 in full summer he arrived with his fifty soldiers and fifty settlers. He built a solid square fort with the usual blockhouse corners, large enough to protect some dozen and a half buildings, a house for himself, barracks, store, church and sacristy, and a few private houses. The fort had a large and small gate.

Cadillac himself had come by way of the Ottawa River and Georgian Bay, since the Iroquois were still technically at war, but peace was made that same summer and in the fall Madame Cadillac journeyed to Detroit by open boat across Lake Ontario and Lake Erie. When advised not to go, she said, "I know the hardships and the dangers of the voyage and the isolation of the life to which I am going. But I am eager to go, for a woman who sincerely loves her husband has no greater attraction than his company, wherever he may be." All the appalling bridge between the civilization of Versailles and the wilderness is in that pretty speech.

Cadillac himself rhapsodized about Detroit. From the site where the Detroit-Windsor tunnel now discharges its international traffic, he wrote home to France: "The climate is temperate, and the air purified through the day and the night by a gentle breeze. The skies are always serene and spread sweet and fresh influence which makes one enjoy a tranquil sleep."

He ruled the settlement well for ten years and left it so strongly established, with settled families and schools, that it survived much Indian hostility and bureaucratic mismanagement in the growing century. Then he was sent down to Louisiana as governor, and disappeared from Great Lakes history.

This is a drawing by Charles V. Kern of Detroit (Fort Pontchartrain in Cadillac's time. It is based on data supplied by C. M. Burton. The stream in the rear was the Savoyard, now a city underground sewer. This is considered the best available conception of the city at that time.
Burton Historical Collection

Portrait of Cadillac.
Burton Historical Collection

FROM
CARTIER
TO CADILLAC

The first extant picture of Niagara Falls, dating back to 1698 when Father Hennepin's book, A New Discovery of a Vast Country in America, was published in London, translated from almost contemporaneous editions on the Continent. The good father wrote of "a vast and prodigious cadence of water which falls down after a surprizing and astonishing manner.... This wonderful downfall is compounded of two great cross-streams of water and two falls with an isle sloping along the middle of the waters which ... from this horrible precipice do foam and boyl after the most hideous manner imaginable making an outrageous noise, more terrible than that of thunder, for when the wind blows out of the South this dismal roaring may be heard more than fifteen leagues off." A spectator is represented as turning away from the sight and covering his ears.
New York Public Library

Chapter 4

Ships of the Great Lakes

IT IS significant that the second large ship launched on the Great Lakes was English. La Salle's *Griffin* had not been followed up by the French. These hardy scouts, soldiers, and fur traders were not generally the householder or marrying type. But the English in their colonies to the south had from the start been establishing homes and families, and their power was growing.

They expanded up the Mohawk to a beachhead on Lake Ontario and, in 1755, foreseeing the American campaign of the European Seven Years' War (just ahead), they rushed through the building of a 43-foot sloop named after their base. The *Oswego* went down the ways 76 years almost to the day after the *Griffin*. It had twelve cannon and five guns.

The shipbuilders continued hard at work that summer and the next and more vessels were launched—among them, the *Ontario*, the *London*, and the *Halifax*.

The French meanwhile were building ships of their own at Fort Frontenac.

The expected war broke out and on June 27, 1756, the first naval engagement was fought on the Great Lakes. Two English ships and a schooner met two French ships and lined up for battle. The French fired the opening salvo, and Captain Broadley, in charge of the English ships, saw that his small guns were outranged. He turned and fled.

He might as well have given battle, for the French shortly afterward captured Oswego and, without a base, Captain Broadley had to surrender.

Copying the French strategy, in 1759, the British officer Sir William Johnson led a force of 2,300 men, with whaleboats, bateaux, and canoes as transport, and captured Fort Niagara, where he forced the surrender of the two French warships, the brig *Outaouaise* and the corvette *Iroquois*.

**SHIPS
OF THE
GREAT LAKES**

The first ship after the Griffin *was also the first British ship launched on the lakes, and so the Oswego has a high historic interest. Notable in her design was the extraordinary sail area that could be spread, if necessary, in proportion to the hull. She was 55 feet long and her single mast was 53 feet tall.* Albertype Collection, Michigan Historical Commission

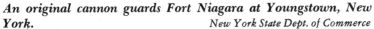

An original cannon guards Fort Niagara at Youngstown, New York. *New York State Dept. of Commerce*

Fort Niagara was built by the French in 1678 and has been restored from original plans made available by the French War Department. This is the Gate of the Five Nations. The fall of this fort in 1759 made no small contribution to the surrender of Canada to the British, for it cut the French off completely from the west.

Forty-nine days later Quebec fell to General James Wolfe and the British in a decisive battle fought on the Plains of Abraham, where both General Wolfe and General Joseph Montcalm, the French commander, were mortally wounded.

This was the end of French power in North America, and Canada was ceded to England at the end of the Seven Years' War in 1763. The British now opened a shipyard at Navy Island on the Niagara River above the cataract, and built the first ships on the upper lakes since the *Griffin.* These were the *Huron* and *Michigan,* which were not much larger than the *Griffin* —eighty tons apiece. Their help was crucial in the struggle with Pontiac, the redoubtable chief of the Indian coalition of the Northwest. They maintained communications and brought supplies and heartened the besieged defenders of Detroit. When Pontiac surrendered, the British were in full control of the lakes.

His Majesty's Schooners **Huron** *and* **Michigan,** *1763, the first British ships launched on the upper lakes.* Albertype Collection, Michigan Historical Commission

The war with their American colonies to the south did not end so well for them. In 1783, the Peace of Paris established the boundary between the new United States and Canada. Oddly enough, the War of 1812, the perhaps needless sequel to the American Revolution, strengthened the peace between the new country and its neighbor. The maritime history of this war goes back to 1763. Between that year and the War of 1812, the British built 28 ships on Lake Ontario, including the 510-ton *Niagara* (first of many to bear this name), which carried a crew of 200 men, the 400-ton *Queen Charlotte,* and the 230-ton *Lady Provost.*

It was to face such a fleet that a 27-year-old native of Rhode Island was sent in March, 1813, to Erie, Pennsylvania. He was Oliver Hazard Perry, and destiny was to make him one of America's greatest naval heroes.

British desire to keep a commanding position in the fur trade led them to be slow in giving up frontier posts along the lakes to the United States after the Revolutionary War. This view of the American Fur Company's buildings at Fond du Lac in 1827 (on the south shore of Lake Superior) is typical of such posts and is not much changed from its appearance during the period between the Revolutionary War and the War of 1812 when the British were pushed back. The post had originally been established by the French. Library of Congress

At the start of the War of 1812, it seemed as if the Americans would easily invade and conquer Canada. The British had hardly five thousand troops in their colony. The rest were busily fighting Napoleon. The tactic would have been to drive determinedly through the Champlain gap on Montreal, and the lakes would have fallen without a blow. Instead, General Hull crossed the Detroit River and called on the citizens of Ontario to revolt and assume "the dignified station of freemen." They did nothing of the kind. They and the British "tyrants" incited the Indians and cleverly cut off Hull's supply ships, and finally throttled him into a state of fear and paralysis. He surrendered Detroit to the British General Brock without firing a shot, and for this he was court-martialed.

Burton Historical Collection

Under Perry's direction, great activity in Erie resulted in the launching by July 25 of two brigs, the *Lawrence* and the *Niagara* (second of that name), as well as a schooner and a gunboat. Additional ships were built or refitted at Black Rock on the Niagara River and hauled by oxen up the river into Lake Erie to join Perry's fleet. The American strength was augmented by the *Caledonia,* which was captured from the British in a surprise night action near Fort Erie, at the mouth of the Niagara River.

With this fleet—nine ships in all—Perry met Commodore Barclay and the British at Put-in-Bay on September 10. Perry's fleet consisted of three brigs, five schooners, and a sloop, with 54 guns and about 400 fighting men.

Barclay had under his command only six vessels—two ships, two brigs, one schooner, and one sloop—but they boasted nine more guns than the Americans and about fifty more men.

Perry's seamanship and daring more than offset the superior British firepower. In the midst of the fierce battle, he crossed in a small boat under the British guns from the disabled *Lawrence* to the *Niagara,* and continued his assault on the British until they surrendered. The American victory was complete and overwhelming. The British were driven off the Great Lakes.

Portrait of Oliver Hazard Perry. Burton Historical Collection

Oliver Hazard Perry

Oliver Hazard Perry was born at South Kingston, Rhode Island, August 23, 1785. He was fourteen when he started in the navy as a midshipman, and in ten years (via the war against the Barbary pirates) he had made his way to the command of the *Revenge,* which two years later was wrecked. The court of inquiry acquitted him of all blame and the next year, at the start of the War of 1812, he left the command of a division of gunboats and headed resolutely for the Great Lakes. When he took command on Lake Erie, General Hull had surrendered and the situation was dark. Furthermore there was no fleet whatever. Perry had to build it.

He came to Erie, Pennsylvania, in March, 1813. By July, he had a workable fleet in operation, literally hewed out of the trees along the Presque Isle peninsula. The British commander, Barclay, seems to have been overcautious. At any rate instead of attacking at once, he gave Perry a month in which to sail here and there and train his men for battle.

There is something about wanting to win. Perry had come of his own volition to the lakes. He belonged to a naval family and his younger brother—just twelve years old—was midshipman on Perry's own ship (and this young boy was later to do something perhaps even more momentous than the older Perry's accomplishments: he was to open Japan to the world). Perry meant the slogan he spread in white across his blue banner—"Don't give up the ship." He fought hard, but he fought with self-belief. "We have met the enemy and they are ours."

His victory was stunning. It was the end of the British naval power on the lakes, and from that time on the lakes were devoted to peace. Forts became museums. When an occasional cruiser noses in from the Atlantic, people stare at it as a curiosity. The Perry monument at Put-in-Bay is truly a Peace Monument.

This is the actual Niagara. After the war it was scuttled in Misery Bay, but was raised in 1913 for the centenary of the battle and was restored. It is now tied up at the foot of State Street in the harbor of Erie, Pennsylvania. This picture was taken just after its first restoration.

Perry crossing under fire from his disabled flagship Lawrence *to the* Niagara. *He has his battle flag, "Don't give up the ship," over his left arm. Having nearly destroyed Barclay's* Detroit, *he now moved in on her with the same relentless assault as before, from the* Niagara. *It was too much. Barclay hauled down his flag.*

Burton Historical Collection

64

Thus ended all warfare on the lakes. Trade and passenger service became the dominant factors in development of Great Lakes shipping.

In 1816, seven farsighted Canadian shippers in Kingston raised £12,000 and built a steamship of 700 tons. The *Frontenac,* described as trim and graceful, was 170 feet long, 32 feet wide at the beam, and carried three tall masts and a funnel.

Not to be outdone, the Americans at Sackets Harbor got to work. Six months after the *Frontenac* was launched, they put in the water a 220-ton steamer, the *Ontario.*

The next year, 1818, saw the launching of the third steamboat, the first on Lake Erie. This was the *Walk-in-the-Water,* a paddlewheeler built at Black Rock. She was 132 feet long with a beam of 32 feet. Her smokestack jutted 30 feet into the sky and was set between two sails that were used when the wind was favorable.

Passengers were able to make the voyage between Buffalo and Detroit in a day and a half, and they paid $18 cabin or $7 steerage for the privilege.

**SHIPS
OF THE
GREAT LAKES**

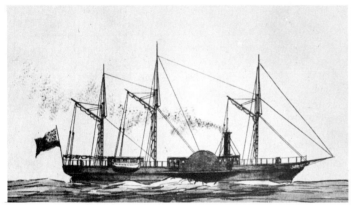

Sketch of the Frontenac, *drawn by Eric Heyl from Van Cleve,* Steamers of Lake Ontario.
The Great Lakes Historical Society, Cleveland, and Eric Heyl, Buffalo

Companion sketch of the Ontario. *The American* Ontario *had only about a third the tonnage of the British* Frontenac.

The Walk-in-the-Water *seems to have been a much-loved boat, even if short-lived. Here it is shown arriving from Buffalo at its terminal point, Detroit, in 1820. No sails are set as it runs into port under its own power with a pennant of black smoke.* Burton Historical Collection

In this view of Detroit five years later, there are four steamers in sight, all paddlewheels.

Burton Historical Collection

But the designer of the *Walk-in-the-Water* apparently had no idea of the storms that could sweep across Lake Erie. Caught in bad October weather in 1821, she was washed into a sandbar twelve miles from Buffalo. All aboard were saved, but only the engine was salvaged from the *Walk-in-the-Water*.

The Chicago Daily Democrat *for May 3, 1842, greets a newcomer: "The steamer* Vandalia. *This little steamer has excited considerable attention in our port, being the first one of the kind which has made its appearance here. She has Ericsson's propellers instead of the ordinary paddle wheel, and travels at the rate of seven miles an hour. In smooth waters, it is said, she could attain a speed of ten miles per hour, but the friction would be injurious to the machinery. She is rigged like a sloop, and at a distance would be readily taken for one. This boat is moved by what is termed the screw paddle, it being something between the buckets of the old paddle wheel and the ordinary augur so that the propellers may be said in some measure to bore their way through the water. The wheels are placed at the stern on each side of the rudder. The paddles are of iron and they work under water. Not being visible, they are admirably calculated for vessels of war, and the water is so slightly agitated that boats propelled by them must, we think, soon be extensively used on our canals. The* Vandalia *is from Oswego, on Lake Ontario, at which place, we understand, three more boats of the same kind are being constructed."*

The Great Lakes Historical Society, Cleveland

In 1822 the *Superior* was launched, and two years later the *Henry Clay*. For the next two decades these two steamers—the first powered by the engine from the *Walk-in-the-Water*—plied the Buffalo-Detroit run. Meanwhile, up and down the lakes, on both the Canadian and American shores, shipyards were busy turning out steamers and sailing vessels.

In 1835, a total of 225 sailing ships put into harbor at Chicago. In 1836, at Cleveland harbor sailing ships greatly outnumbered steamers, although steamers were making quicker trips.

Ships of sail were many and varied on the lakes. There were square-riggers, brigantines, and schooners, of both two and three masts.

Europe was beginning to pour forth thousands who were seeking opportunity in the New World, and the demand for passenger service on the lakes was growing.

To meet this demand, newer, bigger, and faster ships were commissioned. In 1841, the first screw-propeller steamer was built on the lakes. This was the *Vandalia*, which was launched at Oswego.

By the middle of the century, steamers were leaving Buffalo with as many as seven hundred passengers, most of them immigrants bound for the western plains. They went to Detroit, for the most part, or to Monroe for the Michigan Southern Railroad to New Buffalo on the Lake Michigan shore. There they could travel by stage to Chicago, and then go on to the West by rail.

The *Great Western,* the *Western World,* the *United States,* the *Plymouth,* the *Queen of the West,* the *City of Buffalo*—these were but a few of the great steamers of this era. The *Empire* was one of the first of the luxury ships; 1,220 tons, 260 feet in length, she made the run between Buffalo and Chicago.

Then came the *Hendrik Hudson* in 1847, faster yet and more elegant. The traveler could take the train from New York to Buffalo, board the *Hendrik Hudson,* and be in Chicago only five days after departing the Atlantic seaboard.

With its launching in 1841, the *Vandalia* had started the trend from paddlewheelers to propeller-driven vessels.

A directory of 1856 listed 118 propellers in service on the lakes, 120 steamers, and 1,149 sailing ships of various types and rigs.

Photograph of one of the early wood-built propeller steamers, the John C. Gault, *1,212 gross tons, 218 feet long. This was operated originally by the Wabash Railroad Line of Toledo, Ohio.*

Captain H. C. Inches Collection

SHIPS
OF THE
GREAT LAKES

While the "propellers" came on modestly, the side-wheelers got bigger to handle the rush of immigrants to the West. Built in Huron, Ohio, the Great Western *was at first scoffed at because it had an upper cabin above decks which critics said would cause it to capsize. But Captain Augustus Walker brought it successfully into Cleveland on its maiden trip, and it was one of the notable vessels of its class.* Huron, Ohio, Public Library

The Empire, *one of the first of the luxury ships. Though retouched, this photograph gives a good idea of its size and elegance.* The Great Lakes Historical Society, Cleveland

The transition from side-wheel to propeller is dramatically illustrated in this certificate of inspectors dated May and June, 1849, and illustrated by both a side-wheeler and a propeller. But there is a further story connected with this document. It was made out for the steamer Independence, the first steamer on Lake Superior. The discovery of copper, and later, iron (a story told at the end of this chapter), called imperatively for boats on the upper lake. There was then no canal at the Soo. In the autumn of 1845, six schooners and two steamers gathered at the lower end of the mile-long portage to Lake Superior. The Independence was hauled up on land, the capstans creaked, the rollers turned alongside the seething rapids, the horses pulled against their collars, and that first steamer crawled up inch by inch to her new home.

Munson Collection

During the Civil War, Lake Erie saw a naval engagement of a seemingly minor nature, but one that might have had disastrous consequences for the North. Confederate agents planned to capture the sole Federal warship on the lakes, the U.S.S. *Michigan,* and then, with command of the water, burn the lakes cities, using prisoners of war released from nearby camps. Two steamers were captured and sunk during the raid, but the *Michigan* escaped with damage only to its engine room. While the *Michigan* was crippled, agents tried to buy and arm a steamer, the *Georgiana,* to raid and burn Buffalo, but the Canadian government intervened and stopped the plot.

The mining and transport of ore in the Great Lakes region was of crucial help to the North in winning the Civil War. The "Soo" Canal was opened just in time for this vital traffic.

Just preceding the war had come large-scale and rapid development of railroads in the area. These could not replace the lakes freighters, but the passenger vessels were hard hit. They recovered their prestige and popularity to some extent in the 1870's and 1880's, but never again regained their old position.

It remained for the Canadians during this period to take over leadership on the Great Lakes in passenger ships. The Canadian Pacific decided in the 1880's that the lakes were ready for vessels comparable in size to the ocean-going type. The company had them built in Scotland along the Clyde and then sailed to Montreal. There they were cut in two and towed by tugs to Buffalo where they were reassembled. The *Assiniboia*—336 feet long— was one of these Clyde-built steamers.

The Madeira Pet

One of the belles in the history of Great Lakes shipping is the *Madeira Pet,* the first European vessel ever to sail directly to the lakes (and don't think that event wasn't appreciated when it happened). It came about this way. In 1856, a Chicago merchant built a vessel—the *Dean Richmond*—to take advantage of the improved St. Lawrence canals opened in 1848, and sailed it to Liverpool. He made a lot of money, and the British decided they might be able to do the same thing in reverse. They ventured it with the *Madeira Pet,* a small brigantine of 123 tons. It made an eighty-day trip across and on July 14, 1857, tied up at Chicago's North Pier, its destination.

The reaction was spectacular. The Chicago Board of Trade in a special call-to-order voted this the most significant and important commercial event in the history of the city. Captain Crang of the *Pet* was brought before the Board and cheered, and hundreds of people lined the banks and bridges of the Chicago River as the vessel was towed up to a new mooring at the dock at the foot of La Salle Street. The next day there was a city-wide celebration in Deerborn Park, its significance underlined by alternate playing of "Hail Columbia" and "God Save the Queen." When the *Madeira Pet* set off for home with a load of salted hides and calf skins, wild cheers, farewell delegations, salutes, and band music helped her on her way. Chicago, aware of the possibility of "Western eminence," drew up practical plans for deepening waterways. The future was on the march.

ARREST OF MAJOR COLE AT THE BANQUET ON BOARD THE "MICHIGAN".

A contemporary newspaper sketch of the arrest of the Confederate agent who plotted the capture of the Michigan.

Chicago Historical Society

The Canada Steamship Lines also entered into the competition with such ships as the *Hamonic* and the *Noronic*—the latter 362 feet long and about 7,000 tons.

Until the early 1870's, nearly all trade on the Great Lakes, as distinct from passenger service, had been carried on by sailing vessels. A tabulation in 1870 showed 1,737 schooners, 214 barques, and 159 brigs on the lakes.

A few wood boats and metal boats, driven by steam, had put in an appearance in the combined passenger, cargo, and package-freight trade in the late 1860's. The *Onoko,* in 1882, was built of iron for bulk cargoes of iron, ore, coal, and grain.

As good oak grew scarcer and the ships bigger, the 1880's saw a new development known as the "composite." These had metal frames, but were planked on the bottom and up to just below the load line with wood. Above the load line, plates were put on the metal frames.

Only eight or nine of these composites were ever built, and none after 1890, but they did represent the reluctance of Great Lakes skippers to abandon oak completely in favor of metal.

These scenes in Oswego harbor in the 1870's and '80's show the great period of the sailing vessel when over two thousand, including barques and brigs, swept back and forth across the lakes. At Buffalo and Oswego, they transferred cargo to the canal boats with their pretty striped bows waiting to go down to New York.
Captain H. C. Inches Collection

Schooner's End

Great Lakes schooners ranged typically from the small *Jessie Martin* to the large *David Dows,* and there were 1,700 of them in the mid-seventies. The *Jessie Martin* had an over-all length of 90 feet and was built in 1881. She carried lumber, and piles of lumber awaiting loading can be seen at the left of her. She foundered in Lake Michigan in 1908.

Built in the same year as the *Jessie Martin* was the largest schooner ever known on the lakes, the *David Dows,* a handsome but impractical five-master with a 265-foot over-all length and 1,418-ton cargo capacity. In these two vessels, the extremes of the commercial sailing schooner are illustrated. The *David Dows,* built in Toledo, was operated by the Corrigans of Cleveland, but within a year had lost a mast in a storm. It then met a fate typical of these schooners facing the competition of steamers: all the masts were drastically shortened, the rigging was reduced, and she became a tow barge.

When the *David Dows* was in trouble in 1882, the tug *Winslow* went to her rescue and took her in tow. The scene was painted by the famous Great Lakes marine artist, Captain Thomas Chilvers, owner and captain of the ferryboat *Gem* that operated between Detroit and Windsor. In this somber painting, the end of one phase of Great Lakes shipping is dramatized.

The David Dows *in storm.*

Dossin Great Lakes Museum

The tug Champion *and tow.*

Captain H. C. Inches Collection

The David Dows.

Dossin Great Lakes Museum

Unusually complete information is available about another boat which went through the same cycle, the *J. I. Case*, built in 1874 at Manitowoc, Wisconsin, and considered one of the finest schooners on the lakes in its time. It was originally owned by F. M. Knapp and Jerome I. Case of Racine. In the eighties it carried cargoes of grain from Chicago to Buffalo and cargoes of coal from Buffalo to Chicago, 65,000 bushels of grain and 1,600 tons of coal. The crew was ten men and two boys and the sailing time was two to three weeks depending on the weather, the *J. I. Case* being one of the fastest sailing vessels on the lakes. In the early nineties she was made into a tow barge in the same fleet of barges as the *David Dows'*, and was towed behind the *Aurora* in the ore and coal trade.

A famous picture sketched in 1878 gives the story on the towing operation. Here the tug *Champion* is coming past the Fort Gratiot Light from Lake Huron into the St. Clair River, hauling behind her eight schooners: the *James F. Joy*, the *Sweetheart*, the *Emma L. Coyne*, the *Michigan*, the *Elizabeth Nicholson*, the *Wells Burt*, the *Sunnyside*, and the *Francis Palms*. The total cargo of wheat from Chicago to Buffalo in such a line of vessels was 286,000 bushels.

A photograph taken in the nineties shows the *Charles H. Bradley* towing the *Brightie*, the *Mary Woolson*, and the *Goshawk*. So the pride of the lakes was reduced to a line of barges.

The J. I. Case.   *J. I. Case Co.*

The Jessie Martin. *Dossin Great Lakes Museum*

The Charles H. Bradley *and tow.*
Captain H. C. Inches Collection

The age of the schooners was coming to an end. In 1889, the last full-rigged schooner ever built on the Lakes—the *Cora . A*—was launched at Manitowoc.

The same year saw another interesting development. Alexander McDougall had designed a unique type of vessel called the "whaleback." The first was launched in 1889 at Duluth. By 1898, 43 bulk-cargo whalebacks, some barges, 14 steamers, and one passenger vessel of this unusual design had slid off the ways at Duluth and West Superior.

Whalebacks became known on the lakes as "McDougall's Dream." No more were built after 1898, but some can still be seen today along the bustling shipping lanes.

For fifteen years, Captain Herman Schuenemann brought Christmas trees from the woods around Manistique to Chicago, and Chicagoans made a habit of going to the Clark Street Bridge to buy from him. Just a month before Christmas in 1912, he and the Rouse Simmons, *the handsome three-masted schooner shown here, set out from Manistique. The next day, the Coast Guard patrol got a glimpse of a vessel driven before a heavy snowstorm, the deck loaded with evergreens and distress signals out. A big surf boat from Kewaunee hunted for the schooner, got one look at her with her sails in tatters, and then she vanished. Next April, fishermen complained that their nets were filling with unwanted Christmas trees.*
Captain H. C. Inches Collection

"All built here, all gone"—twelve schooners built at Manitowoc, Wisconsin, and later sunk, wrecked, or otherwise "gone." In the upper right-hand corner is the launching of the historic Cora A, *the last schooner built on the lakes.*
Munson Collection

A full view of the Cora A under sail.

Manitowoc at the time when the Cora A was launched.

In the fifties a Scottish couple emigrated to Collingwood on Georgian Bay. Their sea-feverish son, Alexander McDougall, grew up to work as a deckhand to Chicago and later as a Great Lakes master, and dreamed of a new kind of ship, stripped to essentials. This whaleback freighter bears his name to honor the inventor of the type. It never became completely typical of the lakes, but it added its fantastic item of color as its blunt snout bored through the water. Here the Alexander McDougall (oddly enough, the only one of its kind without the blunt nose) passes through the Duluth Ship Canal. Fraser-Nelson Shipbuilding and Dry Dock Co., Inc.

The only passenger whaleback ever built, the Christopher Columbus, was launched in Superior, Wisconsin, in 1893, just in time to run out of Chicago during the World's Fair. Its regular run was Milwaukee to Chicago. Captain H. C. Inches Collection

Three whalebacks of the Buffalo fleet moored together.

Albertype Collection, Michigan Historical Commission

James Davison built the last wooden vessel on the Great Lakes in Bay City, Michigan, in 1898. The era of wood had given way to steel.

During this period the Great Lakes bulk freighter was developing in its own manner, characterized by superstructure fore and aft with the long flat deck in between. Designed specifically to carry ore, grain, or petroleum, these ships grew ever longer and larger.

To keep pace with the development of these ships, George H. Hulett in 1899 developed the unloader which bears his name. First used at Conneaut, Ohio, the Hulett unloader was able to take more than 5,000 tons of ore from the hold of a freighter in half an hour.

The first vessel able to carry 10,000 tons of iron ore from the mines of the Upper Superior ranges to the blast furnaces of Gary and Cleveland, Lorain and Buffalo was launched in 1904. A quarter of a century later, top capacity had grown to 15,000 tons of ore, and in 1952 it went above 20,000 tons.

The **William J. Averill,** *built at Detroit in 1884, and the* **J. C. Lockwood,** *launched at Cleveland in 1889, were among the last of the wooden bulk freighters built on the lakes. The great change to iron and steel was under way. It had begun with the* **Merchant,** *back in 1861, and by the end of that decade the navigation quarters had been put at the extreme bow and the engines aft, and in between was the constantly extending continuous hold. Between 1855 and 1905, the cost of transporting ore dropped from three dollars a ton to sixty cents.* Captain H. C. Inches Collection

Something had to be done about unloading the new freighters. The first solution was the "whirly," a scoop that could be whirled around on its crane to a waiting car or gondola. Here are three whirlies in operation at the turn of the century, unloading ore at the Pennsylvania Railroad docks at Erie, Pennsylvania. Library of Congress

But more had to be done and the hatches yawned, waiting for a more efficient unloader. As the young century started, the Hulett unloader got into operation, and several of these grasshopper-like mechanisms could be put on a single ship, each one taking 15 to 18 tons at a bite. Albertype Collection, Michigan Historical Commission

The ore was dropped into waiting freight cars which filled up, much like the old wheelbarrows, and hurried off to the stockpiles, unloaded, and came back for a refill. United States Steel Corp.

**SHIPS
OF THE
GREAT LAKES**

Today, since the opening of the St. Lawrence Seaway, waters of the Great Lakes are no longer traveled only by "the lakers," ships designed and built specifically for these great inland seas. Now the lakes are aswarm with ships from all corners of the globe, of all designs and flying all flags.

The little *Griffin* that first plied these waters would be dwarfed by modern-day vessels, and the latter are in danger of becoming mere pygmies in the years just ahead. From the University of Michigan comes word of the designing of 1,000-foot ore carriers, three times as big as any now on the Great Lakes. These would be 81,000-ton self-unloading bulk carriers, intended to carry pelletized ore from Escanaba at the upper end of Lake Michigan to the mills of the Chicago-Gary area at the southern end of the lake.

From the 45-ton *Griffin* to 81,000-ton ore carriers in less than three centuries, is indeed a huge stride in the history of ships on the Great Lakes.

Today in a few hours a ship like this U. S. Steel freighter at Conneaut, Ohio, can be emptied of 15 to 20 thousand tons and be on her way back up to her Lake Superior home port for more.

United States Steel Corp.

**SHIPS
OF THE
GREAT LAKES**

In many ports, there is no unloading equipment and there was still less of such equipment early in the century, and so one of the remarkable phenomena of the lakes developed: the self-unloader, a swinging superstructure that could lie over the deck or swing out to shore and unload the ship by itself. Here is an early self-unloader at Collingwood, Ontario, in 1907.

Albertype Collection, Michigan Historical Commission

Here in 1909 is a later and lighter self-unloader, on the Alpena of the Wyandotte Chemicals line.

Albertype Collection, Michigan Historical Commission

A reminder, and a rare picture. In Racine in the nineties there were no unloaders or self-un-loaders, no power hoists, no floating 110-ton cranes. An anonymous schooner at the Pugh State Street coal yard is laboriously unloaded with a bucket made of a halved barrel, raised and lowered by a horse harnessed to a simple rig. The bucket was emptied into wheelbarrows, visible on the narrow runway above the coal pile. It took days to unload, and more days to load, a vessel of between 400 and 500 tons.

Racine County Historical Rooms

Here is the ultimate in self-unloading, the Myron C. Taylor *of the United States Steel limestone fleet. The steady stream of limestone can disgorge the hull in a few hours. The result is that one ship like this can transport a million and a half tons of cargo in one season.*

United States Steel Corp.

The loading story is still more astounding and dumbfounding than the unloading story. Here is a view of a row of ore-loading chutes as one chute goes down and the others prepare to follow. The man on the freighter's deck below shows the comparative size. Munson Collection

Ore to feed the chutes is stored in pockets. Here is a close view of a train of freight cars on the surface of an ore dock at Two Harbors, Minnesota, a half century or so ago, as the ore is dropped direct from the cars into the numerous pockets of the dock. Library of Congress

These four Great Northern ore docks in Superior, Wisconsin, are the largest in the world. Each one is 2,250 feet long and 80.5 feet high. The approaches alone, which carry the trains up onto the docks, are as long as the docks themselves. A total of 1,352 pockets along the docks hold the ore and have a storage capacity of 442,000 gross tons.

The usual train that brings ore from the mine a hundred miles away consists of 180 cars, each carrying 75 tons—a total of about 13,500 tons. Such trains make fifteen round trips daily. The cars go up on the upper part of the dock and their bottoms open, filling the pockets on either side. From these pockets, the ore falls through large chutes into the hull of the boat. Good time for loading a large boat, which can take the full load of an average train of 180 cars, is thirty minutes. This kind of loading enabled Superior to ship 22,200,000 tons of ore in 1961.

Wisconsin Conservation Dept.

A close-up of an ore freighter in loading position, the Arthur M. Anderson of the Pittsburgh Steamship Company at the No. 1 dock, Two Harbors, Minnesota.

Poundstone Studio of Photography, Two Harbors

The Ore that Filled the Ships

It was iron that lengthened the freighters and made the big tonnage, and the story of iron goes back to 1845 when William A. Burt, a government surveyor having trouble with his compass, discovered surface ore that led to the opening of the first iron mine on Lake Superior, the Jackson mine.

The first mines went down deep on the Marquette and Gogebic Ranges, some two to three thousand feet straight down. Then at the end of the eighties the Merritt brothers and nephews, seven in all, changed history by finding the Mesabi Range, where billions of tons of high-grade ore—at first analysis it tested 64 per cent pure—lay open to the shovel and scoop.

A big X on the right-hand lower corner of the Mountain Iron picture shows where the first pit of merchantable ore was found on the Mesabi Range in Minnesota. It was dug in November, 1890, with mining captain J. A. Nichols in charge. The Merritt brothers located many ore "bodies" (as they were called) in this immediate area, and they shipped the first trainload of ore from the Mountain Iron pit on October 17, 1892. They used a small dinkey engine and three-yard capacity cars. Both can be seen in the picture.

First pit on the Mesabi Range, at Mountain Iron.   St. Louis County Historical Society, Duluth

View of the same pit taken in 1962. It was shut down in 1956 and is now filled with water.   St. Louis County Historical Society, Duluth

Miners coming up from a mine shaft in the Great Lakes area at about the time when deep mining was in full progress.

Library of Congress

SHIPS
OF THE
GREAT LAKES

Frank Hibbing.
Hibbing (Minn.) Daily Tribune

The Merritt family as it appeared in Duluth in 1871. Reading from left to right, top row: Leonidas, Lewis J., Andrus, R., Alfred, and the Reverend Lucien. Seated: Cassius Clay Merritt, Hephzibah Jewett, the mother, Lewis H., the father, Jerome, and Napoleon B. Merritt. St. Louis County Historical Society, Duluth

An early picture of open-pit mining at Hibbing, Minnesota, with a five-ton steam shovel and the little four-wheeled cars which were used for stripping. The cars were designed with slanting sides so that the ore could automatically be dropped into the pockets on the docks.

Library of Congress

The Merritts of both generations were lumber men, timber cruisers and lookers. It was hard for them to get backing for their newly discovered mines. Henry C. Frick brushed them off, and they finally started with local backing. When the eastern magnates discovered what they were missing, they moved in in a hurry, and the end result was that the Merritts were dispossessed and beaten out of their holdings. Leonidas, Cassius, Napoleon, and the rest of them—they died poor.

The climax of discovery in the Mesabi Range waited for Frank Hibbing. He was a German immigrant boy who grew up with the timber age and shifted to iron. The big Hibbing area of ore started with the digging of a well where the digging was easy, but heavy, and what came up was tinged with red. A timber-camp foreman carried the news to Captain Hibbing, who came and looked at this small fortune being hoisted up from a well hole. He believed he knew where the center of an unprecedented mountain of ore lay, and he was right. The ore around Hibbing, Minnesota, named for him, was the most spectacular ever found anywhere in the world.

Today the pits that lie open and from which hundreds of millions of tons of ore have been taken defy the imagination.

A comment on ore is the moving of the town of Hibbing itself. When it was found that it lay over the enlarging pit, the whole town was shoved a mile and a half out of the way—houses, church, and even cemetery, which was taken up by scoop shovels.

Large Mallet steam locomotive, the last of the world's largest steam locomotives used to haul ore on the same line, the Duluth and Iron Range. Poundstone Studio of Photography, Two Harbors

The "Three Spot," a wood-burner and the first locomotive to haul ore from mines north of Two Harbors, Minnesota.

Poundstone Studio of Photography, Two Harbors

A present-day view of the Hull-Rust-Mahoning Mine at Hibbing, largest open-pit mine in the world, showing operations in merely one corner. An average of sixty feet of surface material and taconite rock is stripped away to uncover the ore, then twelve-ton-capacity electric shovels load it into railroad cars or trucks. A total of well over a half billion tons of ore have come from this single mine, which covers an area of 1,600 acres. Oliver Iron Mining Company, United States Steel Corp.

The Northwest *was a steel twin-screw passenger steamer, for steel took over passengers as well as freight. The* Northwest *summed up in one career much that can happen to a ship, and more than happens to most ships. She started in 1894 on the run from Buffalo to Duluth, a sister ship to the* Northland. *Originally she had three stacks and 28 Belleville boilers. In 1901/2, the forward stack was removed and the boilers replaced by 10 Scotch boilers. In 1911, she burned at her Buffalo pier and sank. In 1918 she was raised and her hull was cut in two at Buffalo so that she could be hauled through the Welland Canal, whose locks wouldn't take her whole length. While she was being towed across Lake Ontario in two sections, the forward section sank, but the after section arrived safely in Lauzon, Quebec, had a new bow added, and was renamed the* Maplecourt. *The newly christened ship worked out of Sarnia in the wrecking business. It was rebuilt again at Montreal in 1940 for use in World War II, and was torpedoed and sunk off the West Coast of Ireland on a cold day in February of the following year.* Vermilion, Ohio, Marine Museum

That long space between fore and aft on the F. A. Bailey *is used to carry a load of a hundred automobiles.* Munson Collection

The Paul H. Carnahan, *ore-carrier for the National Steel Corporation, is now typical of the largest freighters feasible for the St. Lawrence Seaway or the Soo Canal. It is a converted T-2 seagoing tanker, 730 feet long by 75 wide, with a draft of 39 feet. It can carry 21,000 long tons of cargo.*

Dossin Great Lakes Museum, Detroit

The steamer S. T. Crapo, one of the unique Great Lakes types, is the world's first ship built to the special specifications necessary for carrying cement in bulk. It was built in 1927 at Detroit by the Great Lakes Engineering Works for the Huron Cement Company. She operates out of the company's plant at Alpena, Michigan, ferrying bulk cement to Huron's various storage facilities around the lakes. After delivery, the product is packaged at the various plants for sale and distribution. The S. T. Crapo is 392 feet long and carries 4,769 gross tons.

Canada's Silver Isle is a new maximum 730-footer built in Cobh, Ireland, especially for the Great Lakes trade. It was designed by H. C. Downer and Associates of Cleveland. All the houses are aft, including the pilot house. It uses a gigantic 10,000 horsepower M.A.N. diesel engine, the largest single diesel unit on the lakes. This enormous engine drives the world's largest controllable-pitch propeller (19 feet, 1 inch in diameter), which can be operated either from the wheelhouse or the engine room. With the Silver Isle, the Great Lakes freighter, a phenomenon of bulk transportation unparalled in marine history, reaches at least a temporary peak.

Great Lakes Racing

Mention was made in the first chapter of the beginning of Great Lakes racing (between two racing boats, one a Crolins, on a Detroit River course in 1839). Most races, like this one, have been between boats built for pleasure and speed, but the most famous and colorful race ever run on the Lakes was between two regularly scheduled passenger boats, the *Tashmoo* and the *City of Erie*.

It was worked up by bragging on the part of A. A. Parker, owner of the *Tashmoo*, who one day in the fall of 1900 let it be known via the *Detroit Free Press* that he would bet a thousand dollars that his *Tashmoo* in still water could beat the *City of Erie* or the *City of Buffalo*. T. F. Newman for the challenged steamers wrote: "The only still water in which I can conceive the *Tashmoo* would be on even terms with either vessel would be in a dry dock." This made the race inevitable.

It was scheduled for 9:30 A.M. June 4, 1901, with the *City of Erie* representing the challenged boats. The *Tashmoo* (which means "graceful" in Indian) was cleaned, repainted, and primed for the contest. The *City of Erie* made no special preparations, but finished its regular run to Cleveland the morning of the race. The course was from Cleveland a hundred miles down the south shore of Lake Erie. Millionaire businessmen signed up as deck hands on the *City of Erie*. Betting was rampant. Enormous crowds lined up all along the shore. The interest was so great that carrier pigeons were taken on board to be released at intervals to bring bulletins to the newspapers. The *Tashmoo* by lot received its choice of outer position, and the handicapped *City of Erie* in shallower water for a while fell behind. But as the water deepened, slowly it caught up and at last pushed ahead, making its best time of 22.2 miles per hour in the deepest water. When it won by a close 45 seconds, in a cloud of black smoke, the exultation of loyal backers, including its engineer who had

Finish of the Tashmoo—City of Erie *race, the* City of Erie *ahead on the right.*

Great Lakes Historical Society, Cleveland

SHIPS
OF THE
GREAT LAKES

personally put up a bet of a thousand dollars, was boundless. Seldom had there been such partisan feelings or such strong emotions over a race anywhere in recorded history.

Perhaps some of the passions of the *Tashmoo-Erie* race were revived in an annual tugboat race which was run for about ten years in the Detroit River, for this too engaged loyalties of working crews. Contesting in the International Tugboat Race for the William W. England Trophy, there was what seemed like a dead heat in the 1960 race with, left to right: the *Oregon* of the Great Lakes Towing Company, the *John Roen III* of the Roen Steamship Company (a several-time winner), and the *Mark Twain* of the LaSalle Oil and Coal Company.

International Tugboat Race, 1960.
Dossin Great Lakes Museum, Detroit

Burt Smalley's Robin.
Robert E. Mann, Chicago

The annual Inter-Lake Yachting Association Regatta, held at Put-in-Bay (the Bass Islands), Ohio, is the most important sporting event on the Great Lakes in the opinion of many, and is certainly the largest. Yacht racing at Put-in-Bay goes back to 1872, when four South Bass Islanders headed by John Doller decided to hold a race to try out their yacht, the *Phantom,* against competition. They lost to the *Coral* of Toledo, but later won so many races that the *Phantom* was asked to eliminate herself.

The first regatta after the organization of the Inter-Lake Yachting Association was held in 1885, following a preliminary regatta at Lake St. Clair. In 1894, Inter-Lake was reorganized and since 1895 the regattas have been held continuously at Put-in-Bay except for two years, at Toledo in 1909 and Erie in 1920.

In 1908, Lee de Forest, inventor of the vacuum tube and a resident of Toledo, broadcast the race results by radio to a receiving station at Monroe, Michigan, from Commodore William R. Huntington's yacht *Thelma.* This was the first time in history that the radio was used to broadcast a sporting event. The success of the venture got De Forest a contract to install radio in naval vessels.

Inter-Lake Yachting Association has grown to 88 member clubs and 23,100 members. The regattas are the climax of the Put-in-Bay summers. All along the shore, contestants are picnicking, drying sails, talking up a breeze. Local homes are opened to regatta-week transients. The boat taxis are in service night and day and calls for help echo across the water. Privacy vanishes. Friendliness reigns over docks and bay. When the regatta is finished, the balance of the summer season seems to have lost its meaning.

The 333-mile Chicago-Mackinac race is the world's longest fresh-water sailing classic, the ranking U.S. yachting event sponsored by the Chicago Yacht Club. It annually now attracts over a hundred entries. Its course from Chicago up to the Straits of Mackinac extends nearly the length of Lake Michigan and often, as in 1963 the going is rough.

The Mackinac race originally was born of bragging, which seems a good way generally to get races going. For a couple of winters in the late nineties, skippers of the Chicago Yacht Club got talking about their fast passage, and in August, 1898, two sloops and three schooners set out to see who could make the best time to Mackinac Island. The *Vanenna* won in 51 hours.

That started it. The great years were the early 1900's when 80- and 100-foot topsail schooners competed and set records. Big Bill Thompson, later mayor of Chicago, won three times in succession, setting the record time of 31:24:06 the third time out with the schooner *Valmore.*

The sister race is the younger 235-mile Port Huron-Mackinac run up Lake Huron, started in 1925 by Detroit's Bayview Yacht Club. The 1963 winner of this race was the *Robin,* owned by Mr. Burt Smalley and sailed by his son Jim, which took all honors.

SHIPS
OF THE
GREAT LAKES

The winner of the 1963 Chicago-Mackinac race was the Schoendorf brothers' *Blitzen* with an elapsed time of 43:22:22 and a corrected time of 40:44:08.

In the public mind, the world's greatest speedboat race is the Harmsworth Trophy. It is at any rate factually the world's oldest unlimited powerboat race. It is a race between countries, not between individuals or their private clubs.

The Miss Bardahl *is fourth from the left in this picture of heat 1-B.*

Detroit News

It was first run in 1903 in Ireland. France won it. The United States won it first in 1907 and was undefeated till 1912. Gar Wood won it back for the United States in 1920. Canada captured it with *Miss Supertest III* in 1959 and defended successfully in 1960 and 1961. An effort is being made to set up a United States challenge for 1964.

The Gold Cup Race was started in the East in 1904 and is a powerboat race between individuals or their private clubs. Seattle has come on strong in the race since 1950, but so far has defended only 7 times and challenged only twice, while Detroit has been its defender 15 times and its challenger 21 times. The 1963 race was held in the Detroit River and Ron Musson, in winning with the *Miss Bardahl,* set a lap record for the three-mile course of 114.650 miles an hour and also a new race record with an average of 105.242 miles per hour. An estimated 300,000 persons watched the race.

Veteran Harmsworth Trophy racer Gar Wood congratulates Ron Musson. Detroit News

The younger generation talks over ice-boat racing on Reed's Lake near Grand Rapids.

Grand Rapids Chamber of Commerce

Map of the courses for the 1963 regatta of the Inter-Lake Yachting Association at Put-in-Bay, Ohio.

Inter-Lake Yachting Association, Dearborn, Mich.

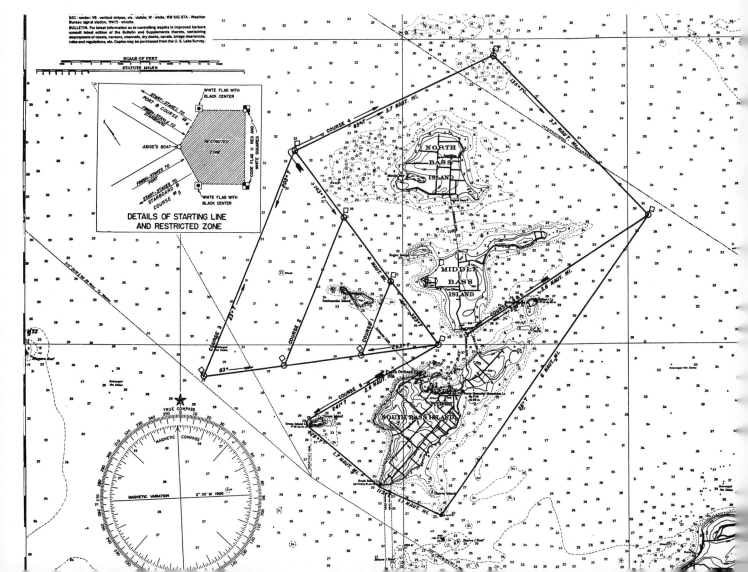

Chapter 5

Wind, Fire, Ice, Collision

SAILORS the world over fear storms, fog, collision, and fire. Great Lakes sailors are no exception. With good reason they fear the November storms with their high winds and ice, which have brought death to more lakes sailors than any other agent.

Shipping losses in the Great Lakes since the *Griffin* disappeared have been great. According to one authority, of the 199 steamships on the lakes between 1818 and 1853, 14 burned, 4 exploded, and 36 were wrecked, a total loss of over 27 per cent. The record of sailing ships probably showed even greater casualties. In 1855, 118 lives were lost; in 1856, 407 were lost. In 1869, 97 ships were lost in a four-day hurricane. In the twenty years from 1878 to 1898, 5,999 vessels were wrecked on the Great Lakes, and of that number 1,093 were total losses of ships and cargo. The losses of men emphasize to the sailor and to his relatives how dangerous his trade is.

The Great Storm of 1913, which lasted from Friday, November 7, until Wednesday, November 12, is most accurately named. In the six-day storm, the greatest recorded in the history of inland navigation, 19 vessels were totally destroyed; 20 were stranded. Of those destroyed, 10 were lost in Lake Huron, 3 in Lake Michigan, one in Lake Erie, and 5 in Lake Superior. Of those stranded, 6 were in Lake Huron, 3 in Lake Erie, 5 in Lake Superior, one in Georgian Bay, one in St. Marys River, one at Simmon's Reef, Straits of Mackinac, one in the Livingstone Channel of the Detroit River, and two in Lake St. Clair.

The value of vessels and cargo lost combined was $10,381,000. Of the total, $5,199,000 was lost on Lake Huron.

*These views of the two-masted schooner, the Jamaica, outbound
and wrecked, from the Captain H. Chesley Inches collection,
dramatize the sudden changes of Great Lakes weather.*

Captain H. C. Inches Collection

*The steamer Algoma was one of the handsome new nearly 400-foot-long ships which the Canadian
Pacific put on the Great Lakes in the early 1880's to upgrade the passenger service from Georgian
Bay to the lakehead cities. This photograph was taken November 7, 1885, after the Algoma was
wrecked in a blizzard off Greenstone Island in Lake Superior.*   *Ontario Archives, Toronto*

A small boat rescues the crew of the schooner Len Higby, *foundered off Frankfort, Michigan, in a late October storm in 1898.*   *Munson Collection, Michigan Historical Commission*

The Hudson *of the Western Line foundered with all hands off Eagle River at Keweenaw Point, Lake Superior, in September, 1901.*   *Munson Collection*

WIND

FIRE

ICE

COLLISION

At Ludington, Michigan, the Pere Marquette 3 *in the early morning hours of January 17, 1902, went hard aground on the sandbar north of its pier and about 600 feet from shore. Coming in, the rudder had failed and Captain Dority reversed engines to avoid hitting the pier, but the ship ran onto the bar. A mortar shot a line to the steamer and, as the day dawned, a breeches buoy was rigged and began the rescue of nine passengers, including three women, and all the members of the crew. The boat rolled, dipping the rescued below the surface of the icy water, making the operation particularly hazardous. One woman had just made it to the pier when the hawser broke and a new one had to be rigged up, but eventually all were saved. A man is here shown making the dangerous trip to shore.*

Only three weeks before, the Pere Marquette 16 *had gone aground on the same bar, with one man lost.*

Great Lakes Historical Society, Cleveland, and Thomas B. Dancey

In the Great Storm of November, 1913, eight vessels totally disappeared with all hands lost. In the first picture, upper row, the Charles S. Price *and the* Regina; *lower row, the* Wexford *and the* H.B. Smith.

Marine Review, Dec., 1913

Two hundred and forty-eight lives were lost; tonnage lost was 220,486. Eight of the ships wholly disappeared with all on board. It is not known what happened to them except that one, the *Charles S. Price,* turned turtle and remained that way for several days before she sank. The ships that were destroyed were built mainly in American shipyards. Two were built in British shipyards.

The consensus among the owners of the vessels and among the masters who survived is that the vessels were gradually pounded into the trough of the great waves. There they rolled, were gradually shaken apart, and foundered.

The *Marine Review* for December, 1913, commented on the storm as follows:

"It must be borne in mind that the situation which existed on Lake Huron was unprecedented. Since the lakes have been commercially navigated, no such condition has ever been met with before and centuries may go by before such a phenomenon may again be experienced.

"When all these vessels entered Lake Huron, there was nothing to indicate that the passage of the lake could not be made in reasonable safety. The barometer was unusually low, but aside from that, the weather conditions were not unusual for the time of the year. A northwest gale had been blowing on Lake Superior since early Saturday morning, November 8, and vessels were generally governed by it. On Sunday morning, November 9, this gale died down with only a 15-mile breeze blowing from the northwest across Lake Huron. Even with a low barometer there would be nothing in such a condition to prevent a prudent master from undertaking the passage of Lake Huron. Even a stiff breeze from the north-

In the second picture, upper row, the **Hydrus** *and the* **Argus**; *lower row, the* **John A. McGeau** *and the* **Isaac M. Scott**.   *Marine Review, Dec., 1913*

west is not a dangerous thing on the course that vessels take in crossing this lake, as they are under the lee of the land. As the morning progressed, however, the wind increased, shifting to the north and northeast until by noon it was blowing from the northeast with great velocity. The obvious thing for an upbound ship to do would be to head into it, in the hope of reaching the shelter of the east shore, and that is probably what they all did. They were probably defeated in doing so by the continued and unprecedented violence of the elements. As a rule, wind of that velocity does not last over four or five hours, but the wind of Sunday, November 9, blew steadily for nearly 16 hours at an average velocity of 60 miles an hour with frequent spurts reaching a maximum of 79 miles an hour, making tremendous seas, which followed each other in quick succession, usually three waves coming along one right after the other, and the battering that the ships received from these quick successive blows must have been terrific. The vessels that ran with it had their after-quarters crushed and their engine rooms filled with water from the following sea; vessels that headed into it had their forward quarters smashed, and in one instance at least, with consequent derangement of the steering gear."

The *Marine Review* then mentions the *Howard M. Hanna, Jr.* Nothing makes the storm so immediate as Captain Hagen's account of the struggle his ship made to survive.

"We left Lorain, bound for Fort William, Ont., on Saturday, November 8, 1913, at about ten o'clock A.M., loaded with 9,120 tons of soft coal, and with a full complement of officers and crew, 25 men, including myself. . . . On leaving, the vessel was in ideal trim for encountering heavy weather. The cargo had been loaded so that it was up flush with the hatch coamings, with the exception of 6, 7, and 9, and the way the cargo had been loaded, there was no chance of cargo shifting. The hatches had been battened down. . . . Everything mov-

The **Charles S. Price** *photographed as it lay bottom side up before it sank in the November, 1913, storm.*
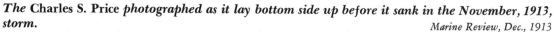
Marine Review, Dec., 1913

able had proper lashings and the vessel was as staunch and seaworthy as possible. . . . We passed Fort Gratiot lightship at 5:12 A.M., of Nov. 9. The weather continued fair and clear until after passing Harbor Beach, but had shifted, first S.E. for a few minutes, then N.E., then N.N.E., and then continued about that direction with increasing velocity. At three o'clock it began to snow. . . .

"As the wind increased, we had hauled more to the northward to hold her head to the wind.

"Between 7 and 8 P.M., with it snowing so we couldn't see the land and could not tell just where we were and could not tell just how fast we were going, but we were possibly 15 miles above Point Aux Barques. The wind and sea had increased so that the vessel began dropping off her course, although the engines were being worked at full speed ahead. Tremendous seas were coming over our bow and our starboard quarter and over the whole vessel in fact, and the seas had carried away part of our after cabin and had broken in our pilot house window and had torn off the top of the pilot house.

"Then shortly after 8 o'clock she dropped off so that she came around into the trough of the sea. We had been taking seas over us right along and had been using our siphons and pumps. After she got into the trough of the sea, she commenced to roll and tumble and the seas were washing over her, and on account of throwing her propeller wheel out of the water and losing her headway, it became impossible for us to bring her back so as to head into the sea. . . .

"Shortly before 10 o'clock we could see Port Austin light and as we saw that we were pretty close to Port Austin reef, I ordered the first mate to drop our anchors to try to bring her head to the wind. She didn't come up only about a point and in a very short time, about 10 o'clock P.M., she drifted broadside onto Port Austin reef, and as she lay on the rocks, she was headed N.W. x W., and the light was bearing S.W. The port side fetched up on the rocks first and the seas and wind pounded her until the vessel went up onto the reef, leaving a list to starboard of about a foot, and in a very short time she filled with water. The water was right up to the deck and the hatches were all washed off.

**WIND
FIRE
ICE
COLLISION**

The **Howard M. Hanna Jr.,** *before the November, 1913, storm.*
Marine Review, Dec., 1913

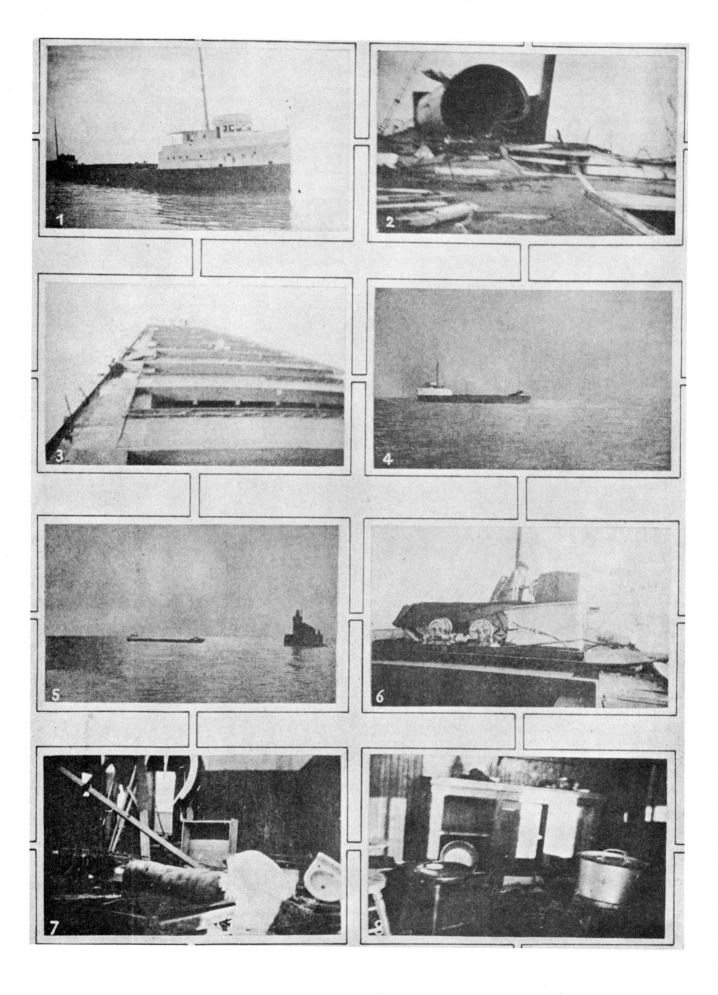

This series of photos of the total destruction of the Howard M. Hanna, Jr. *shows (1) the freighter on the Port Austin reef, the after-structure already largely gone, (2 close-up of the demolished after-quarters, (3) all the hatches stripped, (4) the* Hanna *on the rocks, (5) the* Hanna *stuck about 900 feet off the Port Austin Light, (6) view of the cabins aft, (7) the owner's room, (8) the galley.*   Marine Review, Dec., 1913

"After we went on, the forward crew all came up into the texas to get shelter and remained there until about 2 P.M. the afternoon of the 10th. The after crew all remained aft in the mess room and kitchen, and we had no communication with the other end of the boat until Monday forenoon, when the weather moderated somewhat and the third engineer worked his way forward with food. In the afternoon, the forward crew were able to get aft and we remained there with the after crew until Tuesday morning, Nov. 11. After daylight, the mate went up on the after cabin with some of the crew and they cleared the ice and water out of the port lifeboat, and at about 7:30 they got the lifeboat lowered and started for shore to procure assistance for the rest of the crew. They got ashore and landed on the beach near Port Austin. By the time our lifeboat got ashore the life saving crew started out and got to our boat about 10 o'clock.

"When we left, the vessel was broken in two about the after side of No. 7 hatch; you could see the crack across the deck and down the side. The smokestack was gone; also the life rafts and the starboard lifeboat had been washed away. . . . The houses forward were all stove in, the windows and doors knocked off, the top of the pilot house gone, the bulwarks forward were all driven in, and, in my opinion, the vessel is a total loss."

In the same storm, the steamer *J. H. Sheadle* was saved by brilliant navigation. Starting from the upper end of Lake Huron, she was going with the wind which whipped up 35-foot waves that followed each other in rapid succession and with terrifying impact. The

The J. H. Sheadle, *which survived the great storm.*   *Great Lakes Historical Society, Cleveland*

first wave that hit washed the supper off the table, piling up and smashing the dishes. Water poured into the engine room through the skylights, but the engines were kept going. Captain Lyons used the lead constantly and found his way by these soundings. When he knew he was well off to the west shore, at ten o'clock the night of the 9th, he increased the speed of the ship to enable him to bring her around head to. The vessel steamed back into the throat of the storm. It took six and a half hours to make back the distance they had gone in two hours with the wind. Early on the morning of the 10th, he turned the ship again, and as he held the handles of the steering wheel, he was lifted horizontally into the air. After this turn was made, they were able to go with the wind until the sea went down.

This was the worst storm, but the rages of the wind persist, and even with present-day lights, buoys, and improved weather warnings and communications, the toll of disaster continues.

The steamer Leafield, *built at Newcastle, struck rocks on Angus Island and foundered in deep water with all on board.* Marine Review, Dec., 1913

The steamer James Carruthers, *which foundered in Lake Huron in the great 1913 storm.* Marine Review, Dec., 1913

At Marine City, Michigan, the big whaleback steamer Atikoken *was thrown up on the shore just three months prior to the great storm.*   Munson Collection, Michigan Historical Commission

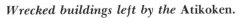*Wrecked buildings left by the* Atikoken.   Munson Collection

The Seiche

The lakes have something approximating a tidal wave, a phenomenon called a *seiche,* pronounced *saysh.* A seiche can raise the lake level at the shore front by six to eight feet. This sudden rise of water takes place when a very long flat wave moves against the shoreline and piles up water because of its momentum. The wave is formed by the pressure surge associated with a line of thunderstorms.

In the summer of 1963, such a seiche caused a rise of more than six feet in the level of Lake Michigan at Waukegan, Illinois, and a rise of two to six feet along the Chicago lake front. Police closed the outer drive to traffic and ordered everybody off the lake front during the danger period. The north branch of the Chicago River rose about eight feet.

A rare and dramatic picture of a seiche was taken at Grand Island, Munising, Michigan, on August 19, 1921. The first picture shows a pier and some of the lake shore at 11:30 that morning, and the second picture shows the same scene at 11:50 on that same morning, twenty minutes later.

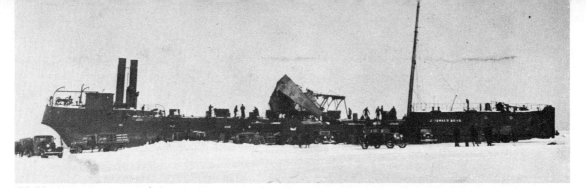

The gasoline tanker J. Oswald Boyd *was wrecked on Simmons Reèf, Straits of Mackinac, in December, 1936, with a million gallons of gasoline aboard. Far from fearing an explosion, automobiles and trucks drove out over the ice to "fill her up."* Munson Collection, Michigan Historical Commission

WIND
FIRE
ICE
COLLISION

On November 18, 1958, the *Carl D. Bradley,* a 623-foot limestone carrier with 35 men aboard, broke in two and sank twelve miles west-southwest of Gull Island in northern Lake Michigan, seventy miles southwest of the Straits of Mackinac.

Ships that tried to reach the disaster area fought winds of 50 to 65 miles an hour and waves 20 to 25 feet. Temperatures were in the thirties.

The *Carl D. Bradley* had a capacity of 14,800 gross tons and was sailing empty from Buffington, Indiana, near Gary, to her home port, Rogers City, on Lake Huron.

Two men survived the disaster. First mate Elmer Fleming and Frank Mays, a deckman, clung to an 8-by-4-foot life raft for fourteen hours, until a Coast Guard vessel rescued them. Two other men who had joined them on the raft perished during the night. Both survivors were washed overboard frequently, but managed to struggle back onto the raft. The wind and high seas had carried them twenty miles from the sunken vessel by the time they were rescued.

The *Bradley* was a self-unloading carrier. After a stern section of the boat broke off and sank, her boiler exploded. Captain Roland Bryan shouted, "May Day," the distress cry of the sea, into the ship's radio as she perished.

A former captain of the *Bradley,* Forrest F. Pearse, believed metal fatigue and a tidal wave caused her to break apart. He said, "On the Great Lakes there are certain small areas during a storm that have a lower barometric pressure than the surrounding area.

Proudly the steamer Carl D. Bradley, *then the largest on the lakes, went through the MacArthur Lock at its dedication on July 11, 1943. Fifteen years later it broke in half and sank in northern Lake Michigan, not far from the Soo.* Munson Collection

A full-length view of the Bradley, *self-unloader and pride of the limestone fleet.*
Munson Collection

"Because of the differences, a few waves often build up to twice the height of other waves.

"Usually there are two or three such giant waves in succession. We were told that waves out there were 25 or 30 feet high. The tidal waves might have been from 45 to 60 feet high.

"The ship might have been caught on two of these waves, with the bow and the stern high on the waves and the midship just hanging in air. That could have caused the break up.

"I've experienced those tidal waves many times in the fall. They are just there. There's nothing to be done about them. You just have to weather them."

Rogers City received the news of the tragedy much as a mining town receives word that there has been a mine explosion. The twenty-three crewmen who lost their lives left forty-eight children fatherless.

A text on this contemporary lithograph of the "Burning of the Steam-Boat Erie," after describing the breaking out of the fire, continued:

"The Steam-Boat Dewitt Clinton *had just left Dunkirk on her upward course when, discovering the flames of* The Erie, *hastened to her relief. She came up about 11 o'clock, and picked up 27 persons—some hanging to her wheels and braces, others floating on the small boats, boxes, wood, etc. Two others were picked up by a small boat from shore."*

The American dead were listed and, "Besides, 120 Swiss passengers, shipped by Messrs. Parsons & Co. Buffalo, emigrating west."

Second only to storm is the threat of fire. A horrible disaster involving fire happened to the *Erie* in the summer of 1841. She was bound for Chicago out of Buffalo with two hundred passengers and a crew of thirty. One hundred and forty people aboard were Swiss and German immigrants. Six of the passengers were painters on their way to Erie to paint the S.S. *Madison*. The painters placed their demijohns of turpentine and varnish on the boiler deck immediately above the boilers. At eight o'clock in the evening, when the ship was eight miles off Silver Creek, the first demijohn exploded. In no time flaming turpentine and varnish set fire to the whole ship. All but twenty-nine aboard were burned to death or were drowned.

A major disaster took place November 21, 1847, when the *Phoenix* burned completely in Lake Michigan, six miles off Sheboygan. The *Phoenix* was a wood-hull, propeller-driven steamboat that carried passengers and freight. Built in 1845 at Cleveland, she was a 302-ton vessel, 155 feet long, and was one of the first twin-screw steamers on the lakes.

The *Phoenix* left Buffalo on November 11, 1847, with three hundred passengers aboard, one-third Americans and two-thirds Norwegian immigrants. After she left Mackinac on November 17, rough weather caused the steamer to put in successively at the Beaver Islands and at Manitowoc. From November 13 to the time of the disaster, the ship was in charge of the mate, Captain Sweet having suffered a serious fall with injury to his left knee that kept him immobile in his cabin.

Although no official explanation of the cause of fire was ever recorded, the consensus was that the boilers ran dry, became red hot, and ignited the woodwork about them. There

An old print of the burning of the Phoenix, *from Lloyd's* Steamboat Directory.
James T. Lloyd & Company, 1856

Ship arriving in port heavily loaded with ice.   *Munson Collection*

were only two lifeboats, with room for forty passengers. The two boats made it to shore with forty-three passengers, the captain being one of them. Three other men including the engineer, a clerk, and one passenger were picked out of the water by a boat from the steamer *Delaware* which put out from Sheboygan to lend aid. All the rest were lost.

November brings with it not only high winds but the possibility of sudden frost and ice. When a ship passes through a fog frost it is coated with ice so thick that hundreds of tons are added to its weight. In storm, some ships have been known to go down from the overload of ice.

A quick freeze can hold one ship or hundreds imprisoned for a few days or a whole winter. The water in Lakes Michigan and Superior will freeze to a depth of forty feet and more in a severe winter.

*Ice near Detroit, Michigan,
typical of the yearly freeze.*
Detroit Edison Company

The steamer Benson Ford *went aground in West Neebish Channel in 1949 and stopped down-bound traffic at Sault Ste. Marie. The blocked fleet of freighters dropped anchor.*
Materna Studio, Sault Ste. Marie, Mich.

The winter surface of Lake Superior gives some idea why the Great Lakes are closed to traffic an average of four months of the year.
Michigan Tourist Council, Lansing

Ice-breakers (first called "ice crushers") built to free freighters from early-winter or early-spring ice were first announced to the lakes by the Al-gomah when she went down the ways at Detroit in 1881. A young mechanic named Henry Ford helped build her strong engines.
Munson Collection, Michigan Historical Commission

In 1927, in early December, 98 ships loaded with ore and grain reached the Sault on their last voyage down; 149 upbound ships met there on their way to Lake Superior. A sudden freeze gripped the area and the ice froze so thick that automobiles drove out to bring supplies to the ships. There were 5000 sailors stranded on the 247 ships.

Winter usually finds the ships tied up one against another, securely anchored. They are often tied in groups of thirty or more in the various harbors from Duluth-Superior to Detroit and Buffalo.

The greatest tragedy involving a single ship that has occurred in the region of the Great Lakes happened in the narrow channel of the Chicago River at the Clark Street Bridge dock on July 24, 1915. The steamer *Eastland* was tied at the dock to receive 2500 employees of the

**WIND
FIRE
ICE
COLLISION**

At Manitowoc, an old picture of skating on the canal alongside the ships, icebound for the winter.
Munson Collection

Typical winter scene at Sault Ste. Marie, Michigan.
Munson Collection

Twenty-six freighters frozen in for the winter. In a bad winter, in 1926, ice remained in Buffalo harbor till May 25.   *Munson Collection*

Western Electric Company who were taking a holiday excursion across Lake Michigan. The *Eastland* was a 1900-ton three-decked ship that had been in service for ten years. The passengers crowded aboard at 7:00 A.M. The ship immediately began to list and swayed first toward the dock, righted when the seacocks were opened to trim the ship, then listed and swayed dangerously toward the river. There was consternation among the passengers who lost their balance and were thrown against one another and the sides of the vessel. Panic seized them as the captain tried to steer the ship into the river channel. People began to jump overboard. At 7:30 the *Eastland* turned over, her starboard side turned topside above the water. People were trapped below decks in their cabins. Eight hundred and fifteen people died.

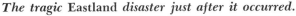

The tragic Eastland *disaster just after it occurred.*   *Munson Collection*

Later photograph of the Eastland *before raising.* *Munson Collection*

The Eastland *after raising.* *Munson Collection*

The freakish action of the *Eastland* was never officially explained. She was converted to a naval training ship and renamed *Wilmette*.

Collisions (like other serious disasters) often take place not on the stormy sea or in the grip of wind and weather or when ships are proceeding under full power. They occur between ships when they are cautiously or incautiously moving away from a dock into a ship channel. The night of July 30, 1962, the British freighter *Montrose* sank in the Detroit River under the Ambassador Bridge after colliding with a cement barge. She was salvaged and put back in operation.

WIND
FIRE
ICE
COLLISION

The **Montrose** *being righted preparatory to being towed to a* **Toledo** *dry dock for examination of her hull.* Detroit Free Press

Ships survive terrible disasters; they are patched and sometimes rebuilt to continue their usefulness. The steamer *Henry Cort* and the *Ann Arbor, No. 4,* a car ferry, are examples.

The steamer *Henry Cort* was built at Superior, Wisconsin, in 1892. She was one of Alexander McDougall's patented whalebacks, and was originally christened the *Pillsbury,* but the name was later changed. In December, 1917, she was sunk at the mouth of the Detroit River in a collision with the steamer *Midvale.* She was completely frozen in and when spring came she was carried out with the ice into Lake Erie. When the ice melted she dropped to the bottom where a diver found her. She was raised and repaired. She sank again in Detroit at her dock in December, 1933, when ice had cut her open on the last trip of the season. She was repaired but struck the Muskegon breakwater in a December storm in 1934. After standing at Muskegon and breaking apart, she was cut up by acetylene torches and sold for scrap.

The whaleback steamer Henry Cort *stranded at Muskegon. A member of her crew is being saved by a lifeline strung from the ship to the Muskegon breakwater.*   *Munson Collection*

The *Ann Arbor, No. 4,* a railroad-car ferry running between Menominee and Frankfort across Lake Michigan, had a long history of disaster. She had twice run ashore near Kewaunee, Wisconsin, and once near Manitowoc. She had capsized in Manistique Harbor in 1909. On the night of February 4, 1923, she ran into an 80-mile-an-hour snowstorm, and coal cars on both sides of the ship broke loose and threatened to wreck her. Still she managed to reach Frankfort piers before she sank, and all the crew were saved. She froze in, but the following spring she thawed and was salvaged.

Car ferry Ann Arbor No. 4 rolled over in Manistique, Michigan, in 1909, when heavy iron-ore trainways were run aboard her on the port side. *Munson Collection*

A view between decks of the Ann Arbor No. 4 in the February, 1923, disaster. *Munson Collection*

Another view between decks as the winter ice moved in.
Munson Collection

Exterior view of the Ann Arbor No. 4 as she rested on her bottom at the Frankfort, Michigan, pier, in the winter of 1923.

Munson Collection

View across the frozen deck taken at the same time.

Munson Collection

The Ann Arbor No. 4 after she thawed out the following spring.

Munson Collection

The Cities

Chapter 6

From the Founding to the Present Day

Cities are people, and each place where people live manages from its situation and its ways of working (and playing too) to become distinctive. The Great Lakes has an extraordinary variety of towns and cities, of language and continuing national groups, of traditions, legends, and memories. It lives in peace, the whole area works together, and there are associations of ports and cities that symbolize this friendship. It draws from the past. It looks to the future. Its communities are a notable sign of what a climate of freedom and common interest can achieve.

The communities along the Canadian shoreline are listed below as one would meet them entering the country by the St. Lawrence Seaway.

On the St. Lawrence River

QUEBEC, in the province of Quebec, is on the north bank of the river above the Island of Orleans, 180 miles below Montreal. It has an excellent harbor and is a port of entry for Atlantic steamers. The early settlers

General view of the city of Quebec, on its rocky promontory overlooking the St. Lawrence.

Hunting Survey Corp. Ltd., Toronto

In 1830, R. A. Sproule painted this monochrome watercolor of the marketplace in Upper Town, Quebec. In those days meat was hung in the open and the customer indicated what cut he would like. Behind the market is the old Jesuit church begun in 1666 and given a new facade in 1730. Like so many Quebec buildings, it was considerably damaged during the siege, and was completely rebuilt in 1807 except for the south tower. The Anglican Cathedral spire appears over the housetops at the right.

In 1860, the Prince of Wales (later Edward VII) crossed the Atlantic to make the first royal state tour of Canada. There were no photographers. Instead, the Illustrated London News sent an artist, G. H. Andrews, and while he sketched the approach to Quebec, a Canadian named C. Williams sat beside him and also sketched. They did almost identical views. The one shown is by the Canadian, a lively watercolor of the historic event. The British man-of-war Hero carried the Prince, escorted by the Ariadne and the Flying Fish. "The Gibraltar of America," Quebec's rock, crowded with spectators, loomed over the scene. Flags fluttered everywhere. The Citadel, Durham Terrace, and the Grand Battery fired salutes from guns some of which had not been shot in thirty or forty years. *National Gallery of Canada, Ottawa*

James Pattison Cockburn, a career army officer who also painted, was posted to Canada about 1823 and stayed there thirteen years. This is a watercolor sketch he made of the Mickmac Indians at Point Levis, Quebec. Their wigwams and canoes were both covered with white birchbark. The main body of the tribe lived mostly in Nova Scotia and New Brunswick; a writer of that time mentioned that their cheekbones were "high and set wide apart."   National Gallery of Canada, Ottawa

named it from an Indian term, *kebec,* meaning "the river narrows here." The river narrows at "the rock" and widens to its ever-busy wharves. "The rock" made itself famous (or infamous) when the British scaled it in 1759 to defeat the French and end their colonial power in Canada. But modern Quebec with a population of 171,979 is still 90 per cent French. Its streets resemble those of provincial France and are as narrow.

One, Sous-le-Cap, is reputed to be the narrowest on the continent. The Citadel, Laval University, provincial government buildings, the Chateau Frontenac, churches and cathedrals—the Church of Notre Dame des Victoires—give the city of Quebec a handsome and timeless look within its old walls. It exports cattle, timber, and grain from docks that smell of the tidal sea.

J. Crawford Young, a British army officer stationed in Quebec in the Citadel garrison during the 1820's and 1830's, used his free time to paint. He liked to do watercolor sketches of scenes in and around the city, and particularly to paint Indians. This excellent example of his work shows an Indian family, probably in the village of Lorette. The wife, with a papoose and two other children, is saying good-by to her husband before setting off for the white settlements to sell her baskets and brooms to the local Europeans.   National Gallery of Canada, Ottawa

Smelt fishing on the Quai de la Traverse, Quebec. Children as well as men are fond of the pastime—in fact, few persons in the villages near the river have not, at one time or another, had the experience of fishing for smelt (l'éperlan) in the cool autumn weather. Office Provincial de Publicité, Quebec

Sous-le-cap Street, in Quebec, in 1901.
Library of Congress

Looking up at Quebec from the deck of a St. Lawrence cruise ship. The majestic Chateau Frontenac towers above the massive wall that was part of the early fortifications.
Canadian Government Travel Bureau Photo

A typical old section of Quebec, seen against a background of modern grain elevators. The large building in the foreground is the Post Office. Behind it, to the left, is the oldest part of Laval University, including Quebec Seminary. In the center background is the Archbishop's Palace.

Provincial Publicity Bureau, Quebec

The remains of the old Citadel at the top of the rock in Quebec. The walls are surrounded by a dry moat. In the foreground is a Cross of Sacrifice honoring the war dead. The beginnings of the Plains of Abraham can be seen at the right. *Office Provincial de Publicité, Quebec*

Montreal, Canada's largest city, is a business and banking center as well as an important port for both inland and ocean-going shipping. Its name comes from Mount Royal, the hill in the center of the city.

Canadian Government Travel Bureau Photo

MONTREAL, Quebec, occupies an increasing part of Montreal Island, where the Ottawa River meets the St. Lawrence. It takes its name from Mount Royal, the hill which was named by discoverer Jacques Cartier—a sizable eminence (753 feet high) now in the center of the city and of a large park. Montreal is the largest city in Canada and the world's largest inland seaport —although a thousand miles from the sea. In its early days, it was the site where Champlain, near his friends, the Hurons, dreamed of exploration and set out for Lake Huron. It seemed predestined to commercial growth. Today, Montreal ships a third of Canada's entire output, exporting a large list of products from flour and cheese to furs (on which its original pros-

One of the newest additions to Montreal's rising skyline is the cruciform Royal Bank of Canada Building, at the left in this picture. At the right is the Marie-Reine-du-Monde Cathedral, a half-size replica of St. Peter's in Rome. Between them stands the Queen Elizabeth Hotel. The three buildings are typical of the contrasting architecture in downtown Montreal.

Canadian Government Travel Bureau Photo

THE QUEEN ELIZABETH

Dominating this 1829 painting of the Place d'Armes in Montreal by R. A. Sproule is one of the oldest churches in Canada, La Paroisse ("the Parish Church"), built by the Sulpician Fathers in 1672, which follows the lines of Saint-Sulpice in Paris. Behind it is the "new" Notre-Dame, which was opened for use just as this picture was being painted; its towers were still unfinished. A street-corner playbill in the right foreground advertises a play starring Clara Fisher (Madden), an actress who was the talk of Montreal at the time. National Gallery of Canada, Ottawa

R. A. Sproule's painting of Notre-Dame Street in Montreal, around 1829. Nelson's column was long a familiar landmark. It was erected in 1809 by joint French and English efforts, with some heavy contributions from Scottish merchants. The chain at the base is supported by cannon to which, it is said, offenders were sometimes tied and publicly whipped. The "New Market" in Jacques Cartier Square is still held at the same location. To the right of the column, on the corner, is a building put up in 1720, which was at one time James McGill's town house. At the end of Notre-Dame Street can be seen the old Parish Church and the uncompleted towers of Notre-Dame Church that were the subjects of Mr. Sproule's painting of the Place d'Armes.

Montreal's Place d'Armes and the Notre Dame Church.
National Film Board, Ottawa

Notre Dame de Bonsecours, in Montreal.
Office Provincial de Publicité, Quebec

A circa-1870 view of Montreal from the height of Mount Royal.　*Ontario Archives, Toronto*

Night view of the Montreal skyline.

National Film Board, Ottawa

perity was based). It is the gateway to the St. Lawrence Seaway. All Canadian transportation funnels into the city and both of Canada's transcontinental railways have their headquarters there. Though busy, the city keeps much of its old charm—from Mount Royal it looks like a mosaic of church spires and chimney pots, old gray stone buildings and modern skyscrapers. The Catholic Cathedral of St. James is a smaller replica of St. Peter's Basilica in Rome. Montreal is a great center of education. Just below Mount Royal is Mc-Gill University, on whose shady grounds cricket is often played, and on the other side of the hill are the ultra-modern buildings of Montreal University, a vital focus of French culture. The population of this cosmopolitan city is 1,191,062, of which 60 percent is French.

Kingston on Kingsriver, Ontario, probably in 1850. In the foreground a company of troops marches at Fort Henry. Across Haldimand Cove Fort Frederick can be seen, with its long barracks and high walls. The bridge across the Cataraqui River was constructed in the late 1820's. The large building in the background, on the heights above the river, is probably the Roman Catholic Cathedral of St. Mary, not begun until 1844 and still unfinished when this view was made.

I. N. Phelps Stokes Collection of American Historical Prints, New York Public Library

On Lake Ontario

KINGSTON, Ontario, near the head of the St. Lawrence River, is not only an important lake port, but its nearness to the Thousand Islands and the Rideau Lakes district makes it a popular holiday center. It has one of the best harbors on Lake Ontario, is an outlet for traffic on the Rideau Canal from Ottawa, and at the peak of its prosperity from 1841 to 1844, it was the capital of Canada. Frontenac built a fort there in 1673 that stood for 85 years. Today the city is perhaps best known as the home of Queens University, one of Canada's great institutions of higher learning. Kingston manufactures locomotives, textiles, and machinery. It is an important military training center, and Tete du Pont, at the site of the old French fort, has been renamed Fort Frontenac because of the military schools there. The city's population is 53,526.

A view of the Royal Military College at Kingston, Ontario.   Ontario Dept. of Travel and Publicity, Toronto

A British soldier, probably garbed like the young man in this photograph, doubtless manned Martello Tower (at the left) in 1812. It was part of old Fort Henry at Kingston, Ontario, which was built as a protection against attack from the United States.

Canadian Government Travel Bureau, Ottawa

The business section of Belleville, Ontario: a typical Canadian small-city main street.
Ontario Dept. Travel and Publicity, Toronto

BELLEVILLE, Ontario, on the Bay of Quinte, is 51 miles west of Kingston. It was founded in 1790, and Upper Canada's first brick house was built there in 1794. Much of its economy has depended on its situation as an important terminal point for the Canadian National Railroad. It now has well-diversified manufactures, and being located in a large dairying region, has become noted as a cheddar-cheese center. It has two residential educational institutions—Albert College and the Ontario School for the Deaf. Its population is 30,655.

Belleville circa 1830, as sketched by Capt. Thomas Burrowes.
Ontario Archives, Toronto

Albert College, Belleville, Ontario.
Ontario Dept. Travel and Publicity, Toronto

COBOURG, Ontario, 71 miles east of Toronto on Lake Ontario, has a population of 10,646. It is a popular resort town and an agricultural center, but it also does some manufacturing: plastics, prepared food, carpets, chemicals, furniture, rifles, gelatin, machinery. The town was first settled in 1798. It had several names in succession, including the nickname Hardscrabble be-cause of the kind of soil it had, but in 1819 it took its final name—to honor the marriage of the Royal Princess Charlotte to Prince Leopold of Saxe-Cobourg. It was long the site of Victoria College, now part of the University of Toronto. Cobourg has an army ordnance depot and several schools and a hospital.

Cobourg, Ontario, around 1842, from a steel engraving by W. H. Bartlett.
New York Public Library

OSHAWA, Ontario, on Lake Ontario 35 miles east of Toronto, is a modern industrial town, the home of General Motors of Canada and other automotive plants. It has foundries and woolen mills and manu-factures glass, pottery, leather, steel products, and radio supplies. Oshawa was first settled when a military road was built there from Kingston in 1795. Its first name, Skae's Corners, was changed to the Indian name of Oshawa, meaning "salmon creek" or possibly "ferry line over." It was incorporated as a town in 1879 and as a city in 1924. The present population numbers 62,415.

Oshawa, Ontario. At the lower left in this photograph is the large North Plant of General Motors of Canada. Curving across the top of the picture, not far inland from the shore of Lake Ontario, is Highway 401.
Hunting Survey Corp., Ltd., Toronto

The harbor of Toronto, with the business district of the city in the background.

TORONTO, Ontario, with two thirds of a million people, is the second largest city in Canada. It occupies about ten miles of the Lake Ontario shoreline near the western end of the lake, and has a fine natural harbor at the mouth of the Humber. In the seventeenth century it was a Seneca village, the terminus of a trail from Lake Huron, and by 1797 it still had no more than a dozen houses. Its development into a great city started only about eighty years ago. Port facilities were reorganized in 1911 and are outstanding. The Canadian National Exhibition (held every year since 1879) in its 350-acre park is said to be the largest annual fair in the world. Toronto is the national center of book and magazine publishing and of music and opera. There is a well-attended local opera festival each summer, and the Metropolitan Opera Company of New York plays for a week to audiences of 10,000 a night. The University of Toronto, the Royal Conservatory of Music, the Royal Ontario Museum, and the Ontario College of Art are all notable in the cultural life of Canada. The city crest celebrates "Industry, Intelligence, Integrity"—qualities characteristic of this great, sprawling, growing city.

View of Toronto probably in 1850, drawn by August Kollner, then made into a lithograph by Deroy. The two gentlemen and the lady in the foreground are walking on College Street; University Avenue is at the right. Beyond is the harbor.

I. N. Phelps Stokes Collection of American Historical Prints, New York Public Library

Aerial view of the port of Toronto, Ontario. In the foreground is the western channel, the main entrance to the harbor; at the right are the Toronto Islands.

Parliament buildings in Toronto, the capital of Ontario Province.

Ontario Dept. of Travel and Publicity, Toronto

"The Pit" in the Toronto Stock Exchange on Bay Street.   *National Film Board, Ottawa*

A section of the beach at Sunnyside Amusement Park in Toronto, Ontario.   *National Film Board, Ottawa*

This air view of the Toronto Islands shows the surrounding waters dotted with scores of small sailing craft.   *National Film Board, Ottawa*

In Canada, as elsewhere, the postwar years have seen a great influx of population into the major cities, and—in turn—a tremendous increase in the creation of subdivisions and the building of suburban homes. Cliffside Subdivision, a part of which is shown in this photograph, is in East Toronto on the bluffs that form the shore of Lake Ontario, land formerly occupied by a golf club. This medium-price development was one of Canada's pioneering experiments in community planning.   The Photographic Survey Corp. Ltd., Toronto

Toronto, the Dominion's second largest city, is a center of education and culture as well as industry and commerce. Seen in this photograph are the roundhouse and a section of the railway yards. The huge Royal York Hotel rises in the center distance.   National Film Board, Ottawa

A drawing of Hamilton, Ontario, in the 1850's.   *Library of Congress*

HAMILTON, Ontario, is at the head of Lake Ontario. The fine triangular-shaped harbor is completely protected by a straight gravel bar formed in the time of the glaciers. The city occupies a sloping plain at the foot of "the mountain" (the Niagara escarpment). Settlement was begun in 1778 by two pioneers who did much to give the city its present form, including the donation of Gore Park. Railways and the Burlington Canal helped the city's growth, and it now ranks third in Canada in industrial production (there are over 500 manufacturing plants) and third also in port tonnage handled. At Hamilton the raw materials for the iron and steel industry may be assembled easily. Limestone comes from the local escarpment, iron ore from the Lake Superior region or the new Labrador trough mines, and coal from the Lake Erie ports. Fruit-farming is important in the area. The city has one of Canada's larger educational institutions, McMaster University, and a population of 273,991.

View of Hamilton, Ontario, with its well-protected harbor.   *Ontario Dept. of Travel and Publicity, Toronto*

The entrance to Hamilton harbor from Lake Ontario, 300 feet wide between the piers. The Skyway Bridge carries Queen Elizabeth Way traffic 120 feet above the water.

The Hamilton Harbour Commissioners, Hamilton

The Gore, Hamilton, Ontario.   *Canadian National Railways*

Guelph drum band marching in the Niagara grape festival parade at St. Catherines, Ontario. St. Catherines is in the center of a fruit-growing region.
Ontario Dept. Travel and Publicity, Toronto

ST. CATHERINES, Ontario, is near the Welland Ship Canal, not far inland from Lake Ontario, south of Toronto and east of Hamilton. Known as the Garden City, it is in the center of the famed Niagara fruit belt and has a large food-processing industry. It also manufactures textile, metal, paper, and wood products.

Mineral springs make the city a noted health resort, and it is the site of a sanitorium for tubercular patients. Ridley College is located here. The two major annual events are the Canadian Henley Regatta and the St. Catherines Horse Show. The population is 84,472.

On the Niagara River

NIAGARA FALLS, Ontario, is on the left bank of the Niagara River opposite the falls. The famous Rainbow and Whirlpool Rapids bridges connect it with its United States counterpart. It had the name of Elgin from 1853 to 1856, then was called Clifton, and finally Suspension Bridge until 1881, when it took its present name. The town began to grow with the building of the bridge completed in 1855 designed by John Roebling (builder of the Brooklyn Bridge). Its main interest is the falls themselves and it is visited by many of the two million annual pilgrims to this

attraction. Alongside the falls is Queen Victoria Park and the Oakes Garden Theatre, a remarkable arrangement of lily-ponds, terraces, rock gardens and flowerbeds with miniature falls and other ornaments. The famed Carillon Tower has 55 bells ranging in size from 9 pounds to 10 tons. Niagara Falls produces electric power and manufactures fertilizers, railroad and electrical equipment, domestic appliances, and other products from castings to cereal foods. Many American firms have Canadian branches there. The population is 22,351.

Looking up at the Horseshoe Falls from the observation plaza below, on the Ontario side of the river.
Ontario Dept. of Travel and Publicity, Toronto

The view from Burning Springs Lookout, on the Canadian side. The American Falls are at the left, the Canadian at the right.   National Film Board, Ottawa

Niagara Falls, Ontario. Sightseers ride across the boiling whirlpool in the Niagara River gorge by means of an aero car operated by the Niagara Parks Commission.   National Film Board, Ottawa

On the Welland Ship Canal

WELLAND, Ontario, population 36,079, is on the Welland Ship Canal and the Welland River, 38 miles southeast of Hamilton. The diverting of the Welland River underground, beneath the canal, sometimes considered a feat of modern engineering, actually originated in the early days with a wooden aqueduct. In fact, the whole community was then called The Aqueduct, not receiving its present name until later. Welland is not only a canal port but an important steel town (mill and foundries). It also has a carbide works, an agricultural-machinery plant, a pipe mill, a shoe factory, and cordage and cotton mills. The canal dates back to 1824 and is still the most striking feature of the local geography.

Aerial view of the city of Welland, Ontario. In the lower left foreground, the Welland River flows under the Welland Canal through six 22-foot-diameter siphon culverts that go 75 feet underground—a triumph of modern engineering. The canal extends on to Port Colburne and Lake Erie, dimly visible in the far distance, passing under the lift bridges in the center of the photo, one of which is raised for the passage of a ship. Chamber of Commerce

On Lake Erie

PORT COLBORNE, Ontario, is at the south entrance to the Welland Ship Canal, on the northeast shore of Lake Erie. The first settlement, at the time of the building of the canal in 1832, was called Gravelly Bay. The later town was named for Sir John Colbourne, then governor-general. It is a great transshipment center between Montreal and the west, and has large grain elevators, a nickel plant, a cement plant, and flour mills. The population is 14,886.

The Eviliz, passing under the lift bridge on the Welland Canal near Port Colborne, Ontario. This Lake Erie port at the end of the canal is a nickel-refining center and has grain elevators, flour mills, and blast furnaces. Ontario Dept. of Travel and Publicity, Toronto

BRANTFORD, Ontario, is 65 miles southwest of Toronto, on the Grand River. The Indian chief Joseph Brant, the head of the Six Nations, made it his headquarters in 1784 after the American Revolution, and gave the place his name. King George III honored Brant by building a chapel in the village in 1785. This chapel is now the oldest Protestant church in Ontario and the only Indian Royal Chapel in existence. Brantford's other main historic distinction is that Alexander Graham Bell made the experiments for the invention of the telephone there in 1874. Bell's residence has become a public museum, and in 1917 the city erected a monument to him, designed by Walter S. Allward. In the 1840's the town was connected to Lake Erie by a canal. Today, with a population of some 55,000, it is an important railroad center and a center of paper milling and lumbering. It manufactures a large range of commodities from electrical and athletic equipment to farm machinery. Its more than 150 plants place it twelfth in Canada in the gross value of its manufactured products. It has two collegiate institutes and a government school for the blind. Besides 14 parks, it has one of the largest public swimming pools in the commonwealth.

The famous communion service presented by Queen Anne to the church of her Indian subjects in New York State in 1712. It was later brought to Brantford by the Six Nations Indians. Brantford Board of Trade

The home in Brantford to which Alexander Graham Bell moved with his father in 1870, where his failing health was restored. It was here that "the telephone idea originated and became complete" in his mind—on July 26, 1874. A monument and plaque identify the house as a historic site.

The Bell Memorial at Brantford, Ontario, commemorates the invention of the telephone. With the inventor himself in attendance, the memorial was unveiled by the Governor-General of Canada in 1917. Mr. Bell is show here standing on the steps. Bell Telephone Co. of Canada

PORT DOVER, Ontario, is on Long Point Bay, an inlet of Lake Erie about fifty miles west of Port Colborne. It is the shipping point for a large farm and industrial region, and is said to have the largest fresh-water fishing fleet in the world. It was named for Dover, England, and appropriately is a summer resort. The first white men visited Lake Erie's north shore here in 1669. Population 3,064.

In the 1860's and 1870's, a picnic-excursion on the Port Stanley railway must have looked something like this.   T. T. Ferris, London, Ontario

Beach scene at Port Dover, Ontario, located on an inlet of Lake Erie.
Ontario Dept. Travel and Publicity, Toronto

PORT STANLEY, Ontario, named for Lord Stanley, is at the mouth of Kettle Creek nine miles south of St. Thomas. It serves as the port for St. Thomas and London. With large docking installations and storage facilities for grain, coal, and oil, it is the chief Canadian harbor on Lake Erie, although its permanent population is only about 1,500. It is an active fishing center and a popular summer resort.

The harbor at Port Stanley, Ontario, on Lake Erie.   *Ontario Dept. of Travel and Publicity, Toronto*

ST. THOMAS, Ontario, county town of Elgin County, on Kettle Creek, eighteen miles south of London and eight miles north of Lake Erie. It dates from 1810 and was named in honor of Sir Thomas Talbot, who was a leader in the early settlement of the district. Roads and railroads converge in this city of 22,469, to cross the rather difficult and deep-set Kettle Creek. Here, too, there are railroad workshops and foundries, meat-packing and textile manufacture, flour, flax, and planing mills. The surrounding country is notable for its orchards.

The business section of St. Thomas, Ontario.

LONDON, Ontario, at the forks of the Thames River, is about halfway between Toronto and Windsor. It was named for London, England, because it was originally planned as the capital of Upper Canada. This scheme fell through completely and no buildings at all were put up until 1826. In 1848 London became a village and in 1855 a city. As railroads came in, it grew steadily and today is a great center of industry, commerce, and finance in a rich agricultural area. It

An aerial photograph of the downtown section of London today.
Chamber of Commerce

A view of London, Ontario, in 1845.
Ontario Archives, Toronto

has over 300 well-diversified manufacturing plants: aircraft assembly, knitting mills, breweries, and facilities for making steel, leather, brass, and chemical products. The main educational institution is the University of Western Ontario, with a Faculty of Medicine on the south side of the city. There are several affiliated colleges, including Huron College. London's public library and art museum are outstanding in their services. The city is the seat of the Anglican and Roman Catholic bishops. The population is 169,569.

An old photo of the Dundas Street Bridge in London, Ontario. In the foreground is the Victoria, *in process of construction.*
Ontario Archives, Toronto

The docks at Leamington, Ontario, can accommodate either lake or ocean freighters.
Ontario Dept. of Travel and Publicity, Toronto

LEAMINGTON, Ontario, is thirty miles southeast of Windsor. Though mainly an agricultural center with greenhouses and a large canning business, it also has a dock that handles lake and ocean freighters. It is the gateway to Point Pelee National Park. Leamington's population is 9,030.

AMHERSTBURG, Ontario, is on the east bank of the Detroit River where it enters Lake Erie, fourteen miles south of Windsor. Fort Malden was built there in the late 1790's by the British, and from this base British troops attacked and captured Detroit in the War of 1812. The fort was maintained until the 1850's and now is the site of two museum buildings. Nearby salt and limestone deposits are the basis of a soda-ash industry. There are also a distillery, a tomato-processing plant, a metal-stamping plant, and a bakery. The town is further notable for marine salvage operations. It has a population of 4,452.

One of the museum buildings on the site of Fort Malden in Amherstburg, Ontario.
Ontario Dept. of Travel and Publicity, Toronto

WINDSOR, Ontario, is opposite Detroit and closely connected with it by the Ambassador Bridge, a vehicular tunnel, a railroad tunnel, and railway car ferries. With a population of 114,367, it is Canada's largest city on the international border and its chief automobile manufacturing center. The first settlement dates back over two centuries to pioneer French farmers. A town site was laid out in the early 1830's, and in 1836 the new community was named after Windsor, England. Incorporated as a village in 1854, it became a town in 1858 and a city in 1892. Its business development was rapid, and it now has over 490 industries, including Ford and Chrysler plants, and is an important railroad terminus. Windsor is Canada's leading port of entry for United States visitors—about 17,000,000 persons cross the international boundary there annually.

Aerial photograph of Windsor, Ontario, which grew to encompass three adjacent suburbs—East Windsor, Sandwich, and Walkerville—in 1935.   The Photographic Survey Corp. Ltd., Toronto

A view of busy Ouellette Street in Windsor, Ontario, with Detroit's skyscrapers (across the river) forming a background.
Canadian Government Travel Bureau, Ottawa

Assumption College, Windsor, Ontario.
Ontario Dept. of Travel and Publicity, Toronto

Chatham, in Canada's Ontario Province, sets inland from Lake St. Clair in the center of a farming and fruit-raising region, but it is a busy industrial city, with canneries, factories, and mills.

The Photographic Survey Corp. Ltd., Toronto

CHATHAM, Ontario, 45 miles east of Windsor, is the head of navigation on the Thames River, which connects it with Lake St. Clair sixteen miles to the west. The community was laid out in 1795 and the first log cabin was built in 1800, making Chatham one of the earliest settlements in western Ontario. Now, with a population of almost 30,000, it is the center of a thriving agricultural area specializing in fruit and livestock, and its industries are largely canning, packing, milling, and otherwise processing food products. The Chatham-Kent Museum has a wide range of art and historic interests.

On the St. Clair River

SARNIA, Ontario, is across the St. Clair River from Port Huron, to which it is joined by the graceful Blue Water Bridge and by a railway tunnel and ferries. The first French settler in the area arrived in 1807. The English came in a quarter of a century later, the accredited founder of the community being Malcolm Campbell, who came from Perth, Lanark County, in 1833. The area south of Sarnia along the shore is known as "Chemical Valley"; it contains Canada's greatest concentration of petro-chemical industries. The harbor limits include the entire eastern shore of the St. Clair River, a distance of thirty miles. Sarnia's rate of growth has been so fast that the population doubled in the seven years between 1946 and 1953; it now stands at 50,976.

The feed preparation units at Polymer Corporation's plant in Sarnia, Ontario, give a Christmas-tree effect to a night-time photograph.

Sarnia Chamber of Commerce

Sarnia, Ontario, is located on Lake Huron at the mouth of the St. Clair River. The high-level international bridge over the St. Clair, shown in the background here, joins Sarnia on the right to Port Huron, Michigan, at the left. Polymer Corporation and Dow Chemical both have plants in Sarnia, which is an important transshipment point for lumber, grain, coal, and other products.
The Photographic Survey Corp. Ltd., Toronto

A grain elevator at Sarnia, Ontario.   *Ontario Dept. of Travel and Publicity, Toronto*

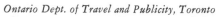

On Lake Huron

SUDBURY, 35 miles north of Georgian Bay on Lake Huron, is a recent city, its beginnings going back only to 1883 and the discovery of copper and nickel. At first the nickel was considered merely a detriment to the copper ore. Then separation techniques were developed, and before long nickel came into wider demand for use in hardening naval armor plate in the First World War. The fact that most of the world's nickel was concentrated in this part of Canada was influential in the growth of Sudbury. By 1945, over a billion dollars' worth of nickel ore had been extracted from mines some of which go down over 5,500 feet. In the area there are also important quantities of copper, silver, lead, zinc, and gold, as well as platinum, palladium, cobalt, and other minerals essential to industry. The mines have been rich, the mining extensive, and there is much smelting and refining. The result is a community where workers are well paid and the income level is high, with good homes, schools, and recreation facilities. During the Second World War there was a particularly rapid growth; the present population is 80,120.

The downtown area of Sudbury, Ontario, a city that has grown up largely within the present century.
The Sudbury Daily Star

A pre-1948 view of the locks at Sault Ste. Marie, Ontario. *National Film Board, Ottawa*

On the St. Marys River

SAULT SAINTE MARIE, Ontario, is at the falls on the north shore of St. Marys River, opposite Sault Sainte Marie, Michigan. This city and its American sister city are famous for the five ship canals, one Canadian and four American, that lie between them. Because of the vast amount of shipping that passes between the St. Marys River and Lake Superior, the canals are referred to as "the Miracle Mile." The Canadian "Sault" includes among its industries shipbuilding, pulp and paper mills, and iron smelting. The Algoma Steel Corporation's production unit there is one of the three largest steel plants in Canada. The community is a port of entry and a railroad center. The International Bridge, opened for use in October, 1962, joins the two "Saults" as well as Interstate 75 Freeway of the United States and the Trans-Canada Highway. The city's population is 43,008.

View of the St. Marys River and Sault Ste. Marie, Ontario. *Ontario Dept. of Travel and Publicity, Toronto*

General view of Port Arthur and Fort William, Ontario, showing the massive grain elevators and also the long breakwater that protects the harbor.   The Photographic Survey Corp. Ltd., Toronto

On Lake Superior

PORT ARTHUR, Ontario, on the northwest shore of Lake Superior, on Thunder Bay, is three miles north of Fort William, its twin city. The two communities are known together as "the Canadian lakehead." Port Arthur, the Hill City, originally spread along the lakeside hummocks as an adjunct to a silver-mining operation. The Dawson Road was built to reach the water route to the prairies in 1869, and in 1882 the western railway was completed to Selkirk. The first Manitoba wheat was shipped from Port Arthur the following year, on the steamer *Erin.* For many years the two communities were rivals, competitively dredging and building breakwaters, but in 1906 the federal government joined them in a general harbor unit. The harbor is now protected by nearly five miles of breakwaters; which recently have undergone extensive work to prepare the harbor for the St. Lawrence Seaway trade. Sixteen large grain elevators, including the largest water-shipping one in the world, can store up to 50,000,000 bushels. There are important shipbuilding yards, and pulp, paper, and lumber mills located in Port Arthur. The predominant stock is British,

but 9,000 Finns make this "the Finnish capital of Canada." Population, 45,276.

FORT WILLIAM, Ontario, is at the outlet of the "Kam," the Kaministikwia River, which has a tendency to fill that part of the harbor and to require dredging. Nevertheless, the harbor formed by the three channel mouths of this river is one of the finest on the Great Lakes and is the transfer and bulk-breaking point for the export and import trade of western Canada. An earlier fort was named for the river. The present fort (still surviving), named for William McGillivray of the North West Company, was built in 1801 when the company moved its headquarters from Grand Portage, which was found to be in United States territory. Both the Canadian National and Canadian Pacific railways have terminal facilities at Fort William. The Canadian Pacific has one of the largest coal docks in the world there. The two port cities are the westernmost Canadian ports on the Great Lakes waterway. They have an almost identical population count. Fort William's is 45,214, only about sixty persons less than Port Arthur's at the last census.

This aerial photograph of Port Arthur clearly shows some of the docking facilities.

National Film Board, Ottawa

Cutting ice on Boulevard Lake at Port Arthur, Ontario.

Ontario Dept. of Travel and Publicity, Toronto

At High Falls, near Fort William, Ontario.

Ontario Dept. of Travel and Publicity, Toronto

U. S. A. Shoreline

The cities along the American shoreline are given in the order met by a traveler following the water route which begins at the lakehead in Silver Bay and Two Harbors, Minnesota.

On Lake Superior

SILVER BAY, Minnesota. From this new harbor, privately owned and developed and capable of sheltering the largest ships on the Great Lakes, taconite—called "the million-dollar marble"—is shipped. Taconite is what is left in the Mesabi and Vermilion ranges after the high-grade iron ore pockets have been mined. The University of Minnesota devised a method by which taconite, "a flintlike rock containing granules of iron oxide," could be reduced to dust and then fused by heat into small, coarse gray pellets the size of a glass marble, a concentrate of 63 percent iron. Reserve Mining Company built a $190,000,000 plant, the Davis Works, at Silver Bay in 1955, which in its first year of operation produced two million tons of taconite pellets. The plant is owned by Republic Steel and Armco. Another Reserve plant is at Babbitt, Minnesota, 45 miles west of Silver Bay. At Hoyt Lakes, Minnesota, Erie Mining Company, owned by U. S. Steel, Youngstown Steel, and other steel companies, has built a taconite plant with an annual production capacity of 7,500,000 tons of pellets. Silver Bay is the shipping point for all taconite now being smelted. The population is 3,723.

TWO HARBORS, Minnesota, 26 miles northeast of Duluth, was originally called Spear-by-Moonlight in Chippewa. After several other designations, in 1884 it was finally named Two Harbors for its two bays. The first load of ore from the Minnesota mines was shipped from here in that same year. At one time its iron-ore dock was one of the largest in the world, 1,338 feet long and 59½ feet high. It has shared also in the general pulpwood and lumber trade of the area. The United States Coast Guard has a base here. Population, 4,695.

An air photo showing newly developed residential areas of Silver Bay, Minnesota, a community that has expanded greatly in the last few years as the result of the construction of taconite plants in the area.   Reserve Mining Co., Basgen-Photo

The ore docks at Two Harbors, Minnesota, in circa 1870.   *Minnesota Historical Society*

DULUTH, Minnesota, is the westernmost port of the Great Lakes, at the west end of Lake Superior where craggy volcanic rocks rise 600 to 800 feet above lake level. It shares a spectacular 24-mile-long harbor with Superior, Wisconsin. The third largest city in the state, Duluth has a population of 106,884. Landmarks are the crescent of Minnesota Point, the Aerial Lift Bridge spanning the ship canal in the harbor, and of course the clifflike shore itself. Duluth summers are short and cool, winters are long. Duluthians say, "Nine months of winter and three months of poor sledding." Local history goes back to the 1650's when the first French explorers arrived. Sieur Duluth, for whom the city is named, came in 1679 to make peace among the Indians. George P. Stuntz is generally believed to be Duluth's first permanent settler, in 1853. Right after that the copper and iron ore boom got under way. Duluth and Superior today run their total annual harbor tonnage up close to New York's in spite of being closed down a third of the year.

Duluth harbor basin, with the city in the background. In the center of the photo are the public marine terminal and Duluth's grain elevators.   *Duluth Chamber of Commerce, Basgen-Photo*

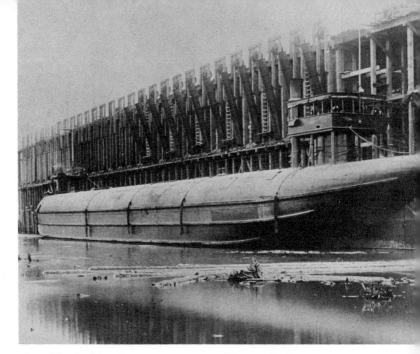

A nineteenth-century photo of the first dog-team mail delivery to Duluth. In their early days, many Great Lakes communities had great difficulties with land communications, bordering as they did on the wilderness.

Duluth Herald and News-Tribune

An old whaleback steamer at an old ore dock.

Duluth Herald and News-Tribune

Sightseers used to ride on Boulevard Drive in Duluth in conveyances like this one. Library of Congress

The harbor shared by the two cities is protected by a long, narrow harbor bar. Originally, boats from Duluth had to go seven miles to the only natural break in the bar, at its southeastern end, opposite the more favorably situated Superior. In 1871, the people of Duluth felt that this handicap had continued long enough and the time had come to cut through the near end of the bar and get their own exit. They put a steam shovel to work at Minnesota Point, digging openly and expecting no trouble. The word came that Superior had petitioned Washington for an injunction.

Duluth heard about it on a Friday evening and was transfixed. The injunction was due Monday morning.

Shocked, indignant, but legally advised that the right to dig still existed, thousands of citizens hurried to the harbor bar with spades and shovels and dug in shifts day and night until, early Monday morning, the way through to the lakes was open. The tug *Fero* greeted the arriving injunction by blasting its lashed-down whistle from one end of the new channel to the other, expressing the general triumph and delirium.

A 1908 photograph showing the **D. O. Mills** *going through the ship canal at Duluth, Minnesota.* Library of Congress

160

SUPERIOR, Wisconsin, is in a common harbor with Duluth where the St. Louis and Menadji rivers enter Lake Superior. In 1634, local Chippewa Indians canoed east and visited the French, and the French came back to trade furs. Fur trading and copper prospecting filled the time for more than two centuries; then George R. Stuntz laid out both the township lines and the Wisconsin-Minnesota state boundary. For a few years there was a land boom, with sales going sometimes at the rate of $200,000 a week, but in 1857 came a crash and the population dropped to a mere 500 during the sixties and seventies. In 1883, the first iron-mining operations in the Gogebic Range brought a real explosion in Superior's growth. It became the second largest city in the state. Dozens of whalebacks were launched from the local shipyards. Scandinavians, Finns, and Poles crowded in and Superior became "the consumer cooperative center of the United States." From its commanding terminal position, the city developed the largest dry docks on the Great Lakes. Superior has a State Teachers' College and a Vocational School. Its population is 33,563.

The "city" of Superior, Wisconsin, at the western end of Lake Superior, opposite Duluth, as it was in 1856. Superior grew rapidly after the discovery of iron ore in the Gogebic Range.

Library of Congress

The grain elevators at Superior, Wisconsin, 290 feet in height, are reputed to be the world's tallest.
Wisconsin Conservation Dept., Madison

An aerial view of Superior, Wisconsin, showing the largest ore docks in the world (lower left), the breakwater, and the fine natural harbor.
State of Wisconsin Dept. of Resource Development

The Fraser-Nelson Shipbuilding & Dry Dock Company at Superior, Wisconsin, boasts the largest dry docks on the Great Lakes (center foreground). This shipyard originated in 1890, when Capt. Alexander McDougall built his famous whaleback steamers and barges. It is located on an arm of the Duluth-Superior harbor. In the background of this photograph are grain elevators, coal docks, and ore docks. The new Duluth-Superior high bridge (also in the background here) was opened late in 1961.

Ashland harbor on the receiving end of a large float of Canadian pulp wood.

Founded in 1892, Northland College in Ashland, Wisconsin, has been expanding rapidly in recent years.

Chamber of Commerce, Ashland

ASHLAND, Wisconsin, is 58 miles east of Superior, on Chequamegon Bay. In 1659, the first arrivals, the French, had to be portaged across the spit by Indians. In 1854, Asaph Whittlesey decided to settle here, and as the first tree he cut down to build a cabin was a large ash, he petitioned Washington to use the name Ashland for his new-born community. The arrival of the Wisconsin Central Railroad in 1877 started a rapid development, added to by the discovery of iron ore in the area. For a while, Ashland was a major supplier of brownstone for houses in growing American cities. When that phase passed, it shifted to polished black granite. Today it receives pulpwood floated across the lake from Canada and manufactures paper products. Ashland is the home of the musically oriented Northland College. Nearby, the twenty famous Apostle Islands with their cliffs and natural arches decorate the deep blue of the lake with their strange stonework. The city's population is 10,132.

This picture was taken in Ashland, Wisconsin, in 1894, at a historical meeting of the chiefs of the Sioux and Chippewa Indians, who made "lasting peace" under the auspices of Lt. W. A. Mercer, agent for the Chippewas, and Buffalo Bill (he is seated in the center of the group). Among the chiefs present were Chief Cloud, Chief Blackbird, and Chief Buffalo of the Chippewas and Chief Flat Iron of the Sioux.

U.S. Signal Corps Photo, National Archives

Ontario

PORT ARTHUR
FORT WILLIAM

Minnesota

Canada

L A K E   S U P E R I O R

TWO HARBORS

SAULT STE.MARIE

DULUTH
SUPERIOR
ASHLAND

MARQUETTE
MUNSING

SAULT SAINTE MARIE

Michigan

MANISTIQUE

ST. IGNACE

L A K E   H U R O

ESCANABA

MACKINAW CITY
CHEBOYGAN

ROGERS CITY

ALPENA

Wisconsin

MENOMINEE
MARINETTE

TRAVERSE CITY

L A K E   M I C H I G A N

KEWAUNEE
TWO RIVERS
MANITOWOC

MANISTEE

LUDINGTON

SHEBOYGAN

Michigan

BAY CITY

MUSKEGON

PORT HURON
SAR

Iowa

MILWAUKEE

GRAND HAVEN
GRAND RAPIDS
HOLLAND

Mt. CLEMENS

RACINE
KENOSHA

DETROIT
WIND

WAUKEGAN

SOUTH HAVEN

AMHURSTBURG→
MONROE

BENTON HARBOR
SAINT JOSEPH

EVANSTON
CHICAGO

MICHIGAN CITY

TOLEDO

Illinois

GARY

Indiana

SANDUS

Ohio

The Great

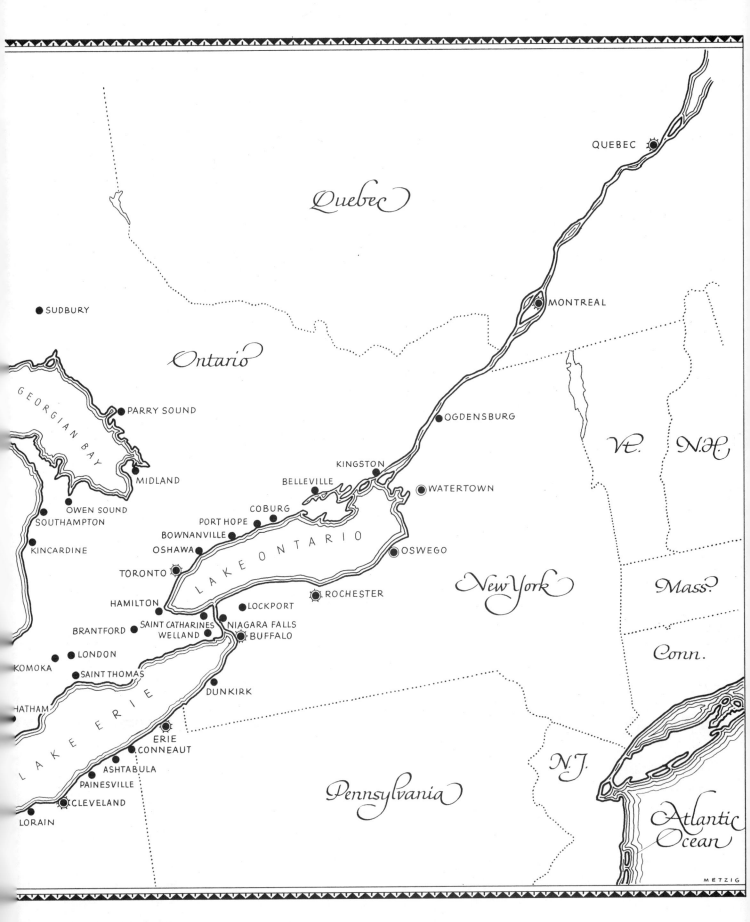

QUEBEC

Quebec

MONTREAL

SUDBURY

Ontario

PARRY SOUND

OGDENSBURG

GEORGIAN BAY

KINGSTON

BELLEVILLE

WATERTOWN

Vt. *N.H.*

MIDLAND

OWEN SOUND

COBURG

SOUTHAMPTON

PORT HOPE

BOWNANVILLE

OSHAWA

LAKE ONTARIO

OSWEGO

KINCARDINE

TORONTO

New York

Mass.

HAMILTON

ROCHESTER

LOCKPORT

BRANTFORD

SAINT CATHARINES

NIAGARA FALLS

Conn.

WELLAND

BUFFALO

LONDON

KOMOKA

SAINT THOMAS

DUNKIRK

CHATHAM

LAKE ERIE

ERIE

N.J.

CONNEAUT

ASHTABULA

Pennsylvania

PAINESVILLE

CLEVELAND

LORAIN

Atlantic Ocean

METZIG

Lakes Region

An old photograph of ore trains on the docks at Marquette, Michigan.
Vermilion, Ohio, Marine Museum

MARQUETTE, Michigan, on the high rocky south shore of Lake Superior, is one of the main shipping points of the Upper Peninsula. Its natural harbor is lined with crescent-shaped beaches, and the waterfront docks roar with iron and coal pouring into Great Lakes freighters. Chemicals and metal and wood products come from the local plants. Tradition has it that Father Marquette visited here, and the community was renamed for him in 1850. A disastrous fire destroyed the business district in 1868, but it was rapidly rebuilt and in 1871 Marquette was incorporated as a city. Its pleasant climate helps to make it a popular summer resort that attracts many artists. Presque Isle Park is the summer community playground. Nearby ski runs provide winter recreation. Marquette is the site of Northern Michigan University and of a branch of the State Prison, which has an unusual sunken garden maintained for the public by the prisoners. The city has a population of 19,824 persons.

Air view of the harbor at Presque Isle (northeastern Michigan) showing a boat being loaded with ore. At the right is the famous Presque Isle Park, a scenic spot with wooded trails and drives and facilities for swimming, boating, and various outdoor sports.   Marquette Chamber of Commerce

Near the cascades of the St. Marys River in 1842.

On the St. Marys River

SAULT SAINTE MARIE, Michigan, is at the falls on the south shore of the St. Marys River, between Lakes Superior and Huron. It is connected by a railroad bridge and—since October, 1962—by a vehicular bridge with its sister city of the same name in Ontario, Canada. The Michigan community was the first permanent settlement in Michigan, and is the third oldest surviving community in the United States. Etienne Brulé, sent by Champlain to scout a possible Northwest Passage, reached its present site in 1618 and named it Sault de Gaston for King Louis XIII. But another story has it that when Jesuit priests first gazed at the falls, they said, "Sault!" (falls) and added "Sainte Marie" to express their reverent admiration. At any rate, the Jesuits had a mission there in 1670 under the care of Father Marquette. The first small premonitory canal, with a nine-foot lock, was built in 1797. Today the town is the port of entry for the great canals joining Lake Superior with the St. Marys River and Lake Huron. The United States Fort Brady, built in 1823, was in use until 1941. That and the house of H. R. Schoolcraft, the house of John Johnson, fur trader, and the site of Father Marquette's mission are notable historically. The population is 18,722.

Looking south from Sault Ste. Marie, Canada, toward Sault Ste. Marie, Michigan. In the foreground is the Canadian plaza and approach to the bridge that spans the ship and power canals and the St. Marys River on its way to the American shore. Locks here lower or raise ocean vessels 21 feet (in from 6 to 15 minutes), so that they can pass between Lake Superior and Lake Huron.

Materna Studio, Sault Ste. Marie, Michigan

On the Straits of Mackinac

MACKINAW CITY, Michigan, is on the south shore of the Straits of Mackinac. The straits were the early path of Indians, *coureurs de bois,* and Jesuit missionaries on their way between Lake Huron and Lake Michigan. The famous Fort Michilimackinac, which shifted its position many times during the early wars, was located here when the British took it over from the French in 1761, and also when most of its garrison was massacred by the Indians in Pontiac's Conspiracy a few years later. A rebuilt stockade of the fort can now be seen in the nearby state park. (Michilimackinac meant "Big Turtle" in Chippewa.) From Mackinaw City (population, 942) a ferry goes to nearby Mackinac Island, long a popular summer resort.

Michilimackinac in 1842. Today there is a Michilimackinac State Park, with an authentic restoration of the original French and British fort.

Library of Congress

An old view of Michilimackinac with the American flag flying over the fort.   *Library of Congress*

Old Fort Michilimackinac on the tip of Michigan's lower peninsula stands almost in the shadow of the towering but graceful Mackinac Bridge—a study in contrasts. The bridge was opened in 1957; the historic fort was the site of the bloody Pontiac massacre nearly two centuries ago.

Michigan Tourist Council, Lansing

Monument to Father Marquette in St. Ignace, Michigan.
Library of Congress

ST. IGNACE, Michigan, on the north shore of the Straits of Mackinac directly across from Mackinaw City, is the second oldest settlement in Michigan. It dates back to Father Marquette's chapel, built in 1671. St. Ignace was eight years old when La Salle's *Griffin* put in there on its way to Green Bay. It has long been a fishing town, setting its nets for whitefish and trout. Today it is a popular resort town. In Marquette Park is the final grave of Père Marquette, who wanted "to return to his little chapel in the straits" and was carried to St. Ignace and reburied there by his Indian friends. The town has a population of 3,334 persons.

ESCANABA, Michigan, is an important iron-shipping port on Little Bay de Noc. The first iron-ore dock was built in 1863, and in the next quarter-century shipments jumped from a few thousand to well over a million tons annually. Escanaba manufactures chemical and paper products. In 1936, it supplied 100,000 square feet of bird's-eye maple for the *Queen Mary* (almost all the world's bird's-eye maple is concentrated in the Escanaba area). Fishing runs to the millions of pounds a year. By a long tradition, the Upper Peninsula State Fair is held annually in Escanaba. The population is 15,391.

Aerial view of the city of Escanaba on the northern shore of Lake Michigan. *Photo by B. F. Schultz*

The marina at Menominee, Michigan, is one of the best small-craft anchorages in the Great Lakes.

MENOMINEE, Michigan, is on Green Bay at the mouth of the Menominee River. Its many manufactures are powered by the river's hydroelectric plant. First settler Louis Chappée built a fur-trading post here in 1796. A sawmill and dam followed in 1832. When lumber gave out, the local economy turned to dairying, fishing, manufacturing, and resort services. There are fine local parks and beaches. The year-round population is 11,289.

GREEN BAY, Wisconsin, is on the south end of Green Bay, at the mouth of the Fox River. It had fur traders living there as early as 1718, and Augustin de Langlade settled there in 1745, so it is the oldest settlement in Wisconsin. Green Bay has one of the finest harbors on the Great Lakes and is a port for river and lake steamers. It has meat-packing plants, fisheries, shipyards, and limestone quarries, and manufactures paper.

The Neville Museum has the silver ostensorium of Nicolas Perrot, a *coureur de bois* in the service of the Jesuits, who came to the region toward the end of the seventeenth century and became the French commandant and a great figure in the area. In late years the city has gained wide recognition through its professional football team, the Green Bay Packers. Its population is 62,888.

A very early drawing of Fort Howard and its environs, just up the Fox River from Green Bay, Wisconsin (the community of that name did not then exist). At the lower left is the fort itself, and at the upper left is a sketch of the view that could be seen from the windows of the fort in 1818. The map at the right points out the location of various houses, a mill, and of Indian lodges and cornfields.

U.S. Signal Corps Photo, National Archives

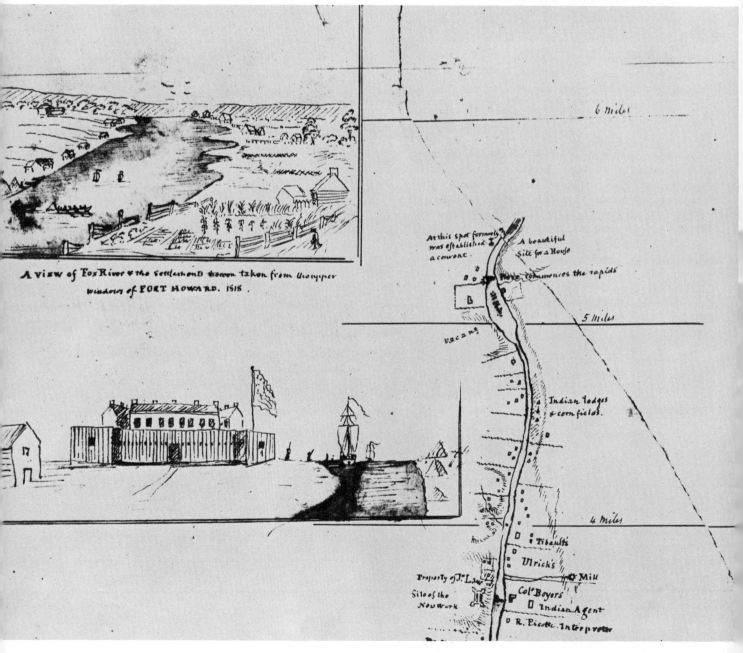

Looking inland, at Green Bay, Wisconsin, in the northeastern part of the state. A trading center as early as 1669 and the oldest settlement in the state, Green Bay today handles several million tons of cargo a year. The city is outstanding in the production of paper and cheese—and famed also for its professional football team, the Green Bay Packers. Lefebvre-Luebke, Green Bay

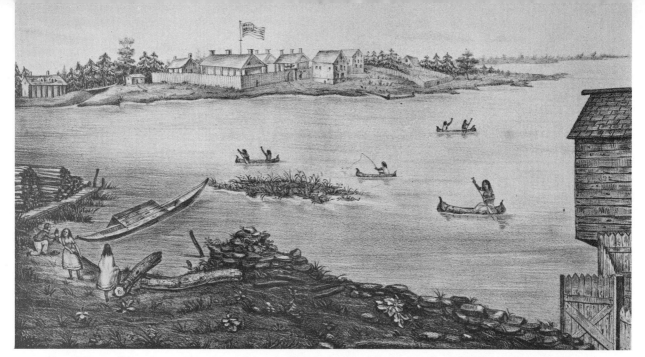

Fort Howard on "la grande Baie verte" well over a century ago. The Fort Howard Hospital Museum in present-day Green Bay has many fascinating relics of the past.   Library of Congress

The Tank cottage in Green Bay, oldest standing frame building in Wisconsin, built in 1776 by a French fur trader who married a Menominee Indian woman. In 1850 the cottage was bought by Nels Otto Tank, a Norwegian Moravian missionary who had married a Dutch girl, and thereafter was called by their name. In 1908 it was moved from its original location to Tank Park, a tract of land given to the city by Madame Tank. (This photo was taken before the cottage was moved.) The cottage now has been refurnished with much of the original furniture. One of the most interesting pieces is a marquetry dressing table given to Madame Tank's mother by Queen Caroline of Holland. A wardrobe contains a court dress worn by her mother when she was first lady-in-waiting to the queen.
Neville Public Museum, Green Bay

Tanker on Fox River, near the entrance to Green Bay harbor.   Lefebvre Luebke

An old view of Manitowoc harbor (Wisconsin). Captain H. C. Inches Collection

MANITOWOC, Wisconsin, is at the mouth of the Manitowoc River 25 miles north of Sheboygan. In the early nineteenth century, it was still little more than an Indian fishing village, but it boomed with lumber, as did so many lakeside towns, and then was hit by two cholera epidemics in the fifties that just about wiped it out. By 1860, it was back on its feet building ships, and it continues to be a leading shipyard of the lakes. In 1960, it launched the lakes' largest ore carrier to that date, the *Edward L. Ryerson*, 730 feet long, of the Inland Steel Company. In 1962, it finished construction of a 700-ton dredge destined for Switzerland and loaded it on board the German freighter *Ophelia*. So the occupations of a community change. The city also does flour-milling and vegetable-canning and produces aluminum goods, malt, and Portland cement. It has a fine library, museum, and recreation program sponsored by the community. The population is 32,275.

In Manitowoc, Wisconsin, shipbuilding has always been an important industry; this photo shows a launching. Manitowoc also is noted for its manufacture of aluminum ware and its canneries.
Great Lakes Marine Museum, Vermilion, Ohio

SHEBOYGAN, Wisconsin, 51 miles north of Milwaukee, spreads out along the shore of Lake Michigan around the mouth of the Sheboygan River. German-Americans predominate, and the English spoken in the countryside has long been much influenced by German dialects. Sheboygan really got started only in 1843 with the building of a general store. Three years later it was granted a village charter. The population grew tremendously when promoters' pamphlets were distributed far and wide in Germany at a time of religious oppression. Lutherans came and, later, members of the Dutch Free Separate Reformed Church. The Germans cleared land and the Yankees (and later Germans too) went into business. By 1856, the new town had an export trade of $700,000 annually. Hiram Smith began the manufacture of cheese. Interest in choral music was responsible for annual *Sängerfeste*. German plays were performed at the Turn-Halle and the Opera House, and famous artists and actors from the East spent their vacations here. At one time, Sheboygan was referred to as the city of "cheese, chairs, children, and churches." Population, 45,747.

Sheboygan, well before 1850.   *Library of Congress*

This fascinating view of Milwaukee in the early 1850's shows a monument that was never erected. It was usual to make prints of projected monuments as a means of raising money for them, and sometimes, as in this case, a project never got beyond the planning stage. The monument was to have celebrated a truthful small boy beaten to death by his foster-father because he would not admit he had lied. "Pa, I did not lie. Pa, I told the truth," the boy is reputed to have said. The monument is beautifully portrayed in this drawing. In the background the spire of St. John's Roman Catholic Cathedral on Jackson Street dominates the city skyline.

I. N. Phelps Stokes Collection, New York Public Library

MILWAUKEE, Wisconsin, is the largest city in the state and the eleventh largest in the country, with a population of 741,324. It has an excellent and most beautiful harbor located at the point where the Milwaukee and Kinnickinnic rivers join and enter Lake Michigan. Another river, the Menominee, and many canals fill the city with waterways and bridges. Metal trades and meat-packing are the main industries. Once the *Deutsch Athens* of America, Milwaukee has changed in recent years. Where the German group used to be over two-thirds of the population, it is now a minority. The first settlers were three men, a Frenchman, a New Englander, and a Virginian, who between them owned all of Milwaukee. By 1845, the population was up to 10,000. A year later, the city charter was ratified, and the original settler Solomon Juneau was elected mayor. In 1848, defeated revolutionists from Germany arrived and formed a great leaven of intel-lect and culture. Among them was Carl Schurz, later to be United States Secretary of the Interior. The Civil War brought increased trade, and by 1875 the city was the primary wheat market of the world. Labor unions were strong and Victor Berger gathered support for a native Socialist party, which grew strong enough to take office in 1910. Clean local government has made Milwaukee one of the safest cities in the country, with phenomenally high records for fire and crime prevention and good health. Interwound with this history and with the ups and downs of Prohibition was the "beer that made Milwaukee famous." The city's numerous educational institutions include Marquette University, Milwaukee-Downer College for Women, Mount Mary College for Women, Wisconsin State Teachers' College, Alverno College for Women, and the University of Wisconsin at Milwaukee.

Milwaukee shorefront in the late nineteenth century. Shipping in the Milwaukee River can be seen at left center. The sidewheel excursion steamer Sheboygan *of the Goodrich Line is at the center right of the picture.*

Library of Congress

An aerial view of Milwaukee's outer harbor area shows the junction of three rivers: the Milwaukee, the Menominee, and the Kinnickinnic. Long an important lake port because of its good harbor, Milwaukee is on the way to becoming a major seaport as a result of the building of the St. Lawrence Seaway.

Board of Harbor Commissioners, Milwaukee

A loading operation on the open dock terminal, Milwaukee.

Board of Harbor Commissioners

Milwaukee harbor, showing the bridge crossing the Kinnickinnic River.   *Board of Harbor Commissioners, Milwaukee*

Loading a cargo carrier at Municipal Transit Shed No. 1, Milwaukee.
Board of Harbor Commissioners

The City of Racine of the Goodrich Line, which made daily excursion trips to Milwaukee in the 1890's.
Racine County Historical Rooms

RACINE, Wisconsin, the second largest city in the state, has a population of 89,144 persons. The Root River cuts the community approximately in two and gives it its name, since the French name for the snaggy river was Racine, meaning "root." The first settlement dates to 1834. When, in 1840, the first bridge was built across the river, local citizens responded civically by pulling 120 oak stumps out of Main Street. The village was incorporated the following year. The city government dates to 1848. Racine long had trouble with sand in its harbor; then the federal government spent more than a million dollars erecting a mile-long breakwater. Industries have steadily grown, the chief products being farm machinery, printing and lithography, malted milk, and floor wax. A showplace in the city is the unusual glass office and research building of the Johnson Wax Company, which was designed by Frank Lloyd Wright. Wright also designed the Sporer house, a private residence overlooking the lake, which, when it was first seen in 1906, many considered to resemble a steamer. The public library houses the famous Hoy bird collection found within ten miles of Racine.

The side-wheeler Sheboygan on her first trip to Racine in 1874. She carried freight and passengers between Chicago and Milwaukee in the seventies and early eighties. In this photograph she is shown lying on the south side of the river in front of the warehouse where the great fire of 1882 started. The fire spread to Racine's main business section, destroying everything between Third and Fourth on Main Street before brought under control.
Racine County Historical Rooms

Looking north from the State Street Bridge in Racine in 1895, when river business was heavy. In the left foreground are the Joses and the Caledonia.   *Racine County Historical Rooms*

The Research Center and Administration Building of S. C. Johnson & Son, Inc., at Racine were designed by Frank Lloyd Wright. In the foreground is a giant plastic globe 12 feet in diameter, which serves as a directory of the worldwide operations of the company. The Administration Building at the right is considered to be one of the finest examples of modern business housing. Built entirely without windows or glass brick, it utilizes 43 miles of glass tubing for both artificial and natural lighting and boasts shadowless illumination day or night. The Research and Development Tower (150 feet high) is reputed to be the tallest building ever built without foundations directly under the side walls, which are constructed of 17 miles of glass tubing held in place by stainless steel wires.

182

KENOSHA, Wisconsin, is ten miles south of Racine, its lights clearly visible from Racine harbor. It is heavily industrialized and manufactures springs, mattresses, metal products, and brass, copper, and knit goods. Rambler automobiles are made here, and Kenosha also produces fire engines. The original settlers came from the neighborhood of Oswego, New York, and seem to have been an energetic group. One of them transplanted a field of corn overnight (to the amazement of his neighbors) in an effort to substantiate a land claim, and other disputes and maneuvers enlivened the community's early days. Later, culture settled in and Kenosha claims to have opened the first public school west of the Alleghanies and did certainly publish the state's first literary magazine, *The Garland of the West.*

The harbor at Kenosha, Wisconsin, in 1897. *Kenosha County Historical Society*

Kenosha harbor 65 years later, in 1962, at almost the same location. The two pictures show clearly not only the development of Kenosha's shipping facilities but also the improvement in photography. *Kenosha County Historical Society*

WAUKEGAN, Illinois, is the seat of Lake County; its present busy manufacturing operations are all on the site of a seventeenth-century Indian village. La Salle and Hennepin are reported to have thought well of this village for a trading post. When the French built it, it was called Little Fort. Indians, under a treaty with the U. S. Government, held the area until 1836, but by 1841 white settlers had taken over, and several years later the community had "three commodious public houses, seven stores, two blacksmith shops, one chair and cabinet factory, one pier, and a second being constructed, and two brickyards." It was incorporated as a village in 1849 when the townspeople voted to change the name to Waukegan. Ten years later it organized as a city, and to it came Abraham Lincoln, who spoke at Dickinson Hall in his campaign of 1860 and was interrupted by a fire alarm. "Well, gentlemen," he said, "let us all go, as there really seems to be a fire, and help to put it out." Today one of the few permanent naval training bases in the United States is located just south of the city—it trained more than a million naval recruits during World War II. Waukegan's industries include wire and wire products, chemicals, asbestos products, and a variety of machines and pharmaceuticals. Its population is 55,719.

The court house and soldiers' monument at Waukegan, Illinois. *Library of Congress*

EVANSTON, Illinois, fifteen miles north of Chicago, is the seat of Northwestern University, Seabury-Western Theological Seminary, Garrett Biblical Institute, National College of Education, and Kendall College. Until some time into the nineteenth century, the Potawotomi Indians inhabited Evanston's "bay shore," which was so lovely it was called "Beauty's Eyebrow." They had a village where Evanston Hospital now is. The first two white inhabitants seem to have been a gambler and a ne'er-do-well counterfeiter, but they didn't stay and they were not typical of Evanston's later days. In Evanston in 1874, Frances E. Willard founded the Women's Christian Temperance Union and Evanston was and still is its headquarters. The city is also headquarters for International Rotary. One of its celebrated latter-day daughters is Mary Jane Ward, author of *The Snake Pit*. Evanston is a community of old elm trees and old residences and, incidentally, of good city management. Its Northwestern University, founded as a Methodist school, has become one of the great educational centers of the country, with 15,000 students. The city's population is 79,283.

Evanston, Illinois, circa 1874. The large buildings in the foreground are "North Western University."
Evanston Historical Society

A busy intersection in Evanston during horse-and-buggy days.
Evanston Historical Society

Street scene in Evanston, Illinois, in the days when autos first became really common. Behold My Wife, a 1920 movie, is advertised on the theatre marquee.
Library of Congress

CHICAGO, Illinois, at the base of Lake Michigan and connected to the Mississippi by the Illinois Waterway, is the second largest city in the United States (population 3,550,404) and the eleventh largest in the world. Roaring, young, and powerful, it has been enthusiastically aware of its drive for a commanding position among the cities for more than a century. The name Chicago itself derives from an Indian term for anything "strong," particularly wild garlic. The early French left little mark on Chicago. An amazing fact is that the first U. S. settler and the builder of Fort Dearborn (named after the Secretary of War in Jefferson's cabinet, Henry Dearborn) was Captain John Whistler, grandfather of the famous painter. Before Whistler, the local population consisted of three Frenchmen and a Santo Domingo Negro businessman, Jean Baptiste Point Sable. Even as late as 1833, Chicago had only 200 inhabitants. Then the population explosion was on. In 1833 alone, 20,000 immigrants swept into and through the newly incorporated town. By 1847 there were more than 450 stores. Between 1840 and 1850, the population increased sixfold. During the Civil War, Chicago grain shipments almost doubled in a period of two years and McCormick and other agricultural-implement factories flourished. A building boom started. Almost all the construction was done with wood, and by 1871 solid blocks of combustible pine spread over seven-eighths of the city. After months of drought, a devastating fire left 3½ square miles of Chicago a pavement of ashes.

The city was rebuilt more sanely, and its triumphant progress resumed—centered around the harbor, the railroads, and the inland waterways.

"The Chicago Harbor consists of the Chicago River and its branches to their respective sources and all slips adjacent to and connecting therewith, the Ogden Canal, the Calumet River and its branches and slips, the waters of Lake Calumet including its piers and basins and breakwaters, the Drainage Canal and the waters of Lake Michigan, including all breakwaters, piers and permanent structures therein for a distance of three miles from the shore between the north and south lines of the city extended, to the extent that the above named waterways are within the territorial limits of the city"—Excerpts from the Municipal Code of Chicago.

The enormous size and vast scale of the city's trade and of its industrial operations were symbolized in the World's Columbian Exposition of 1893. The "tool maker, stacker of wheat" created several world-famous libraries, the Chicago Art Institute, six universities, including the University of Chicago, liberal arts colleges, teachers' colleges, and Hull House, the famous settlement house founded in 1899 by Jane Addams. The city has 1,885 churches and 418 parks. As to trade, it owns Navy Pier, which can accommodate six vessels at one time, and a dock area at Lake Calumet, which can handle approximately 17 vessels at once. Lake Calumet has two grain elevators with a total storage capacity of 13,500,000 bushels. A quarter of a billion dollars will be invested in the next few years to make Chicago the best integrated port on the Great Lakes. Little wonder that Illinois is the largest exporting state in the nation.

A lithograph view of Chicago in 1849, by H. Camp after a painting by A. Kollner. The position of the masts of the ships in the background suggests that the vessels were resting on the ground (rather than in the Chicago River) at the time—doubtless during the great flood of 1849. The street from right to left in the foreground is Superior Street, then called Wolcott Street. In the extreme left background is the lighthouse built in 1832. Only one copy of this picture is known to be in existence.   I. N. Phelps Stokes Collection of American Historical Prints, New York Public Library

Chicago in 1820, the earliest-known view of the city. At the left of the Chicago River is Fort Dearborn, and to the right is the house of John Kinsie, often called the Father of Chicago, who arrived in the spring of 1804. The cabin a considerable distance to the south of the fort belonged to John Dean, an army carpenter; it was built in 1815. Lake Michigan shipping belonged to the Indians in those days. I. N. Phelps Stokes Collection of American Historical Prints, New York Public Library

Chicago's famous Navy Pier, with the downtown skyline in the background. The five ships tied up at the pier give some idea of its capacity. It can accommodate six in all, and has a total of more than 500,000 square feet of storage and wharfage area, the largest part of it under roof.

Chicago Association of Commerce and Industry

Colonel Wood's Museum, with its street banner advertising the "largest woman in the world—weighing near 900." *Library of Congress*

The Rush Street Bridge, as seen from State Street. *Library of Congress*

A contemporary lithograph of the great Chicago Fire of 1871, which broke out in a barn on De Koven Street. Fanned by a gale, it devoured about 18,000 buildings in two days of uncontrolled holocaust. Whole areas of the city were abandoned, schooners burned in the Chicago River, and walls and bridges collapsed. The fire was one of the great disasters of modern times, the damage estimated at almost $200,000,000.   I. N. Phelps Stokes Collection, N. Y. Public Library

A view of Chicago, taken a year after the devastating fire.   Library of Congress

The Chicago lakefront, with Grant Park and Michigan Avenue in the background. The end of the Grant Park bandshell can be seen at the extreme left, and in back of it, the Conrad Hilton Hotel. The Prudential Building is at right center.   Chicago Association of Commerce

Aerial view of Chicago's world-famous Soldiers Field. Meigs Field can be seen in the distance at the upper left.   Chicago Association of Commerce

An outstanding figure on the Chicago scene was Marshall Field, who was born in Conway, Massachusetts, in 1835, the son of a farmer. Field came to Chicago as a young man and worked in a wholesale drygoods house. He was given an interest in the concern, but withdrew to join Potter Palmer in organizing the firm of Field, Palmer, and Leiter. When Mr. Palmer dropped out in 1867, the firm became Field, Leiter, and Company, and when Leiter retired in 1881, it became known by its present name of Marshall Field and Company. It is one of the great mercantile establishments of the world. Mr. Field was unassuming and sympathetic, close to the people. His rule: "Never borrow, never give a note, never speculate in stocks, and buy for cash." He was a leading philanthropist, giving to Chicago University, the Columbian Museum Fund, and many other institutions and charities.

The Bettmann Archive, Inc.

Navy Pier, built by the city of Chicago in 1916, as it appears today after rehabilitation and improvement. It is used for amusements and expositions as well as for docking.

CALUMET CITY, Illinois, twenty miles south of Chicago is at the Indiana border on the Calumet River which flows into the fast-developing Lake Calumet area. The new Cal-Sag Channel will tie this harbor system integrally into the Illinois Waterway. The main local industries are steel works, chemical manufacturing, and meat packing. The population is 25,000.

Lake Calumet Harbor (Chicago Regional Port District development at Lake Calumet). Since this picture was taken, ground has been broken for a 177-acre tank farm to be constructed to the right, at the entrance to Lake Calumet. Calumet Studio

The grain elevators at Lake Calumet Harbor have a storage capacity of 13,500,000 bushels.
Chicago Association of Commerce and Industry

Suit Against Chicago

In 1927, New York and other states brought suit against Illinois and the Sanitary District of Chicago for lowering the water level of the Great Lakes. The water level was down a foot and a half, it was claimed, because of the thousands of cubic feet a second being diverted into the Sanitary and Ship Canal. Newton D. Baker, former Secretary of War, presented the plaintiff's case before the Supreme Court and called the water loss "a tribute leveled against all Lake States," a menace to navigation, and an act unfriendly to Canada. Even some of the then-recent Mississippi flood was blamed on the defendants.

Chicago's Mayor Thompson had his invitation to attend the New York State Fair canceled because he sided with Chicago in the controversy. And just as feelings were at white heat, Chicago came out with an announcement that its citizens bathed "more often and more diligently" than those of any other city, 278 gallons a day being used for every man, woman, and child. Shrieks of agony promptly arose from other lake cities, noting this additional drain on lake water.

The suit dragged on until 1930, when the defendants were censored by the Supreme Court for "persisting in unjustifiable acts" and ordered to decrease water diversion gradually until December 31, 1938, after which they were allowed only 1,500 cubic feet a second. Chicago noted that heavy rains had meantime restored the lake level and was gratified not to have the flow of the Chicago River reversed, as the plaintiffs had petitioned. The court conceded that that would have been "excessive."

Recently, contradictions have multiplied. Chicago fill-in has been blamed for raising the level of the lakes as owners of low-lying property along the shores of the various lakes have—with shocked amazement—noted the said property disappearing beneath the water. But at the same time, six states—New York, Michigan, Ohio, Wisconsin, Pennsylvania, and Minnesota—are again suing Illinois and the Metropolitan Sanitary District of Greater Chicago to stop all Illinois drainage of the lakes, claiming that the St. Lawrence Seaway and its power plants present a new situation where the loss of water is of far greater importance, and all available water is now needed.

Judge Albert B. Maris has been appointed a special master for the Supreme Court to go through 30,000 pages of testimony and 1,000 exhibits and report back to the court. Decisions in these matters are not entered into lightly, and it will probably be two years before the Supreme Court will give its verdict.

Bear Trap Dam at Lockport, Illinois, site of the lock and dam marking the end of the Chicago Sanitary and Ship Canal in the Illinois Waterway System.   *Library of Congress*

GARY, Indiana, is at the very southern end of Lake Michigan, 24 miles southeast of Chicago. Midway between the iron-ore deposits of the Northwest and the coal fields of the East and Southeast, Gary smelled of its destiny, steel. Judge Elbert H. Gary, head of the United States Steel Company, for whom Gary is named, built the city from the ground up, starting in 1905. It is one of the few cities entirely built by one industry. There was nothing there when it started but sand. The engulfing sand was moved, trainloads of topsoil were brought in, a river was moved 300 feet. At first there were tar-paper shacks, next large buildings; then, in 1921, most of these buildings were pulled down and the whole city was redesigned and rebuilt. Gary has many fine parks and roadways and a progressive school system that has interested educators from all over the world. Under Dr. William Wirt, it divided the child's day into work, study, and play, and tried to make school more attractive than the streets, not stopping at aquariums in the playground. The population of Gary in 1905 was zero. Today it is 178,320. Needless to say, after the success of steel, other industries came in—all of them large.

Gary, Indiana, on Lake Michigan has long been one of the world's greatest steel centers. It is strategically located midway between the sources of iron ore in the north and the coal mines of the east and southeast. This photograph shows ore, coke, and limestone being carried in skip cars to the top of a blast furnace, in an automatic loading operation.

The Chicago Association of Commerce

A 1908 view of the Gary works of the Indiana Steel Co.   *Library of Congress*

MICHIGAN CITY, Indiana, is forty miles southeast of Chicago, at the mouth of Trail Creek. It was founded in 1832 as the northern terminus of the old Michigan Road. It has a fine lakefront and beach and is a popular summer resort. At one time, it was a port rivaling Chicago. It still has good harbor facilities, and these are in prospect of taking on new importance with the building of a Bethlehem Steel Company facility twelve miles away that will have an eventual capacity of 10,000,000 tons of tin, plate, and hot rolled steel. This new billion-dollar operation will be near National Steel Company's Midwest Mill. Michigan City has a symphony orchestra, an Art League, and choral and theatrical groups. Nearby are the world-famous 100-acre International Friendship Gardens with garden plots of different nationalities and an outdoor Theater of Nations where operatic and symphonic concerts are given. Michigan City's population is 36,653.

A bird's-eye view of Michigan City, Indiana, as it appeared in 1869. The cluster of buildings in the foreground consists of a railroad roundhouse and machine shops.   Library of Congress

Every year thousands of visitors come to the International Friendship Gardens at Michigan City, Indiana. Here, in an area of approximately 100 acres, are flowers and plants from many lands, some donated by famous people, some contributed by foreign governments—truly, a world garden.

Michigan City has an outstanding symphony orchestra of 75 pieces. Its six annual programs add much to the cultural life of the community.

The winning float in the 1962 Summer Festival Parade at Michigan City, Indiana.
William T. Swedenberg

Aerial view of Michigan City, on the shore of Lake Michigan in northern Indiana. This city not only manufactures furniture and railroad cars but is something of a lake resort, as evidenced by the boat basin in the center of the picture. Nearby attractions are Indiana Dunes State Park and the International Friendship Gardens.
Northern Indiana Public Service Co.

ST. JOSEPH, Michigan, forms an economic unit with *BENTON HARBOR* across the St. Joseph River, 48 miles southwest of Kalamazoo. Both cities are surrounded with flourishing orchards and depend considerably on fruit canning. St. Joseph manufactures machinery and rubber goods, and its mineral springs and fine beaches make it a popular tourist center. Its population of 11,755 unites in an annual Blossom Festival with Benton Harbor's 19,136 citizens. Benton Harbor is somewhat more widely renowned because of the headquarters there of the House of David, a religious colony. Israelite City, a rival of the House of David, is also located there. The city has a widely known Municipal Fruit Market covering 16 acres, and the annual Blossom Festival in May that attracts 200,000 visitors. Besides canning, Benton Harbor manufactures metal products.

A circa-1890 view of Michigan's twin cities, Benton Harbor (left) and Saint Joseph (right), which are located in the southwestern part of the state on Lake Michigan. Both are thriving cities today, central points in the state's fruit-growing district and also the producers of an increasing variety of manufactured products.　　　　　　　　　　　News-Palladium, Benton Harbor

Benton Harbor is the site of the communistic religious colony known as the House of David, which was organized in 1903. Pictured here are some of the leaders of the Colony.
　　　　　　　　　　　　　　　　　　　　　　News-Palladium, Benton Harbor

The House of David runs Colony Park, an amusement area that boasts lovely gardens and an unusually complete miniature railroad, designed and built by House of David engineers. Sightseers can take a mile-long ride on the small-scale train, with a Colony member at the throttle.
　　　　　　　　　　　　　　　　　　　　　　News-Palladium, Benton Harbor

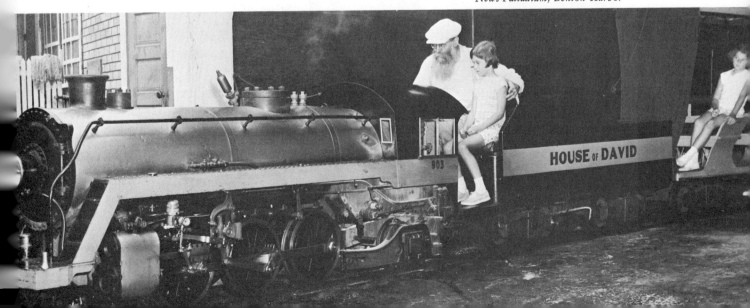

A whaleback excursion steamer at the entrance to Saint Joseph Harbor (circa 1898). Originally grain ships, these whalebacks were converted to carry passengers. They carried thousands at a time, far in excess of safe capacity, but no one of them ever met disaster while in passenger service. The steamer shown is the Christopher Columbus, *the greatest of its kind, 1,511 gross tons, 360 feet by 42. It was built in 1892, scrapped in 1936.*   News-Palladium, Benton Harbor

Scene in Benton Harbor's fruit market—the largest cash market for small fruit in the world.
News-Palladium, Benton Harbor

SOUTH HAVEN, Michigan, at the mouth of the Black River on Lake Michigan, is a customs station and an important port. It is also a manufacturing center (pianos and organs), and a supply center for many neighboring resorts. It has five miles of exceptionally fine white sandy beach, and circling it are forty inland lakes. Michigan State University has a horticultural station here. The population numbers 6,149.

The harbor at South Haven, Michigan, in the early 1900's. The two ships in the foreground are the Eastland *and the* Soo City *(left to right).*
News-Palladium, Benton Harbor

HOLLAND, Michigan, is at the mouth of the Black River on Lake Macatawa, a six-mile Lake Michigan inlet. In many ways it is like a corner of Holland in the United States, its people being predominantly of Dutch descent. At the time of the May Tulip Festival, many put on native costume and even the children take part in the celebration, which includes floral parades, pageants, and Dutch displays. The Dutch wave that settled here in 1846 came (as so often in earlier history) as a result of religious troubles. These people built a tidy, beautiful new-world Holland, and in 1871 (the same catastrophic dry year of the Chicago holocaust), fire in two hours razed their city. They rebuilt it, even more beautifully, from neighboring sandstone. The local Calvinists established two institutions of higher learning, Hope College and Western Theological Seminary. Paul de Kruif, the writer, was born in nearby Zeeland. Holland has a number of local industries, including a wooden-shoe factory. Its population is 24,777.

The steamer Puritan, *which touched at lake resorts* circa 1911, *is shown here at Holland, Michigan.*
Michigan Historical Commission

In the Muskegon and Holland areas of lower Michigan, the population is predominantly of Dutch descent. (In the city of Holland itself, 90 percent of the residents are of Dutch extraction.) Following the tradition of their homeland, they raise fine tulips, and a little girl in native costume like this one is a common sight in tulip time.

Michigan Tourist Council, Lansing

This aerial view of Holland, Michigan, shows Hope College and Western Theological Seminary in the foreground.

Holland Chamber of Commerce

GRAND HAVEN, Michigan, at the mouth of the Grand River northwest of Grand Rapids, is twelve miles south of Muskegon. It ships hundreds of thousands of crates of celery and of grapes and other fruits annually, mainly to Chicago. Its celery shipments alone run to the millions of dollars. It manufactures printing presses, tools, and plumbing fixtures. Along a drive that parallels the deep-water channel between Grand River and Lake Michigan runs beautiful Grand Haven State Park and its wooded dunes and a magnificent beach. There is a United States Coast Guard station at Grand Haven, as well as a Soldier's Home, and the city is proud of its "world's largest" musical fountain. Population is 11,066.

Soldiers' Home at Grand Haven, Michigan.

Library of Congress

The Musical Fountain at Grand Haven, Michigan, is the largest in the world. Columns of water, colored lights, and music are all synchronized.

GRAND RAPIDS, with a population of 177,313, is the second largest city in Michigan and is nationally renowned for the manufacture of furniture. Twenty-five miles up Grand River from Lake Michigan, it was originally the site of a Baptist mission to the Indians. In 1826, Louis Campau settled here and named the place for the rapids. As early as 1837, steamboats were making a regular run between the rapids and Grand Haven on the lake. Lumber rode in on the river, and during the sixties, Campau Square was a notorious gambling and red-light district. In 1883, after prolonged rain, 150,000,000 feet of logs broke away and tore a path of destruction through the city. Disastrous floods have been frequent. But the same unruly river provided the first hydroelectric plant in the Midwest. Grand Rapids furniture first attracted national attention at the Philadelphia Centennial Exposition in 1876. Buyers from the East began going yearly to the Michigan city, and it eventually set the furniture style of the country. Today there are over 80 large plants making furniture. A museum in the mansion of former timber tycoon T. Stewart White (father of the popular novelist, Stewart Edward White) traces the evolution of furniture from Colonial times to the present through a series of rooms. Many of the designs are by master local craftsmen.

A furniture craftsman doing hand-carving in a Grand Rapids plant.

Furniture being hand-painted by a group of girl artists in the thirties.

View of Grand Rapids from Brush Factory looking northeast. Note the timber in the river and the covered bridge. No date given. Copied from a stereograph by Schuyler C. Balwin, Photographer.   Michigan Historical Commission, Lansing, Mich.

The architect's model of the new City-County Center, now rising in the heart of the Downtown Redevelopment Area of Grand Rapids.   Grand Rapids Chamber of Commerce

Aerial view of Grand Rapids, showing the new expressway.   Grand Rapids Chamber of Commerce

MUSKEGON, Michigan, has an exceptionally fine harbor at the mouth of the Muskegon River, 35 miles northwest of Grand Rapids. Its name comes from the Indian *muskego* (river-with-marshes). Muskegon's main national group is Holland Dutch, but there are Poles, Slavs, and Scandinavians. The early settlers were French traders; then came the roaring days of the lumber trade when red-sashed woodsmen cut down the tall timber that Jean Nicolet had noticed some two centuries earlier, and made Muskegon the "Gambling Queen" of west Michigan. At one time there were 47 sawmills in operation at once. Lumber died in the glare of a sawdust conflagration that burned the city to the ground, but both the city and its economy were rebuilt. Motors (the Continental Motors Corporation)

helped and, oddly, a pocket of oil was discovered under the city and was pumped and refined. Industries were diversified and Muskegon steadied into the twentieth century, making airplane engines, machinery, office equipment, refrigerators, cables, and billiard tables. The *Milwaukee Clipper*, which can carry 900 passengers and 120 automobiles, travels daily during the summer between Muskegon and Milwaukee, crossing the lake in six hours. Within the city limits is a state-protected Indian cemetery and one of the earliest municipal art galleries (the Hackley Gallery) in the country with excellent paintings from Goya and Hogarth to John Steuart Curry. The city's population is 46,485.

An 1868 print of Muskegon, Michigan.
Library of Congress

A modern view of Muskegon, Michigan, which claims to have the Great Lakes' finest natural harbor.
Muskegon Chamber of Commerce

LUDINGTON, Michigan, at the mouth of the Pere Marquette River, is a leading Michigan port. Pere Marquette Lake gives it a large safe harbor for passenger boats, railway car ferries, and freighters. A monument here (a large lighted cross) honors Father Marquette's first burial place (1675) before his re-mains were removed to St. Ignace. The community is named for James Ludington, a lumberman of the eighties, on behalf of whom the original name of Marquette was dropped. There is year-round ferry service from Ludington to Manitowoc, Milwaukee, and Kewaunee. The population is 9,421.

A car ferry being loaded at Ludington, Michigan (circa 1912).   *Michigan Historical Commission*

MANISTEE, Michigan, is both a resort and industrial town at the mouth of Big Manistee River where it enters Lake Manistee. It has one of Lake Michigan's finest beaches. The city's name is that of the village of 1,000 Chippewas who originally lived here. The lumbering era rode roughshod through the local area, and it now has a notable interest in reforestation and ad-joins the 350,000-acre Manistee National Forest. A yearly Manistee National Forest Festival is held here in July to promote conservation of this tract. Manistee produces salt pumped from deep mines and makes box boards and boats. Its population is 8,324 persons.

A photograph of Lake Michigan taken at twilight from the Fifth Avenue pier, which, incidentally, is a famous spot for perch fishing.
Manistee Co. Board of Commerce

The Lake Manitee pulp and paperboard mill of the Packaging Corporation of America is the largest wood-utilizing facility in the Midwest. Its multimillion-dollar annual payroll is influential in the economy of northern Michigan. Manitee Chamber of Commerce

An old photograph of the steamer Pere Marquette No. 3, *passing the novelty works at Manistee, Michigan.* Michigan Historical Commission

TRAVERSE CITY, Michigan, has a remarkable site at the base of both arms of Grand Traverse Bay with Old Mission Peninsula projecting north out of the city. It is the center of a cherry orchard area numbering over a million trees. French trappers who lived here almost 300 years ago left evidence of cleared land and apple orchards, but the land was wilderness again for nearly two centuries. It had the usual lumbering pyrotechnics and was saved from the post-lumber-boom collapse by growing its big cherry crop. Traverse City now produces farm tools, leather goods, and coffins, furniture, and other wood products. Cool, pollen-free lake breezes, good fishing, and many other vacationist attractions make it a popular resort. Its year-round population is 18,432.

An aerial view of Traverse City, Michigan. *Traverse City Chamber of Commerce*

Across the Leelanau Peninsula from Traverse City, Michigan, are Sleeping Bear Dunes, a 600-foot sheer rise of sand overlooking Lake Michigan. Some people slide down the dunes on sand skis, some take off in gliders, and others just visit the spot as one of the great natural wonders of the region. *West Michigan Tourist Association*

On Lake Huron

ROGERS CITY, Michigan, thirty miles northwest of Alpena, ships large quantities of limestone quarried nearby and carried by lake freighters. The town became widely known when one of these freighters, the 16,000-ton *Carl D. Bradley,* sank off Charlevoix. Most of the thirty-three seamen who drowned lived in Rogers City (see the chapter "Wind, Fire, Ice, Collision.") The site of the future town seems to have been wilderness up to about 1869; a few settlers incorporated as a village in 1872, only to find they were not legally incorporated and their elected mayor, Charles Pfanneschmidt, was consequently illegal. It was all done over again legally in 1877, except that a new mayor was chosen. Rogers City was named after William E. Rogers of New York, who owned the land on which the new village was platted. An account in the *Presque Isle County Advance* says, "Mr. Rogers, so far as we know, may never have seen the place. Certainly he contributed nothing to the village other than his name, and possibly his blessing." Interest in limestone dates to about 1860, and the current quarrying operations are said to be the largest in the world. Other local interests are commercial fishing and the manufacturing of woodenware. The population is 4,722.

A winter log train at Rogers City, Michigan.

Indies Collection

The vast size of this limestone quarry near Rogers City, Michigan—the world's largest—is clearly apparent from the air. The enormous reserves of the quarry can be seen in the background. The plant is the Michigan Limestone Division of the United States Steel Corp.

ALPENA, Michigan, on Thunder Bay, is fifty miles north of the mouth of Saginaw Bay. When it was surveyed in 1839, no member of the surveying party would accept an offer of the township as full payment for his summer's work. In spite of this discouraging start, Alpena on its hilly site became a flourishing center of lumber and flour mills, tanneries, fisheries, limestone quarries (rivaling those near Rogers City), and cement and paper plants. It has a municipal beach and camp grounds. With a population of 14,682, it is the largest community north of Bay City on the Lake Huron shore.

A horse-and-buggy-days scene on Second Street in Alpena, Michigan. Michigan Historical Commission

BAY CITY, Michigan, is on the Saginaw River, near its mouth on Saginaw Bay, thirteen miles north of Saginaw. A single sawmill, torn down in 1936, was the sole reminder of the roaring days of lumbering at the end of the last century. At that time the river was hidden by piled-up ramparts of wood that departed on all kinds of vessels to build the down-lakes cities. When logs stopped coming down the river, a fifth of the city's population departed. Soft-coal mines in the neighborhood were developed and today there are fishing, boat-bulding, beet-sugar refining, and the production of automobile parts and heavy machinery. The house of the first settlers, Joseph and Mader Tromble, still stands on the northeast corner of 24th and Water Streets. Bay City's population is 53,604.

Aerial view of Bay City, Michigan, on the Saginaw River at the head of Saginaw Bay. Once largely a lumbering center, Bay City now has varied industries, including fishing, boat-building, and manufacturing. Greater Bay City Chamber of Commerce

SAGINAW, Michigan, is a leading port and industrial community south of Bay City on the Saginaw River. Louis Campau, a French fur-trader, was the first known settler. He built a post near the foot of the present Throop Street and cooperated with Governor Lewis Cass in negotiating a treaty with the Chippewas, in 1819, three years after he arrived. Saginaw became one of the great centers of the lumbering industry. Timberland sold for $1.50 an acre and the lumber from it brought hundreds of times that. Moreover, it was a common practice to buy a tract and then steal everything around it. The sawmills moved in like an army. In 1834, Saginaw's first steam sawmill started operating, and fifteen years later there were 558. Little wonder that it took only some fifty years to clean off the seemingly inexhaustible woods. In one year, Saginaw shipped a billion board feet of lumber. When the woods gave out, luckily coal in quantity was discovered by prospectors drilling for salt. With coal handy, the city was set to become an iron producer and now has one of the world's largest gray-iron foundries, a plant of the General Motors Corporation. It also produces graphite, measuring instruments, and bakery equipment. Schuch Hotel, built in 1868, is claimed to be Michigan's oldest in continuous operation. The population of Saginaw is 98,265.

In 1905, Genesee Avenue in Saginaw, Michigan, looked like this.   *Library of Congress*

On the St. Clair River

PORT HURON, Michigan, stretches over seven miles along the St. Clair River where it flows out of Lake Huron. The river carries a gaudy traffic of freighters, ferry boats, speed boats, passenger liners, tankers, tugs, yachts, and an occasional naval vessel. The Blue Water Bridge and an electric railway tunnel cross it to Sarnia, Ontario.

Port Huron is one of Michigan's oldest settlements. It was fortified in 1686 to protect the French fur trade, but the stockade was burned two years later. The first permanent settlement dates from 1790. In 1814, Fort Gratiot was built on the site of the old stockade, and it survived the shocks of war and peace until 1882. Port Huron was incorporated as a city in 1857. Its electric street railway and electrified railway tunnel were among the first ever built, and so it seems appropriate that Thomas A. Edison was a boy and young man here. For a time he had a baggage-car laboratory on the Port Huron–Detroit run of the Grand Trunk Railway—until a slight explosion and fire stopped his traveling experiments. Today Port Huron's economy is based on salt, oil, and gas, and on wood industries, paper manufacturing, boat-building, and the making of automobile parts. The population numbers 36,084.

Port Huron, at the Lake Huron end of the St. Clair River, in 1960.   *Calvin M. Lakin*

On Lake St. Clair

MOUNT CLEMENS, Michigan, on a ridge above the Clinton River, has long been a health resort, "Michigan's Spa," smelling bracingly of sulphur. The water, pumped from a depth of 2,600 feet, contains about thirty different chemical elements. It is bottled and shipped all over the world, the locality's leading industry. By contrast, the town raises roses. Fleeing Moravians founded the community, calling it originally New Gnadenhutten (New Huts of God), and there is still a Moravian Drive that runs along an old Indian trail to the southwest. The population of Mount Clemens is 21,016.

A 1903 photo of the famous Colonial House in Mount Clemens, Michigan, a town noted as a health resort because of its mineral waters.   *Library of Congress*

On the Detroit River

DETROIT, Michigan, is on the 29-mile-long Detroit River between Lakes St. Clair and Erie. It is the largest city in the state, the fifth largest city in the country, and the center of the world's automobile industry, producing a decisive portion of our twelve-billion-dollar annual total of cars and trucks. This stunning lead was the result of an early talent for carriage building and of the inventive genius of Henry Ford and others. Superb Great Lakes and associated transport facilities help send these cars all over the world. No small part of the dollar value of the new St. Lawrence Seaway traffic comes from Detroit.

Two vehicular tunnels, a railroad tunnel, and the Ambassador Bridge join the city with Windsor, Ontario, which by a freak of geography is south of Detroit.

Detroit was founded July 24, 1701, by Antoine de la Mothe Cadillac, in the service of King Louis XIV. The British captured it during the French and Indian War, were reluctant to give it to the U.S. after the Revolutionary War, and did not relinquish it until 1796 when General Anthony Wayne put strong military pressure on them. Detroiters rather welcomed their release from the British, for they were ruggedly independent; they gave women the vote in 1802, and held what is believed to have been the first town meeting in the Midwest.

The city's population doubled every decade from 1830 to 1860 as the great immigration wave came in. After the Civil War there was a rapid growth of industry, and with the invention of the automobile the city vaulted in a few years from fourteenth to fifth in

Walk-in-the-Water, *the first steamboat on Lake Erie, with a view of Detroit in 1820 in the background. Noah Brown supervised the building of the boat and Robert Fulton the mechanical installations. Ship's captain was Job Fish. Starting in 1818, the* **Walk-in-the-Water** *made the run from Buffalo to Detroit in two days or better, with intermediate stops at Erie and Cleveland. Never before had Michigan been so near the eastern states. The passengers may here be seen waving from the deck. Their quarters were all below deck, the ladies forward, the gentlemen aft; there was a small smoking room near the baggage room and a small dining room next to the gentlemen's quarters. Note the still sparsely starred U.S. flag. The boat's engine had a curious history; after powering both the* **Walk-in-the-Water** *and the* **Superior,** *it was used to run the first sawmill in Saginaw. The original of this drawing was done by Major George Washington Whistler, father of James Abbott McNeill Whistler, the famous painter. The large house at the extreme left was the residence of Lewis Cass, governor of Michigan from 1813 to 1831. The house just above the bow of the* **Walk-in-the-Water,** *the Campau house, is said to have been built on the site of the original headquarters of Cadillac.* Dossin Great Lakes Museum

the nation. Present-day industries include a wide range from seeds to salt. The combined demand of some 5,000 factories in Detroit makes the city the world's largest user of finished steel.

Two universities, Wayne State University and the University of Detroit, are the largest of its educational institutions, which also include Detroit College of Law, Marygrove College, the Detroit Institute of Technology, and the Detroit Institute of Musical Art. Its Institute of Art, public library, and orchestra are widely known. Among Detroit's 364 parks, Belle Isle in the Detroit River is outstanding, with flower gardens, playgrounds, an imaginative Children's Zoo, and the Dossin Great Lakes Museum. The city has 1,859 churches. Population, 1,670,144.

The Ambassador Bridge, fragile-looking in this aerial view though it casts a substantial shadow on the waters of the Detroit River, connects Windsor, Canada (on the right), with Detroit.

Photographic Survey Corp. Ltd., Toronto

Detroit has been a trading and political center for the Great Lakes region since its earliest days. This drawing of the settlement as it looked in the middle of the eighteenth century is evidence that the riverfront was a busy spot even then.   Burton Historical Collection

Lewis Cass (1782-1866) is considered to have been Michigan's leading public figure. In his long career he served as state governor, U. S. senator, minister to France, secretary of war, and secretary of state. In 1848 he was the Democratic candidate for President, but was defeated by Taylor. This photograph, reproduced from a daguerreotype, shows him as our representative in France.

Michigan's first state fair was held at Detroit in 1849 on a site west of Woodward between Columbia and Vernor Highway. This painting, done at that time by Frederick E. Cohen, depicts a customary sight—the gathering of a crowd to hear who got the premium awards. Secretary Holmes is reading the list. The fair grounds with the prototype of all ferris wheels can be glimpsed through the open door.

Ford Motor Company's first moving assembly line saw Model T's produced partially out of doors. Inaugurated by Henry Ford in 1913, the assembly line procedure paved the way to mass production in many industries.

Ford Motor Co.

Every home needed a stove, and Detroit early set out to supply the demand. From about 1880 on, it was the stove capital of America. This 25-foot-high kitchen range, originally constructed for exhibition at the Chicago Columbian Exposition of 1893, was the latest word in stove design at that time. After the Fair, it remained on display in Detroit at Jefferson Avenue and the Belle Isle Bridge.

Henry Ford was forty years old and his son Edsel was ten when Ford Motor Company was founded in 1903. This 1905 picture of father and son shows them in a Model C, one of Ford's earliest products. *Ford Motor Co.*

The Detroit Yacht Club with its 3,500 members is the largest in the world in membership. The clubhouse, built in 1921 in a Mediterranean style, is situated on the club's island off Belle Isle near the head of the Detroit River. Across the lagoon are a few of the hundreds of sailboats owned by members. Power yachts anchor on the other side of the island. *Jack Grenard, Detroit*

Busy freight yards stretch along the bank of the Detroit River in west Detroit. Note the waiting car ferry.

Detroit Edison Co.

RIVER ROUGE, Michigan, is on the Detroit River at the mouth of the Rouge River six miles southwest of Detroit. The Ford Motor Company has a huge plant here, including a blast furnace and a glass works.

Shipbuilding is important and the community also makes marine engines. It was incorporated as a city in 1921 and now has a population of 18,147.

Aerial view of the River Rouge. The boat slip is at the center of the picture, blast furnaces and coke ovens at the left.

Ford Motor Co.

On Lake Erie

MONROE, Michigan, was originally called Frenchtown and was settled by the French on the River Raisin four miles from where it empties into Lake Erie. Governor Cass hastily renamed it to honor an expected visit from President Monroe. The rather garish early history of the community had it in the center of a fight, between the militia of Michigan and Ohio, for Toledo. A badly drawn state boundary encouraged Michigan to claim Toledo, and when a local war threatened, Congress calmed Michigan down by giving her the (as it turned out) invaluable Upper Peninsula. Monroe is further celebrated for an equestrian statue of General George A. Custer (of Custer's Last Stand), who was a Monroe resident. Today the community specializes in nurseries and has been known as the "Floral City." It also does steel and paper milling, lime quarrying, fishing, and varied manufacturing. Its population is 22,968.

General George A. Custer (inset) and his home at Monroe, Michigan. The house was Mrs. Custer's birthplace.

Michigan Historical Commission

Bolles Harbor, port-of-refuge, located on Lake Erie near Monroe, Michigan. Greater Monroe Chamber of Commerce

TOLEDO, Ohio, runs for many miles along both sides of the Maumee River, which is the largest river flowing into any of the Great Lakes, at the southwestern corner of Lake Erie. This top-ranking Great Lakes port is one of the world's leading shippers of soft coal. It also refines and ships oil piped in from the west. Settlement began in earnest only after the War of 1812, although Toledo's history dates back to 1615 when Etienne Brulé, the French explorer, found the Erie Indians living here. The reason for its name is dim with legend, but with a rare international courtesy Toledo, Spain, has sent cultural treasures to the Toledo Museum of Art and to the city's cathedral. In 1835/6 the "Toledo War" hysteria broke out (see Monroe, Michigan). The era of canals favored Toledo, which was early noted for its trade as well as for being in fifth-ranking place on the pre–Civil War Underground Railroad. In the eighties, cheap natural gas attracted industry and Toledo became a center of glass manufacture, making many important innovations in the craft. In 1890 the Toledo Museum of Art was founded; its first show was held in a downtown storeroom. Today it is one of the country's top ten museums. Also in 1890, the Zoo was started—with a woodchuck, two badgers, and a golden eagle. Willys-Overland greeted the new century with a mass-produced automobile (two a minute by 1921). Local products now include (besides glass, automobiles, and automobile accessories, particularly spark plugs) ships, cement, chemicals, precision instruments, paints, paper, textiles, pig iron, and steel. Toledo's population is 318,003.

Aerial view of Toledo, Ohio, on the Maumee River at the southwestern end of Lake Erie. A major lake port and industrial center, modern Toledo stands on the site of old Fort Industry, built by Anthony Wayne in 1794.   *Abodeely Studios, Toledo*

Over-all view of Toledo around the turn of the century.

Close-up of loading operations on the present-day Toledo waterfront.

A 1909 photograph of the Toledo waterfront. Library of Congress

A photograph of Riverside Park and Boat House at Toledo that shows the 1909 style in cars and clothing too. Library of Congress

Foreign freighters in the port of Toledo.

Toledo Chamber of Commerce

MAUMEE (derived from the Indian name *Miami*), Ohio, is on the west bank of the Maumee River fifteen miles upstream from Toledo. French-Canadians tried to establish a fort there as early as 1680. In 1784 the British built Fort Miami, and during the War of 1812 they slaughtered most of a group of 800 Kentuckians in what was later known as Dudley's Massacre. The earthen walls of Fort Miami still exist on U.S. Route 24 west of Detroit Avenue. Maumee is largely residential, but there are limestone quarries nearby and there is some manufacturing. The population is 12,063.

Fort Meigs Memorial, near Maumee, Ohio. The fort, located at the rapids of the Maumee River, was besieged unsuccessfully by the British and Indians in 1813.
Ohio Dept. of Industrial and
Economic Development

FREMONT, Ohio, thirty miles southeast of Toledo, is a quiet residential community with a sensational past. George Washington sent Samuel Brady here to spy out the strength of the Indians, and there were Indian battles until the Wyandots were forced out by the British. The Americans in turn forced the British out after the Revolutionary War. The British tried to reoccupy the area during the War of 1812 and were heroically and successfully fought off by young George Croghan and his men. The early town had several names, but was finally called after John C. Fremont, the explorer. President Rutherford B. Hayes lived here for several years and is buried here. The city's economy is organized around canning and beet-sugar refining. It also makes auto parts, rubber and electrical products, clothing, and cutlery. Fremont had 17,573 citizens at the last census.

Fort Stephenson Park at Fremont, Ohio, showing memorials to Major Croghan and to Old Betsy, the cannon.
Library of Congress

View, looking south, of the waterfront at Sandusky, Ohio. Its excellent harbor on Lake Erie makes Sandusky an important shipping point for coal, iron ore, grain, and a multitude of manufactured products.

Sandusky Chamber of Commerce

SANDUSKY, Ohio, on Sandusky Bay, fifty miles west of Cleveland, is one of the leading coal-shipping ports of the Great Lakes. Although it has a large number of successful factories, foundries, and clay works, it has the feeling and reputation of being a resort town. This may be in part because of the state park and fine beach across the bay, and the islands to the north. Sandusky's name is from an Indian word meaning "at the cold water," for there were cool springs near the bay in the early days. Lakes boats always stopped here.

In 1826 there were 355 "arrivals," and trade and immigration boomed in the next decade. Charles Dickens visited Sandusky in 1842 and found the place "free-and-easy," noting that his host at The Colt's Exchange Hotel lay down on the sofa with his hat on, to talk with him. In 1849 cholera struck and 400 died. The town recovered, grew, and became noted for sweet, dry, and sparkling wines, for which it won medals in Rome and Paris. It is the seat of the state Soldiers' and Sailors' Home. Its population is 31,989.

A sunny day at the beach, Lake Erie, near Sandusky, Ohio.

Ohio Development and Publicity Commission

PUT-IN-BAY VILLAGE, on South Bass Island offshore from Sandusky, Ohio, is where Perry lay in wait for the British naval force in the Battle of Lake Erie. It is a popular resort and used to be the exclusive playground of statesmen and persons of great wealth. The Perry Peace Monument is here, a clear shaft visible from long distances, a symbol of the good will between Canada, and the United States. The population of Put-in-Bay is small, but the transients run to the thousands over the summer season, particularly during he Inter-Lake Yachting Association Regatta.

Perry Peace Monument at Put-in-Bay, the scene of Commodore Perry's victory over the British in 1813.

Ohio Dept. of Industrial and Economic Development

Passengers disembarking at Put-in-Bay from a Cleveland-Toledo lake steamer in the summer of 1906. Put-in-Bay was then a highly popular resort with a water toboggan (all sliders fully clothed in neck-to-calf bathing suits), yachting regattas, dance pavilions (highly proper), the Round House for tea or ice cream, and visits to Perry Cave and Needle's Eye Rock. Library of Congress

HURON, Ohio, at the mouth of the Huron River, eight miles east of Sandusky, uses its good harbor as a transshipping point for iron ore and coal. This natural harbor gave it an early start. The French apparently had a trading post here in the middle of the eighteenth century. Settlement began in 1805, and shipping and ship-building boomed the town in the early decades of the last century. After a slower period, the economy steadied and now relies mainly on transshipment, fishing, and tourist services. There is still some boat-building and the town produces cement blocks, sauerkraut, and pickles. Its population is 5,197.

A composite picture showing some of the industries of Huron, Ohio, that are located on the Huron River and its slips: fishing (exemplified by the boats, anchors, and ropes in the foreground), shipping (ore piles, railroad cars, freighters laid up for the winter), and "the mill" (Eastern States Farmers' Exchange silos and facilities). Huron Public Library

LORAIN, Ohio, twenty-five miles west of Cleveland, is an important port, with a heavy traffic of incoming ore and outgoing coal. It manufactures iron and steel, especially pipe, chemicals, steam shovels and cranes, heating equipment, metal toys, stud-welding guns, clothing, and other products in 69 industrial plants. It has fisheries and boat-building facilities, and a U.S. Coast Guard station is located there. Lorain's early settlers were mostly from Connecticut because of Connecticut's claim to the Western Reserve. The very first attempt at settlement was by a Moravian missionary, David Zeisberger, with a band of Christian Indians. They were told to move on. The first permanent settlers were Azariah Beebe and Nathan Perry, Jr., in 1807.

Before 1837, the port had built over 300 wooden sailing vessels. At first called Black River and Charleston, the community did not take the name Lorain until 1874. By 1890, the population was 4,800. The influx of great industrial plants, U.S. Steel (National Tube Division), the American Shipbuilding Company, Ford Motor Company, and the Thew Shovel Company, have caused a phenomenal growth. The present population is 66,932.

About ten miles west of Lorain, in the town of Vermilion, is the Great Lakes Marine Museum exhibiting models of celebrated and unusual ships that have sailed the Great Lakes.

Looking south at the Lake Erie shorefront of Lorain, Ohio, at the mouth of the Black River.
Lorain Chamber of Commerce

Cleveland in 1833, looking east from the corner of Bank and St. Clair streets. The towers and cupolas rising above the peaceful, rural-looking scene are, from left to right, those of the Cleveland Academy, Trinity Church, First Presbyterian Church, and the courthouse.

I. N. Phelps Stokes Collection of American Historical Prints, New York Public Library

CLEVELAND, Ohio, a port of entry spreading over nearly 75 square miles of lake shore at the mouth of the Cuyahoga River, is Ohio's largest city and eighth largest in the country, with a population of 876,050. It unloads for its own important iron and steel industry and for other Ohio and Pennsylvania steel districts. It transships coal, grain, and lumber. Its steel mills are among the world's largest. Its economy is diversified by metal-working, chemical works, paint and varnish factories, the manufacture of airplane engines, electric appliances, and clothing, and by meat packing, printing, and publishing. Western Reserve University, Case Institute of Technology, Fenn College, Ursuline College for Women, John Carroll University, the Cleveland Institute of Music, the Cleveland Law School, the Schauffler College of Religious and Social Work,

and St. John College are its educational institutions. Its public library is one of the foremost in the country, its museum of art is widely known, as are its orchestra and the Cleveland Playhouse. Nela Park, research laboratory of the General Electric Company, is located here. Cleveland celebrated its centenary in 1936/37 by holding a Great Lakes Exposition.

Cleveland was platted in 1796 by Moses Cleaveland, who chose his townsite well. The first early settler who stuck it out at the river mouth was Lorenzo Carter. When the *Walk-in-the-Water* nosed in for a visit in 1818, there were less than a thousand inhabitants. The Ohio and Erie Canal arrived in 1832 and Cleveland rapidly established its leadership on Lake Erie. It was chartered as a city in 1836.

An ore freighter being maneuvered by tugs in the Cuyahoga River, inner harbor at the port of Cleveland. Terminal Tower (52 stories), the city's tallest building, is at the left.

Cleveland Chamber of Commerce

An air view that shows both the inner and outer harbor at Cleveland. Cleveland Chamber of Commerce

Cleveland Park in 1858. This view is a lithograph made from a photograph. Since the Perry Monument was not unveiled until 1860 (and did not look exactly as shown here), the lithographer evidently used his imagination in depicting it. The rest is real enough. The tall spire at the left is the Second Presbyterian Church; the one behind it is Trinity Protestant Episcopal. Behind the fountain is the old Hoffman Block. The spire at the right belongs to St. Paul's Protestant Episcopal Church. The hoopskirted ladies and high-hatted gentleman are authentic figures of the time.
I. N. Phelps Stokes Collection of American Historical Prints, New York Public Library

Nela Park, General Electric's lighting institute and laboratory in Cleveland, is an attractive example of the parklike surroundings many industries today provide for their installations. Tours are available to visitors on weekdays.
Cleveland Chamber of Commerce

Sunday sightseers at the Cleveland Museum of Art.
Cleveland Chamber of Commerce

The Arcade, Cleveland, circa 1905. This was the largest of a number of arcades in Cleveland.

Library of Congress

Old west pier and the original harbor light on the Cleveland lakefront, circa 1894. The area has since been filled in for a U.S. Coast Guard Station. *Cleveland Public Library*

A 1905 picture of the Cuyahoga River taken from the viaduct, Cleveland.   *Library of Congress*

Aerial view of Lewis Flight Propulsion Laboratory at Cleveland.   *Cleveland Chamber of Commerce*

Ashtabula's harbor, on Lake Erie at the mouth of the Ashtabula River.   Photo by Richard E. Stoner

ASHTABULA, Ohio, at the mouth of the Ashtabula River, 55 miles northeast of Cleveland, unloads iron ore for the Youngstown-Pittsburgh steel districts. It manufactures oxygen, acetylene, farming tools, communications equipment, leather goods, and hydraulic presses. It also has shipbuilding yards, oil refineries, fisheries, and large greenhouses for raising vegetables and fruit. The first permanent residence in Ashtabula was built in 1803 by George Beckwith on the west flats of the Ashtabula River just south of what is now known as West Fifth Street. In 1809 a log schoolhouse was built and by 1810 there were 75 families. The British fleet, before Perry captured it, was scared away from the port by a wise display of dummy soldiers and broomstick guns and much marching around of the town's small force. Platt Rogers Spencer, who originated Spencerian penmanship, was an Ashtabulan. Many pages of writing by this master of the art are now on file at the Ashtabula Public Library. The town was a fiery center of antislavery sentiment and the famous Hubbard Homestead was a station on the Underground Railroad. Its recent history has been one of steady civic and industrial growth. The population is 24,944.

The modern docks at Ashtabula are equipped with the most efficient machinery for the handling of iron ore and coal.
Baltimore Life Insurance Co., Photo by A. Aubrey Bodine

CONNEAUT, Ohio, is an ore and coal port at the very northeast corner of the state, just next to the Pennsylvania line. The name is pronounced ko'-ne-ot, an Indian term of fluid meaning that may be "fish" or "snow place" or even "it is a long time since they have gone." The ever-present Moses Cleaveland stopped here in 1796 as surveyor for the Connecticut Land Company, but the first actual settlers came in 1799—Thomas Montgomery and Aaron Wright. The community's natural harbor has been its economic mainstay from the earliest time. Today it produces canned goods and the cans for them, farm tools, leather, communications equipment, light bulbs, cutlery, and clothing. It has railroad shops, fisheries, and molding-sand pits. The latest population figure is 10,557.

The steamer Benjamin F. Fairless *being unloaded at Conneaut, Ohio. The city has benefited greatly from its fine natural harbor.*   United States Steel Corp.

ERIE, Pennsylvania, a busy port, is the only outlet Pennsylvania has on the Great Lakes. It is the state's third largest city. It has a commerce of iron ore, lumber, coal, petroleum, grain, and fish, and manufactures boilers, stoves, engines, electric locomotives, gristmill products, aluminum forgings, paper, plastics, and rubber products. Since 1958, it has been the headquarters for the Motor and Generator Division of the General Electric Company. Erie's name derives from the Eriez Indians, who used to live where the city is now. Pennsylvania bought the site from the U.S. Government in 1792 for 75 cents an acre, George

Washington and Thomas Jefferson signing the deed. When the little community was incorporated as a borough in 1805, it had 250 residents.

In the War of 1812, the entire Lake Erie fleet was built here under the most difficult and trying circumstances. The early Erie frontiersmen who created and manned the fleet contributed much to Perry's victory. Erie continued building ships and made the world's first all-iron battleship, the *Wolverine,* in 1843. The community was chartered as a city in 1851. The present population numbers 138,440.

The Duquesne Marine Terminal and other harbor facilities at Erie, Pennsylvania, that state's only port on the lakes.   Lutz Photo, Erie

This blockhouse near Erie, Pennsylvania, is an authentic copy of one built by General Anthony Wayne, who was to a large degree responsible for opening the area to civilization. A sign over the door dedicates the structure to his memory. Wayne died in Erie in 1796.

Pennsylvania Dept. of Commerce

Perry Memorial House and Dickson Tavern at Second and French streets in Erie, Pennsylvania. This was Perry's home in Erie during the building of his fleet. Here, too, the food was prepared for the banquet given General Lafayette when he visited Erie in June, 1825. During the Civil War period, the house was a station on the Underground Railroad.

Mitchell Advertising Agency, Erie

Erie Country in northwestern Pennsylvania has long been noted for its excellent Concord grapes. This photo shows one of the large, well-kept vineyards.

Mitchell Advertising Agency, Erie

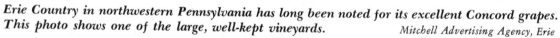

DUNKIRK, New York, is a Lake Erie port in the southwest corner of New York, 35 miles southwest of Buffalo. It is in the midst of a tomato- and grape-raising area and manufactures radiators, boilers, tool steel, glass, machinery, and silk. It was incorporated as a village in 1837 and as a city in 1880, and is the seat of Holy Cross Preparatory Seminary. The population is 18,205.

A view of the Lake Erie shoreline, with the Dunkirk, New York, lighthouse on the point in the background.
                                                                    Dunkirk Chamber of Commerce

BUFFALO, New York, population 532,759, the second largest city in the state and one of the principal ports on the Great Lakes, is at the eastern end of Lake Erie on the Niagara River. A major U.S. industrial complex, it has one of the most diversified economies of any large American city. Its industries include meat-packing, flour-milling, the manufacture of iron and steel, rubber, gypsum products, airplanes, automobiles, furniture, and plastics, and also printing and publishing. Its city hall and Prudential Building were designed by Louis Sullivan, and the Larkin office building by Frank Lloyd Wright. It is the seat of the University of Buffalo. The noted Peace Bridge links it to Fort Erie, Ontario, across the Niagara River.

On August 7, 1679, La Salle's *Griffin* was pulled away from Squaw Island, which is within the present city limits of Buffalo, and was hauled over the short rapids to the lake to start on her fateful voyage. The French made the first settlement in 1758. The British destroyed it the following year. In the latter part of the century, the site of Buffalo was a reservation of the Seneca Indians.

Buffalo, probably in 1852, drawn by J. W. Hill and engraved by Mr. Wellstood for the Ladies' Repository of Cincinnati (a ladies' magazine). The Buffalo River is in the immediate foreground, the Erie Canal at the left. The broad street in the center of the picture is Main Street; parallel to it, at the right, is Washington Street. Sailing schooners, barges, and sidewheel steamers fill the river and are tied up along the docks.
                              I. N. Phelps Stokes Collection of American Historical Prints, New York Public Library

Buffalo seen from Lake Erie, probably in 1835. This scene was painted by W. J. Bennett from a sketch by J. W. Hill. The sailing vessels in the harbor far outnumber the steamers, only two of which are visible, and these were equipped with sails for use in an emergency. A canopied boat propelled by gentlemen oarsmen shows how society toured the lakefront. All the many churches on the skyline were later torn down or converted to various business uses except one, the First Baptist Church, which became a government post office and later part of the Buffalo Medical School.
I. N. Phelps Stokes Collection of American Historical Prints, New York Public Library

An air view of part of downtown Buffalo showing the streets radiating from the McKinley Monument, a memorial to President McKinley, who was assassinated at the Pan-American Exposition held in Buffalo in 1901. *Chamber of Commerce*

The first bulk shipment of grain from Chicago to Buffalo—1678 bushels of wheat, sent on the Osceola in 1839—took seven days to unload. With storage and unloading facilities like those shown in this photo of present-day Buffalo, the same wheat cargo could be unloaded in seven minutes.   Chamber of Commerce

Joseph Ellicott mapped Buffalo for the Holland Land Company in 1799, which offered it for sale in 1803. The British burned the young city in the War of 1812, driving its 500 inhabitants into the woods. The choice of Buffalo as the terminus of the Erie Canal in 1822 brought a period of furious growth. It was visited by Mrs. Frances Trollope in 1828, who commented on the colonnades and porticoes "all in wood," "run up in a hurry." As the century grew, Buffalo's industries increased, and with the coming of inexpensive electric power from Niagara Falls the city's leading commercial position was assured.

In 1881, Grover Cleveland became mayor of Buffalo and was headed toward the presidency. An earlier Buffalonian, Millard Fillmore, was the thirteenth President. In 1901, President McKinley was assassinated here while attending the Pan-American Exposition. The day McKinley died (September 14,) Theodore Roosevelt, who was in Buffalo, took the oath of office as President.

An old view of Main Street in Buffalo, doubtless early in the present century if one judges by the costumes, the architecture, the trolley cars, and the absence of automobiles. The department store of J. N. Adam and Company—advertised in the center of the picture—is still in business today.
Library of Congress

Buffalo's Delaware Park, with Albright Art Gallery in the foreground, State Teachers' College, and the Historical Museum (at the right).   *Chamber of Commerce*

Air view of the new entrance to the harbor at Buffalo, completed in 1961.

On the Niagara River

NIAGARA FALLS, New York, is on the right bank of the Niagara River at the falls, fifteen miles north-northwest of Buffalo. The tourist business, which began early (the falls were even exploited in book form by their discoverer, Father Hennepin), is still flourishing in this community of 102,394. But cheap electric power has given impetus to local industries, which include a wide variety of products from corsets to chemicals, from airplanes to cereals. The local history goes back to the eighteenth century when the French built two forts here, which they burned when the British came to take over in 1759. The importance of the site then was its control of the seven-mile portage around the falls. When the Erie Canal was built in 1825 the portage rights dropped in value, and they became nonexistent with the building of the Welland Canal. Niagara water power ran the first electric generator in 1881.

Niagara Falls from Goat Island, as depicted by Currier & Ives.　　　*Library of Congress*

A recent photograph of Niagara Falls.　　　*Niagara Falls Area Chamber of Commerce*

LEWISTON, New York, is on the Niagara River seven miles north of the falls. According to the estimates of some geologists, it was the site of the falls about 32,000 years ago. Local history began very early when a Franciscan missionary found here a settlement of Attawandaronk Indians, later destroyed by the Sene- cas. The portage trail constructed by La Salle in 1678 and in use for a century and a half went through the site of Lewiston, which was La Salle's base of supplies. Today it is a small community of 3,320, producing crushed stone and chemicals and working a few silica deposits.

Lewiston, New York, seven miles north of Niagara Falls, has two bridges over the Niagara River —an old one and a new.
Photo by David Mitchell

On Lake Ontario

ROCHESTER, New York, 65 miles east-northeast of Buffalo, is on the New York State Barge Canal and the Genesee River. The river, in fact, bisects the city, which is the state's third largest and has a population of 318,611. Rochester is a point of call for passenger steamers and also handles a large volume of lake ship- ping. Among the large companies located here are Eastman Kodak, Bausch and Lomb, and Taylor Instru- ment Companies. The city manufactures thermometers and other instruments, business machinery, chemicals, clothing, glass-lined steel tanks, carbon paper, check protectors, and dental equipment. The Rochester In- stitute of Technology, the University of Rochester (including the Eastman School of Music and Eastman Theater), the Colgate-Rochester Divinity School, and Nazareth College are its chief educational institutions.

The 33 city parks and the many flower nurseries have given Rochester the name "Flower City."

Rochester's first permanent settlement was in 1812. It was incorporated as a village in 1817, as a city in 1834. The first settler had the gaudy name of Hamlet Scrantom and lived in a house on the site of the present Powers Building. When the Erie Canal was opened, Rochester became a leading builder of barges and a leading miller of flour. It was later noted as the home of Susan B. Anthony and as the place where Frederick Douglass carried on his antislavery work. During the last century, Rochester became one of the great shoe centers of the world, with 64 factories making shoes. It still makes fine shoes.

Looking from the east at the Upper Falls of the Genesee at Rochester, New York, probably in 1835. The tall spire at the left of the picture (just right of the dead tree) is Grace Protestant Episcopal Church. This church was erected around 1830 as St. Paul's, became Grace Church in 1833, and was destroyed by fire in 1847. The smaller tower in the center of the picture marks Rochester High School. I. N. Phelps Stokes Collection of American Historical Prints, New York Public Library

Seneca Indian Village Diorama: Represented here is an everyday scene characteristic of life among the Iroquois tribe in the Rochester area before 1600. Harvest-time activities around the community storehouse include storing corn and squash, food preparation, storytelling, and constructing a house.

Rochester Museum of Arts and Sciences

This excellent early view of Rochester (1835) may be compared to the current one taken more than a century later from much the same position, looking east across the Erie Canal where it turns and runs almost parallel to Buffalo Street (now Main Street), which is in the center of the picture. The large white building with a dome on the right side of Buffalo Street is the Monroe County Court House, erected in 1851 and removed to make way for a new one in the mid-nineties.
I. N. Phelps Stokes Collection of American Historical Prints, New York Public Library

This aerial view of Rochester shows clearly the "Inner Loop" that surrounds the central business district. The city is bisected by the Genesee River, in the center of the picture here. The canal, which now runs along the southern edge of the city, is not in the photo.   *Chamber of Commerce*

Diorama of the landing of the Marquis de Denonville from Canada at Irondequoit Bay on Lake Ontario, July 10, 1687. Supported by a large force of Huron Indians and French, he was on a punitive expedition against the Senecas.

Rochester Museum of Arts and Sciences

In this diorama, American farmers are shown viewing the landing of the British at Charlotte (near Rochester) on Lake Ontario during the War of 1812. Tradition has it that the British ships under Commodore Yeo were scared off by militia who pretended they were a large force.

Rochester Museum of Arts and Sciences

The George Eastman House, now a museum of photography.

Division of Public Information, Rochester

The tremendous plant of the Rochester Products Division of General Motors, on the west side of the city, has more than a million square feet of manufacturing space. Among the products made here are automotive carburetors, steel tubing, automotive cigarette lighters, and lock and key assemblies.

Chamber of Commerce

The camera works plant of the Eastman Kodak Company in Rochester is shown in the foreground. This plant manufactures still and motion picture cameras, projectors, and other photographic equipment. In the background is the Tower Building, the company's administrative headquarters.

Chamber of Commerce

OSWEGO, New York, at the mouth of the Oswego River, 33 miles north-northwest of Syracuse, is the northern terminus of the Oswego River section of the New York State Barge Canal. The easternmost Great Lakes port in the United States, it handles oil, coal, grain, lumber, cement, and pulp wood. It has a million-bushel grain elevator, a hydroelectric plant, and freight houses, and is the marketing focus for agricultural products from a large surrounding area.

Oswego has had some notable shipyards—the *Vandalia*, the first steamer to use Ericsson's screw propeller, was built there. The community was settled after the military occupation ceased, following the Revolutionary War, but it had been a base of supplies and a fort for over a century previously. By 1810, it became a busy port. It was incorporated as a village in 1828 and as a city in 1848. Population, 22,155.

An old lithograph of Oswego, New York, showing the Oswego River at its point of entrance into Lake Ontario.   Library of Congress

Aerial view of Oswego harbor showing the famous old Fort Ontario and the modern harbor installations, including grain elevators and coal docks. In the far distance is the electric steam station of the Niagara-Mohawk Power Corporation.   Chamber of Commerce

WATERTOWN, New York, the gateway to the Thousand Islands, is an important industrial city. The Black River, which bisects it, powers factories that make clothing, silk, and numerous other products, including air brakes. The community owes its start to five New Englanders who arrived in 1800, decided the falls would make a good power source, and called the place Watertown. For as long as the spruce trees lasted, papermaking was a leading industry. But Watertown's chief claim to fame is that Frank W. Woolworth here originated the five-and-dime store. A store clerk, during a fair in 1878 he piled surplus items on a counter, captioned them "Any Item 5¢," and sold out in a few hours. Sensing a good thing, he opened his first store in Utica the following year, and the five-and-ten, the Prix Unique, the low-cost department stores of the world were on their way. Population 33,306.

The business section of Watertown, New York, surrounding its tree-shaded Public Square.   *Chamber of Commerce*

SACKETS HARBOR, New York, eleven miles west of Watertown on Black River Bay, is a pleasant summer resort. It was settled in 1801 just after Watertown. In the War of 1812, it fired the first shot of the war at the attacking British fleet, from a single cannon called "The Old Sow." The British fleet withdrew, the mast of its flagship broken. Brigadier General Zebulon Montgomery Pike, discoverer of Pikes Peak, who was killed in the War of 1812, is buried here, and here a certain Ulysses S. Grant was stationed for some time and joined the local Sons of Temperance. The population of Sackets Harbor is 1,279.

A very early view of Sackets Harbor, New York, showing the military post.   *Library of Congress*

Chapter 7

Locks and Canals

And the Men Who Made Them

FOR MANY YEARS after the first white man set foot on the shores of the Great Lakes, dangerous rapids and falls prevented easy passage—or any water-borne passage—between lakes. Canoes could be carried, but ships could not, even though a few were dragged from Lake Huron up to Lake Superior. Goods were portaged and transshipped, but transshipment was a failing answer. As years went by, the whole development of the area was endangered by this lack of interlake transportation.

Even more crucial, the Great Lakes at first had no waterway to the Atlantic, the upper St. Lawrence being blocked off by the Lachine Rapids. An attempt was made to clear rocks out along the river's north bank so that boats could be towed up, and some boats shot the rapids coming down, but often ended up wrecks.

The year 1816 was notable for a plan to bypass the St. Lawrence. DeWitt Clinton, governor of New York, had a dream—a canal 363 miles long from Lake Erie to the Hudson River and so down to the open sea. Scoffers branded the plan "Clinton's Big Ditch."

There were 568 feet of natural barriers in the way. The project was to cost the unheard-of sum of $11 million.

It took ten years—from 1816 to 1825—to build the Erie Canal. Slowly, tortuously the "ditch" inched forward, Irish muscle wielding pick and shovel, 16 feet per man per week.

The canal was 40 feet wide and five feet deep. Eighty-three locks and 18 aqueducts were built to surmount or cross the obstacles in the way.

LOCKS
AND
CANALS

"Working a Canoe up a Rapid" is the title of this steel engraving by W. H. Bartlett from N. P. Willis's Canadian Scenery, published in 1842. Packages from the canoe are already being carried along the portage. Conditions like these are what made locks and canals necessary.

New York Public Library

This is the first lock in America, actually rebuilt on the spot where it first existed at the Soo. It was originally part of a 300-foot canal dug to help get boatloads of fur past the Sault Ste. Marie rapids in 1797, on the Canadian side. The lock was only 38 feet long with a nine-foot lift. The remaining drop in the river was considered negotiable to the boats of those days. Oxen pulled loaded canoes or bateaux through the canal and lock. *Munson Collection, Michigan Historical Commission*

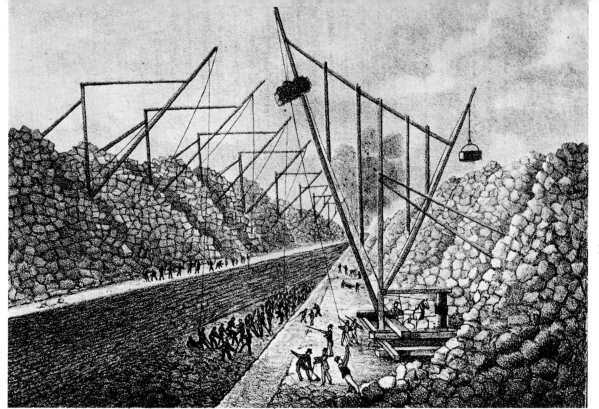

When the Erie Canal was being dug, there were no news photographs. In Cadwallader D. Colden's rare Memoir of 1825 there was this single picture of the digging of the canal, by George Catlin in the period before his fame as an Indian painter. Here are the primitive derricks near Lockport, New York, operated by human or horse power, which pulled the rocks, earth, and mud out of the ditch. In the distance appears to be the explosion of a rock blast. In this crude digging operation, many workmen were killed and injured, but the canal was pushed through by main force.

Courtesy of The New-York Historical Society, New York City

A view of the original five pairs of locks at Lockport, New York. Each had a lift of twelve feet or a total of sixty feet which raised the boats from the Genesee River level to the top of the Niagara escarpment. One tier was used for canal boats ascending, and the other for descending boats. In the center and on either side were stone steps guarded with iron railings, for the convenience and safety of passengers.

The village of Lockport came into being as a result of the Erie Canal. In 1821, there were only two houses there. By 1835, the town had a population of 6,000. This view from a lithograph by Bufford is dated 1836.

Surplus Lake Erie water from the lockages was diverted into a raceway, providing power for manufacturing and milling. With the development of the Niagara region, Lockport became an important marketing center. Courtesy of The New-York Historical Society, New York City

View of the Lockport locks seen from above with a close-up of a Buffalo barge arriving at the top of the escarpment. This view was published in London "by George Virtue, 26 Ivy Lane."

University of Michigan

These historic hand-operated locks on the Rideau Canal at Smith Falls, Ontario, are similar to those used on the early Erie Canal at Lockport. Wesley R. Harkins, Duluth

Terminus of the Erie Canal, at Buffalo harbor, about 1824. The artist is probably George Catlin, who did an almost identical view for Cadwallader D. Colden's Erie Canal Memoir *the next year. This is one of the earliest views of the Buffalo end of the canal, which may be recognized from the two barges floating in it.* Phelps Stokes Collection, New York Public Library

The Erie Canal Is Finished!

The successful completion of the Erie Canal was greeted with unparalleled public enthusiasm. Governor Clinton and retinue rode the first barge from Lake Erie to New York, carrying with them a keg of Lake Erie water to be mingled with the Atlantic Ocean in grave symbolic rites. The keg was painted in green with gilded hoops; it still exists and is on display at the New York Historical Society in New York City. As the governor emptied part of the water into the ocean, he said, "This solemnity at this place on the first arrival of vessels from Lake Erie, is intended to indicate and commemorate the navigable communication, which has been accomplished between our Mediterranean Seas and the Atlantic Ocean, in about eight years, to the extent of more than four hundred and twenty-five miles, by the wisdom, public spirit, and energy of the State of New York; and may the God of the Heavens and of the Earth smile most propitiously on this work, and render it subservient to the best interests of the human race."

At this same moment, the contents of a number of bottles containing water from every part of the world were poured into the sea as "emblematical of our commercial intercourse with all the nations of the earth."

Warships fired off salutes and New York's City Hall erupted into such a display of fireworks, rising from a prepared arsenal on its roof, as had never been seen before on earth. A portion of the Lake Erie water from the famous green keg was put into bottles and into a box made expressly for the occasion by Duncan Phyfe and was shipped to "Major-General Lafayette" who was still dear to the American public.

Oil portrait of Governor DeWitt Clinton by John Wesley Jarvis.
Courtesy of The New-York Historical Society, New York City

The keg of Lake Erie water.
Courtesy of The New-York Historical Society, New York City

*Junction of the Erie and Northern canals, an aquatint by John Hill done about 1838, gives a
good idea of the early canal boats, one being drawn by a tandem team of horses.*

Courtesy of The New-York Historical Society, New York City

In 1825, with great fanfare, the Erie Canal was opened to traffic. Along the canal the
barges began to move, pulled by horses, oxen, even humans who strained along the towpath
built parallel to the canal.

Almost immediately the cost of moving a ton of freight from Lake Erie to New York City
plummeted from a prohibitive $120 down to only $4.

Soon the ever-increasing flow of traffic on the canal forced its deepening to seven feet. In
1916, the Erie Canal was rebuilt and reopened, with 36 locks, each 328 feet long, 45 feet
wide, and 12 feet deep. The 363-mile channel was 123 feet wide at the waterline and 12 feet
in depth.

Across the border in Canada close attention was paid to the planning and the building of
the Erie Canal. Faced with possible diversion of all traffic to the south, Canadians came up
with their own scheme.

They would build a canal to go past Niagara Falls and connect Lakes Erie and Ontario.
This would handle large-vessel traffic instead of the barges that had to be hauled along the
Erie.

*A single canal boat goes through a quiet stretch of country in this picture which united the
talents of H. Inman and Peter Maverick, artists.* *University of Michigan*

This lithograph by D. W. Moody shows the Erie Canal at Rochester, about 1853.
Courtesy of The New-York Historical Society, New York City

This photograph, made in 1904 by the Detroit Photographic Company, shows approximately the same stretch of the Erie Canal at Rochester a half century later, the loaded barges still going through. Library of Congress

Henry Ford's motorship Green Island *had collapsible masts and pilot house so that it could go under the bridges on the New York Barge Canal between the Great Lakes and the Hudson.*
Munson Collection, Michigan Historical Commission

View of the old Welland Canal at Thorold before the improvements of 1873 to 1887 were made.

Ontario Archives, Toronto

View of the Welland Canal during reconstruction in 1881 at Thorold, looking north. This view and the above were taken from Harper's New Monthly Magazine *for August, 1881.*

Ontario Archives, Toronto

A photograph of the Welland Canal at Thorold, taken in the 1890's after the reconstruction was finished.

Ontario Archives, Toronto

Work on the Welland Canal began in 1825. This was to be a 27.6-mile-long lock-canal between Port Colborne on Lake Erie, and Port Robinson on the Chippawa River, which empties into Lake Ontario. The canal runs parallel to and west of the Niagara River. Forty locks were necessary to negotiate the 326-foot lift required to take boats from Lake Ontario (246 feet above sea level) to Lake Erie (572 feet above sea level).

The Welland Canal was first opened to traffic in 1829. From 1873 to 1887 it underwent reconstruction. The number of locks was reduced to 25, which were enlarged in individual size to 270 feet by 45 feet, and deepened to 14 feet.

Work on a new and improved canal started in 1913. The big new Welland Ship Canal was opened in 1932. This consists of four single locks, one flight of three double locks, and one guard lock. Each lock has a lift of 46 feet, is 80 feet wide and 30 feet deep.

Number 5 Flight Lock in the Welland Ship Canal at Thorold, Ontario, today. The steamer **T. R. McLagan** *is downbound, the canaller* **Texaco Brave** *is upbound.* *Wesley R. Harkins, Duluth*

A ship in the Welland Canal at Port Colborne, Ontario.

Ontario Dept. of Travel and Publicity

A railway bridge spanning the Welland Canal is lifted to let a lake freighter go through on its way from Lake Ontario to Lake Erie.

National Film Board of Canada

Contemporary steel engraving of the construction of the Cornwall Canal around the Long Sault Rapids in the 1840's, by W. H. Bartlett.

New York Public Library

When the early stages of the Welland Canal brought water-borne traffic across Lake Ontario to the St. Lawrence, the St. Lawrence was ready with its own improvements. Beginning in 1818, Canadian workmen had been vying with the sweating, barebacked wielders of pick and shovel on the Erie, and were rushing a canal past the foaming barrier of the Lachine Rapids. It was opened in the same year as the Erie, in 1825. It was shallow, and could only take boats of up to 4.5 feet draft. It had to be deepened to nine feet in the busy 1840's, and was enlarged again in 1885 to five locks, each 270 feet long, 45 feet wide and 14 feet deep.

Other canals were built in the area of Prescott and Kingston, the Bay of Quinte and the Thousand Islands, in the bustling and booming 1840's. One, the eleven-mile Cornwall Canal, took navigation around the Long Sault Rapids in the St. Lawrence.

The Williamsburg Canals, more than 26 miles long, floated shipping around Farran's Point, Rapide Plat, and Galops, and included usable parts of the St. Lawrence River itself.

After the success of the Erie and the Welland, the men of the Great Lakes were canal conscious. Other outlets were being hastily constructed to connect the lakes with the Ohio-Mississippi chain of natural waterways.

This might be the same scene taken in an old photograph. It shows a freighter passing the Long Sault Rapids, which are here sufficiently rough but not as rough as Mr. Bartlett's artistry rendered them. *Albertype Collection, Michigan Historical Commission*

There was the Ohio-Erie Canal, opened in 1825, which ran from Cleveland to Akron, and then down the fertile Scioto River valley to join the Ohio River at Portsmouth.

There was the Miami-Erie Canal which linked first Dayton, and later Toledo, with Cincinnati.

Down across Indiana from Toledo went the Wabash and Erie Canal. By 1843 canal boats began to arrive from Lafayette at the Toledo port, which served as joint terminus for the Miami- and the Wabash-Erie canals.

At Chicago, the Illinois and Michigan Canal was pushed forward to completion in 1848. It has been claimed that this waterway and its successors have been the most important single factor in the history of Illinois. By linking Chicago and its Great Lakes trade with a direct water route to the Mississippi and the Gulf of Mexico, it signaled a racing breakaway for this city that had only taken its place in the lakes lineup some two hundred years after its easterly and westerly rivals. The canal also let Chicago outstrip St. Louis as the dominant commercial center of the Midwest.

LOCKS AND CANALS

Lockport Lock, near Joliet, Illinois, handled more than 6,000 lockages in 1962, the largest number of any of the seven locks and dams on the Illinois Waterway. Approximately 21,300,000 tons of cargo passed through this lock, setting a new record. Eight barges, as here, can be pushed simultaneously into the lock and lifted along with the towboat. U.S. Army Engineer District, Chicago

Jolliet had optimistically thought a canal of a mile or two would join the Chicago and Des Plaines Rivers, but La Salle had more realistically estimated a hundred miles would be necessary in dry weather. The first canal bore out La Salle: it was almost a hundred miles long. Later, skilled engineering and the highly controversial diversion of Lake Michigan water cut this distance to about sixty miles.

In 1900, the upper end of the canal was replaced as far south as Lockport by the Chicago Sanitary and Ship Canal. In the years since, the Illinois Waterway has been radically improved by the complete canalization of its route that follows the Des Plaines and Illinois rivers to its junction with the Mississippi at Grafton, 327 miles from Lake Michigan. Throughout its course, the waterway has a minimum depth of nine feet.

The complete canalization has required seven locks. These are all 600 feet long by 110 feet wide and can lift, in a single lockage, a towboat and eight jumbo barges with a total cargo capacity of over 10,000 tons. One diesel-powered towboat may push as many as fourteen barges. This is why, in a single year, the waterway may carry almost a quarter of a billion tons of freight. Illinois is now the largest exporting state in the union.

Dresden Island Lock and Dam, shown in this view, is second among locks of the Illinois Waterway for cargo tonnages handled.
Joliet (Ill.) Herald-News

There is under way and due for completion in 1964 an extension of the waterway, the Calumet-Sag Channel, which will carry the same nine-foot minimum-depth barge traffic right through to the deep-water harbors of the Lake Calumet South Chicago area. The feature of this important new improvement will be the Thomas J. O'Brien Lock and Dam, a lock 1,000 feet long and 110 feet wide.

**LOCKS
AND
CANALS**

There is no toll charge anywhere on the Illinois Waterway, the reason dating back to the Northwest Ordinance of 1787. In that year it was ruled that "The navigable waters leading into the Mississippi and St. Lawrence . . . shall be forever free, without any tax, impost or duty therefor." That ruling has been followed to this day.

This aerial view of the new Thomas J. O'Brien Lock and Dam in the Calumet-Sag Channel gives a good idea of the channel's tie-in with the harbor, visible in the background. The lock's 1,000-foot length and 110-foot width will allow modern-sized tows of eight barges and towboat to enter the lock chamber without time-consuming rearrangement. The wedge-shaped sector gates are open in this picture, but may be seen in withdrawn position at either end of the lock. U.S. Army Engineer District, Chicago

Here is a close view of the distinctive sector gates of the lock.
The lock and dam not only permit control of water levels land-
ward of the lock, but prevent reversals of flow into Lake
Michigan.   *U.S. Army Engineer District, Chicago*

In the 1850's there remained one major obstacle to overcome in interlake shipping.

It was a small falls that blocked the St. Marys River and cut off through-navigation between Lake Superior and the lower lakes. Only nineteen feet did the water tumble down,
but this barrier to transportation provided the major source of employment to the thousand
or so inhabitants of the drowsy village of Sault Ste. Marie up to the year 1853.

Steamers, sloops, and schooners brought their cargoes from Detroit up as far as the barrier at the Sault. From the other direction, ships carried the iron ore and copper that was
being gouged from newly discovered ranges to the west. The discharged ore was piled high
on the Lake Superior side of the falls. The down-lakes cargoes were piled at the Lake Huron side of the falls. The ships themselves, after disgorging their cargoes, turned around
and returned whence they had come.

*View of Indians in 1908 taking a group of passengers down the rapids at Sault Ste. Marie.
Indians shooting the rapids were a common sight in the years before the canal when they often
went hooting and yelling past the young community. In 1837, an English tourist, Mrs. Anna
Jameson, hired an Indian to take her through the rapids, and Henry R. Schoolcraft assured
her she was the first European woman to make the hazardous trip. Mrs. Jameson said it gave
her a sensation of "giddy, breathless, delicious excitement." This excitement, of course, was what
stood in the way of interlake transportation.*   *Library of Congress*

A contemporary view, sketched in 1850, of two pairs of Indians in canoes shooting the rapids.

Munson Collection, Michigan Historical Commission

These cargoes—ore and supplies—were rolled and dragged, pushed and shoved, by perspiring Sault citizens around the falls. It was only a mile, but it was a long, hard mile.

After 1850 the task became a little easier. A tramway of wooden rails and strap iron had been opened that year, and most of the ore was now being handled by horse-drawn cars.

Sometimes the ships themselves were inched along on rollers, or dragged over ice and snow on sledges. Six schooners, one of 110 tons, and two larger steam-driven ships had made this back-breaking portage in the seasons of 1845 and 1847. Five more steamers made the tedious land journey between 1850 and 1853 as new mines along the Superior shore increased their operations and the demand for transport grew.

This was the background in which a young pioneering genius first saw the Sault. Sent there to recuperate from an attack of typhoid, Charles T. Harvey was western agent for the Fairbanks Scale Company of Vermont. During his convalescence his employers asked him to survey and report on the mineral resources of the upper lakes.

This is the principal street of Sault Ste. Marie, Michigan, in 1850, showing the new tramway portage, just put into use. A family of Indians is crossing the street in the foreground.

Chippewa County Historical Society, Sault Ste. Marie

Only the year before, after long prodding by Senators Lewis Cass and Alpheus Felch of Michigan, Congress had granted Michigan a right of way to construct a canal at the Sault, and 750,000 acres of public land to finance the project.

Harvey tramped the banks of the river. In his mind's eye the canal became a reality. He saw the ore piled high, awaiting transshipment from the Lake Superior side to the lower lakes. His sense of the future caused him to reject violently Henry Clay's classic remark uttered during Congressional debate on the canal project: "It is a work beyond the remotest settlement of the United States, if not the moon."

Harvey urged his employers to apply for the contract to construct a canal. They invited other Eastern capitalists—among them August Belmont, Erastus Corning, and John W. Brooks—to join the project.

Agreement between the Fairbanks Scale Company and the State of Michigan for constructing the canal and locks was signed April 5, 1853. Charles T. Harvey was put in charge of the project.

Ground for the canal was broken on June 4. Four hundred men were on the first payroll, but the labor force soon swelled to 1,600. Under summer sun and in winter's biting cold, Harvey drove the men. Company agents met ships at eastern seaports to recruit immigrant laborers to fill the holes in Harvey's ranks caused by men quitting and by cholera.

Equipment and supplies were hard to get, discipline hard to enforce. Once Harvey closed the cookhouse to drive the men back to work. He solved his problems one by one. Construction was completed on schedule.

On June 18, 1855, the governor of Michigan and other high dignitaries made their way north to the Sault to watch the steamer *Illinois* pass through the canal and its locks on the journey from Lake Huron to Lake Superior.

THE MEN
WHO
MADE THEM

When the Sault locks were finished, the first downbound steamer was the Baltimore, *here shown coming into the upper entrance to the canal with seven flags flying. The old horse-drawn tramway portage runs along the side and on either side are the remains of the work of excavation. Ten more ships waited behind the* Baltimore *on that opening day.*

Munson Collection, Michigan Historical Commission

Charles T. Harvey

Charles T. Harvey must be celebrated as the initiator of the world's greatest canal, a canal that helped tip the balance to the North in the Civil War (supplying iron in quantity just in time), and a canal that eventually carried more commerce than all the other important canals of the world combined.

Charles Thompson Harvey was born in Thompsonville, near Hartford, Connecticut, on June 16, 1829. He was therefore just turning twenty-four when he began work on the St. Marys Canal, as it was called then. He had first gone to Detroit to get men. There were scarcely any local workmen available. The few whites living in Sault Ste. Marie and the *voyageurs* and Indians despised the canal project. So Harvey brought a boatload of four hundred men from Detroit and had them in barracks within two days. In four days he took them to the work site and personally shoveled and carted away the first wheelbarrow of dirt.

He lived near the bend of the St. Marys and kept three horses which he galloped back and forth along the extending works, from the portage road to the foremen's offices to the workmen's quarters. By winter he had two thousand men working. Men would drop out to go and homestead or to get the higher wages in the mining camps along the upper lake. Harvey had Irish and German immigrants signed up in New York.

It wasn't the digging that was so hard, it was the blasting. Each blasting hole had to be drilled by hand, one man holding the drill while two others swung sledge hammers. Then into the holes was poured powder that had been brought all the way from Delaware.

To make room for the canal, Harvey ordered a Chippewa graveyard moved, and news was brought to him that Indian *wabeno* drums were sounding along the lake where several thousand Chippewas were encamped. Memories were stirred. This was where bloody massacres had occurred. An old chief came to the excavation, pointing threateningly with a gun and talking loudly in Chippewa. Harvey listened nervously, unable to understand. He called the Indian agent who told him the Indian wanted his gun repaired; the government treaty of 1843 had provided for free repair of tribal guns. Harvey personally fixed the gun.

Harvey finished his job in twenty-two and a half months, less than the required two years. It had cost just under a million dollars. Before the canal was transferred to the government and made free of tolls, it had just about paid for itself. Two years after the canal was finished, he addressed the Michigan House of Representatives and said that while in the first year only 1,400 tons of ore had gone through, in 1856 this increased 800 per cent and the total commerce of the canal, both ways, was $6,000,000. The legislators were satisfied. In fact, they were downright happy.

Harvey's career in transportation was by no means over. He built the first elevated railway in New York City and fifty years after the construction of the St. Marys Canal, he participated in its half-centennial. He died in New York City at the age of 83 on March 14, 1912, within earshot of the elevated rapid-transit system he had helped create.

Charles T. Harvey in early life.   *Late picture of Harvey.*

The canal was one mile and 304 feet long. It was 115 feet wide at the top, 100 feet at the waterline, 64 feet at the bottom, and 12 feet deep. The stone walls were 25 feet high and ten feet thick.

The governor and his party saw two fine locks. Each was 350 feet long, 70 feet wide at the top and 61.5 feet at the bottom. The upper lock lifted or lowered ships eight feet, the lower lock ten feet.

Upper and lower lakes were linked at last.

And the St. Marys Falls Ship Canal Company which had built this great engineering marvel at a cost of $999,802.46—what did it receive? Just the 750,000 promised acres of land,

Here is the lower entrance to the new canal at the time of the opening.   *Munson Collection*

The old State Locks were photographed in 1875 and fortunately the two original tandem locks are here visible as they were just before work started on the new Weitzel Lock that was to replace them. In the two houses on the left lived the lock tenders. The farther house had a lookout tower on top of it.

U.S. Army Corps of Engineers, Detroit

which it judiciously selected to include 39,000 acres in the iron ranges, 147,000 acres in the copper region, and 564,000 acres of fine lower-peninsula timberland.

A month after the opening of the canal, the two-masted brigantine *Columbia* eased her way through the new locks. In her hold was the first cargo of iron ore to make the direct journey from the docks at Marquette to the harbor at Cleveland.

In that first year of operation, 14,503 tons of freight were carried past the now-harmless falls and through the canal. Five years later, the figure reached 153,721 tons. In 1876, it reached the million-ton mark. In 1953, less than a century after the first canal and locks had been dug out of the earth, the Sault handled nearly 129 million tons of freight and cargo. This total is more than the combined figure for the Panama, the Suez, the Kiel, and the Manchester canals.

An early steamer occupies the lower of the two original locks, with rods that supported one-half of the wooden gates visible in the right foreground.

U.S. Army Corps of Engineers, Detroit District

By this time, however, the original canal and locks had undergone extensive modifications and improvements to keep pace with the constantly swelling flow of larger and larger ships. In 1876, work began on a single lock, 515 feet long and 80 feet wide. This was named the Weitzel Lock.

A new feature was incorporated in the new lock. Water had previously been admitted through holes in the gates, but this produced turbulence and made it difficult to keep the ships steady. New openings for taking in and discharging water were made in the floor. Hydraulic machinery replaced manpower.

But even this new lock was not large enough to cope with the flow of grain and copper and iron. Another lock—named the Poe—was completed in 1896. Eight hundred feet long, one hundred feet wide, in its time the Poe was the largest in the world.

Across on the northern shore, the Canadian government constructed a canal and a lock. Nine hundred feet long, and eight inches deeper than the Poe, this was used for the larger ships that sought passage through the Sault until the Davis Lock was built on the American side in 1914.

A view of the single Weitzel Lock in 1887. This lock was named for General Godfrey Weitzel of the United States Army Engineer Corps, who directed work on it. The civilian engineer who designed it was Alfred Noble, who later was a consulting engineer on the Panama Canal.

Munson Collection

A group of vessels wait below the Weitzel Lock after an accident to the lock on August 3, 1890.

The Poe Lock under construction, September 7, 1891. This is a view of the west end of the south wall, looking east. The lock was named for General Orlando M. Poe, who succeeded General Weitzel as Army engineer in 1883. General Poe had served as General Sherman's chief engineer during the Civil War on the Union leader's famed march to the sea. He had later added to his reputation by the difficult feat of building the Spectacle Reef Lighthouse (see next chapter). Now in his new position he pushed hard for a larger lock at the Sault to meet the rapidly increasing size of cargo ships. But when it came to actually tearing down the old State Locks, General Poe admitted a feeling of "great regret. . . . The man who, knowing their history, can see them go, without compunction, is made of other stuff than I am."

Here the floor of the new lock goes deeper. The work in hand was bolt testing and cutting as this view was taken on July 21, 1894. The expense of building the Poe Lock was borne by the U.S. government in the interest of all the states being benefited. There were no further tolls.

U.S. Army Corps of Engineers, Detroit District

A whaleback goes through the Canadian Lock. It was not only one hundred feet longer than the Poe Lock but eight inches deeper. These eight inches were important since for every inch of increased draft over 21 feet, about 150 additional tons could be carried. Munson Collection

*In 1905 Sault Ste. Marie celebrated the half-century anniversary of the opening of the canal.
There was a naval parade, here pictured. Theodore Roosevelt came to attend the ceremonies.
Church bells on both sides of the river greeted each other and the occasion. Crowds of people
walked up and down the canal edge and across the closed doors of the locks, and said that these
locks still were not big enough for the growing size of the freighters.*   Library of Congress

The Davis Lock was 1,350 feet long—350 feet longer than the Panama Canal locks.

Before the Davis Lock was opened, work had already begun on still another lock, laid
down beside the Davis. This was named the Sabin Lock, and it too was 1,350 feet in
length. Thus the Sault had four parallel locks, the Davis, Sabin, Weitzel and Poe.

For thirty years these locks were more than commodious enough to meet the demands
of traffic between the lakes. Then came World War II. Since the old Weitzel Lock was
too small for modern ships, it was removed and replaced by the MacArthur Lock, named
after General Douglas MacArthur. This had the same dimensions—800 feet long and 80
feet wide—as the Poe Lock beside it, with both locks served by the same canal.

*View of the "Indian village" and reviewing stand at the 1905 fifty-year celebration. Silk-hatted
congressmen stared at Chippewas and vice versa. Various parts of the world sent commemora-
tion presents: an obelisk, a Japanese Tori gate, a kiosk.*   Library of Congress

These wood-laden barges going through the Soo are a reminder of the days when lumber melted from the edges of the Great Lakes in billions of board feet, down to the cities.

Albertype Collection, Michigan Historical Commission

The old Union Depot at Sault Ste. Marie with a boat on one side and a train on the other.   Munson Collection

View of U.S. lookout station at Sault Ste. Marie in 1908.
Library of Congress

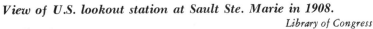

**LOCKS
AND
CANALS**

In World War II the old Weitzel Lock gave way to the Mac-Arthur, which was the same size as the Poe. Here is the steamer C. B. Randall going through the new lock.

U.S. Army Corps of Engineers, Detroit District

In 1963 another new lock was under construction at the Sault. According to the U.S. Army Engineers, this lock will be 1,200 feet long, 110 feet wide and 32 feet deep. It is designed to accommodate vessels 1,000 feet in length and 100 feet in beam.

World War II saw the Sault in its finest hours. Day and night, as long as the water was free from ice, vessels poured through the heavily guarded canals and locks, their holds bulging with wheat, iron, and copper, all so vital to the Allied war effort.

"The Miracle Mile" was the name bestowed on the Sault, and through this mile flowed the sinews of war. Bow to stern the ships went, joining the wheatfields and the mines of the West with the mills and blast furnaces of the East.

An early aerial view of the four locks at the Soo.

Munson Collection

Two views of an ice jam in the Soo, April 17, 1953. In the rear is the open bascule bridge.

U.S. Army Corps of Engineers, Detroit District

An oblique aerial view looking westward, showing from left to right, Sault Ste. Marie, Michigan; the MacArthur, Poe, Davis, and Sabin locks; the powerhouse; and portion of the St. Marys Falls. Whitefish Bay and the Canadian shoreline are in the background. The picture was taken in 1954.
U.S. Army Corps of Engineers, Detroit District

Operator in the control tower at the Soo, 1956.

Michigan Bell Telephone Company

View from a window of the control tower, the Soo. Canada is visible in the distance. *Michigan Bell Telephone Company*

The latest addition to the Sault is the great International Bridge, one of the world's major crossroads of vehicular traffic, which was opened October 31, 1962. It brings U. S. Interstate 75 Freeway (which eventually will connect Tampa, Florida, with Sault Ste. Marie) into touch with the 5,000-mile Trans-Canada Highway. Its building and significance will be discussed in the chapter on bridges. This view of it is looking from Ontario into Michigan with the Sault Rapids in the center. The Canadian canal is in the foreground; the two American canals are on the far side of the rapids.   Materna Studio, Sault Ste. Marie, Mich.

During World War II, the Great Lakes came into their own. There remained just one great obstacle to overcome—the navagational block to large vessels between Montreal and Lake Ontario. When the artificial waterways had been built here, it had been for smaller vessels. Now locks less than 300 feet long with only 14 and 15 feet draft (half that of the Welland locks) were outdated. This was the missing link in the great traverse from lake to ocean. But man's victory in this area lay just ahead, with the opening in 1959 of the St. Lawrence Seaway.

An evening view of the locks in 1957 with the light of the sky shining on the water and a lighted freighter going through.   Michigan Bell Telephone Company

Chapter 8

Lighthouse, Beacons, and Buoys

IN 1804, Canada built the first lighthouse on the Great Lakes, at the mouth of the Niagara River. The United States acknowledged the general usefulness of this effort by sparing this lighthouse during the fighting in the area in the War of 1812.

And in 1810, the American Congress, deciding it was a federal responsibility, voted funds for building two lighthouses on Lake Erie. So began the remarkable story of navigational aids on the lakes where fierce storms and hidden reefs and shoals called for maximum protection. Today there are 150 manned light structures on both the Canadian and American shores (a number equal to nearly half the active light stations supervised by the U.S. Coast Guard in American waters), and these are only part of the defensive operation. Harbors are constantly being deepened, channels dredged, and breakwaters built, and the charting of the lake floors is being extended year after year.

Lightships, buoys, bells, and radio signals spell out in detail the location of shoals, reefs, and other danger points. Fog horns operate through the navigational season to help skippers when conditions of visibility are at their worst. Audio and visual markers of every kind make up a complete system of signals that define shipping and harbor lanes as clearly as if they were highways through the water.

The early mariners on the Great Lakes sailed without benefit of any of these safety devices. For the most part they hugged the protective shoreline, relied on their instinct, and anchored their crafts when night fell.

The U.S. lighthouses on Lake Erie began to shine out in 1818 (the War of 1812 had slowed up the construction of the first two authorized lights). Two years later, the first U.S. light on Lake Ontario was built at Galloo Island. In 1825 a lighthouse was built at Fort Gratiot at the outlet of Lake Huron.

**LIGHTHOUSES
BEACONS
AND BUOYS**

A good deal is known about this first lighthouse erected at Green Bay, Wisconsin, on a point of sand extending into the bay from the town of Suamico. It was built in the summer and fall of 1847 and first used the following year. At its base, it was 25 feet in diameter and its walls were between five and six feet thick. Its height was 84 feet to the stone cap beneath the lantern. It was built by Edwin and Asahel Hart, helped by Daniel W. Hubbard, mason, and by Captain C. B. Hart, then a boy of eight. Young Hart drove the horse around the capstan by means of which the stone and mortar were raised to the mason. The first lightkeeper was John P. Dousman, who was afterward revenue collector at Green Bay. An attempt was made to tear the lighthouse down, but it proved to be unassailable and the structure still remains as a historic landmark at Green Bay.

Marblehead Lighthouse, located at Point Marblehead in Lake Erie, on the northeasterly end of the peninsula enclosing Sandusky Bay on the north, was established in 1821. It was one of the first lights built on Lake Erie, those at Buffalo and Erie preceding it by three years. An automatic aid to navigation, it today consists of a flashing green light of 450,000 candlepower on top of a seventy-foot white conical tower, visible for sixteen miles.

U.S. Coast Guard, Ninth District, Cleveland

Cleveland had its first light in 1829 and Chicago in 1832. Detroit's first light—in 1837—marked Windmill Point at the outlet of Lake Huron.

The same year saw the first lightship on the Great Lakes, stationed at the juncture of Lakes Huron and Michigan. Later a total of twelve lightships were to ride the waters of the Great Lakes, marking spots of extreme danger to navigation. As permanent lighthouses were built, the number of boats was reduced until now there is only one.

Construction of two of the best known lighthouses on the Great Lakes started in 1870. They were the Stannard Rock Lighthouse, lying 23 miles southeast of Manitou Island in Lake Superior, and Spectacle Reef Lighthouse, 10.5 miles from Bois Blanc Island in Lake Huron.

**LIGHTHOUSES
BEACONS
AND BUOYS**

Fort Gratiot Light marks the Junction of the St. Clair River and the south end of Lake Huron. A lighthouse was first constructed here in 1825, this being one of the first lighthouses to be erected in the state of Michigan. The present tower, of brick, was built in 1861. The tower is 86 feet high and displays a flashing green light of 150,-000 candlepower, visible for 17 miles.
U.S. Coast Guard, Cleveland

This is a near view of the Chicago Lighthouse in 1857 (built in 1832). It stood at the mouth of the Chicago River, and an early steamboat with sidepaddle may be seen passing it. To the right is the last remnant of old Fort Dearborn, first established in 1803, destroyed at the time of the Indian massacre, and rebuilt in 1816. The lighthouse, on the south side of the river, was a familiar landmark for many years.
Phelps Stokes Collection, New York Public Library

This view of the old lighthouse at Cobourg, Ontario, is a steel engraving by W. H. Bartlett in N. P. Willis's Canadian Scenery, 1842. *A brig, schooner, and two-masted steamer give the range of contemporary navigation.*

The First Lighthouse on the Great Lakes

After the Revolutionary War, Canadian shipping on the Great Lakes for a while far exceeded that of the United States, so it was logical that Canada should build the first lighthouses. These were to be at Toronto, Kingston, and the entrance to the Niagara River from Lake Ontario.

In 1802, Major James Green wrote a Legislative Council member that "one of those reflecting lamps on a small scale, which are now in general use at home" (for lighthouses) was on the way to Canada. It arrived the following summer and was sent with the needed sperm oil to Fort George on the west bank of the Niagara River, where the first lighthouse was to be built.

On February 29, 1804, Lieutenant Governor Peter Hunter ordered specifications and estimates to be prepared. There was to be no ornament: "You will principally consult utility." The plans called for a stone building forty-five feet high, to cost £178. The cost, in fact, went £22 over the estimate.

Elevation of the first lighthouse on the lakes.

Public Archives of Canada

By June, civilian workmen and soldiers had put up the new building at Mississauga Point and had installed the reflector. It considerably reduced the dangers of navigation at the mouth of the Niagara River. Dominic Henry was appointed lighthouse keeper and tended the light for the next ten years, even through the difficult days of the War of 1812. The Americans destroyed the town of Niagara, but saved the light, and it was only in 1814, when the British wanted to put up a new fort to replace the old Fort George, that the first lighthouse on the lakes was taken down. A plaque on a surviving tower of the fort today commemorates that it was built with stone from the old lighthouse.

The Huron Lightship. *The only lightship on the Great Lakes, the vessel's station is in Lake Huron at the end of the buoy channel of the St. Clair River, near Port Huron. Its light has a walk around it much like lights on shore.*   *U.S. Coast Guard, Cleveland*

Two vessels had been dashed to bits on Spectacle Reef, near the Mackinac Straits, in 1868. Major O. M. Poe, who later built the Poe Lock at the Soo, was charged with planning a lighthouse to mark this dangerous reef, and also with supervising its construction.

He faced formidable problems in putting a lighthouse above a reef in open water, not the least of which was the winter's ice. Many acres in area, and often two feet thick, ice fields for many months each year follow the current through northern Lake Huron and pile up against any obstacle.

Major Poe's solution to the problem was to build a structure against which the ice would be crushed or held fast on the seven-foot shoal, thus creating a defensive barrier against other ice fields. The underwater foundation was laid in a cofferdam protected by a cribwork of twelve-inch timber. This was built much as a ship is built, on ways at Scammon's Harbor, sixteen miles from the reef.

The crib, 92 feet square and 24 feet high, was towed to the reef by ships and then grounded. The cofferdam was pumped out until bedrock was exposed. Masonry courses were then laid on the bedrock.

A heavy storm in September, 1872, almost destroyed the work while it was still in progress, but after emergency repairs construction continued.

The crib, extending thirteen feet above water level, provided space for a landing wharf and quarters for the men to be stationed at the lighthouse.

The tower, shaped like the frustum of a cone, was based eleven feet below the level of the water. This tower is 32 feet in diameter at the base and rises 97 feet above the submerged rock, or 86 feet above the water's surface.

Spectacle Reef Lighthouse, built in the early 1870's on a limestone reef ten miles from land (near the Straits of Mackinac), now consists of a flashing white light of 1,000,000 candlepower and a red light of 250,000 candlepower. The gray conical tower displays the light from 82 feet above the water. Four Coast Guard enlisted men comprise the lighthouse crew. U.S. Coast Guard, Cleveland

The Stannard Rock Lighthouse.
U.S. Coast Guard Ninth District, Cleveland

For the first 34 feet up from the base the tower is solid. Then it becomes hollow, with five rooms, each 14 feet in diameter, situated one above the other. Thickness of the wall varies from five and a half feet at the bottom to 16 inches at the spring of the cornice.

Below the cornice, blocks of stone are two feet thick. The stone was cut so that the blocks interlock. The courses are fastened together by wrought-iron bolts, two and a half inches thick and two feet long. The tower is secured to the foundation by bolts three feet long, which enter the rock 21 inches.

After the severe winter of 1873/74, when the keepers returned to open the lighthouse, they found it literally imbedded in an iceberg. Ice had scaled the tower to a height of thirty feet and it was necessary to cut through the ice to reach the door.

But the tower had stood fast against the ice.

After completion of the Spectacle Reef Lighthouse, all of the equipment used was transferred to Lake Superior for construction of the Stannard Rock Lighthouse. The problem was much the same, and it was approached in virtually the same manner as in Lake Huron, but at Stannard Rock a permanent protective crib was added.

The new light, 102 feet above the approaches to Duluth and Marquette, began shining over the waters of Lake Superior in 1883. Today the light has an intensity of 140,000 candle-power, visible up to fifty miles on a clear night.

Each lighthouse on the Great Lakes can be identified by its individual signal pattern. At Stannard Rock the pattern is a 2.5-second flash of white followed by 12.5 seconds of darkness.

Being a member of the Stannard Rock Lighthouse crew is considered to be one of the loneliest jobs in the whole country. No American lighthouse is located farther from land. The crew is currently made up of four men—two Coast Guard enlisted men and two civilians. The lighthouse is manned from early April until early December, the navigation period on the Great Lakes. The men stand watches in pairs, six hours on and six off. Each man, however, is entitled to one week's leave every month except November, when the lakes experience their worst storms.

For their leaves, two men are taken ashore by Coast Guard launch from Marquette (forty-five miles away) shortly after the first of the month. The other two take their leaves in the middle of the month. When only two are on duty at the lighthouse, they continue to stand watches of six hours, but singly rather than in pairs. The tricky and often fierce weather of Lake Superior can completely disrupt the leave schedule. One crew member once spent ninety-nine consecutive days on the Rock before the launch could make its way out from Marquette to pick him up.

Northeast of Two Harbors, Minnesota, is Split Rock Lighthouse, the highest lighthouse in the United States. Rising from the rugged cliffs of Lake Superior, its 450,000 candlepower beacon can be seen 22 miles away. Chamber of Commerce, Two Harbors

At the lighthouse, the men are isolated, but not to the extent that once prevailed. Today they enjoy both radio and television.

When the crew leaves Stannard in December, a light continues to operate. It maintains the same round-the-clock pattern, but on greatly reduced candle-power from that used during the navigation season.

Many other Great Lakes lighthouses are well known. Split Rock and Rock of Ages in Lake Superior, Little Sable, Big Sable, and White Shoal in Lake Michigan, Marblehead in Lake Erie, the Detroit River Lighthouse—all of these and many others have their own fascinating history and their own signal pattern, easily recognized by Great Lakes veterans.

LIGHTHOUSES BEACONS AND BUOYS

The Rock of Ages Light, located about three miles off the west end of Isle Royale in Lake Superior, is the most powerful light on the entire Great Lakes, with 4,500,000 candlepower. Its foundation is a massive concrete pier, within a steel cylinder, built upon the rock about level with the water. On this pier is the light tower of brick, 130 feet high. The structure was completed in 1908, and its group of flashing lights can be seen from 19 miles away. The station is manned by five Coast Guard enlisted men during the navigational season.

U.S. Coast Guard, Ninth District, Cleveland

Racine Reef, on the Wisconsin shore of Lake Michigan, is one of the few lighthouses maintained the year around. Most are closed down in winter.

When lighthouses were first built on the Great Lakes, they burned oil lamps in their beacon towers. By 1885 kerosene was generally in use, despite the experience of one Lake Michigan lightkeeper who blew the whole lantern from his tower in a kerosene explosion and destroyed the lens.

The oil vapor lamp came into general use on the lakes in 1904, six years after its introduction in France.

Today oil vapor is still used in some of the lighthouses, wherever electricity has proved impractical.

The lighthouses, the beacons and the buoys of the Great Lakes have saved many a mariner's life since the first tower was constructed on Lake Erie. But the savage storms of these inland seas have claimed many lives, despite all the navigational aids that man has been able to devise.

**LIGHTHOUSES
BEACONS
AND BUOYS**

This illustration of an oil vapor lamp was taken from a 1902 booklet of "Instructions to Lightkeepers."
U.S. Coast Guard

A fourth-order French Fresnel lens, used at South Bass Island Light Station. The lens contains four flash panels, making one revolution per minute, giving a flash every fifteen seconds. Either similar Fresnel lenses or rotating airway beacons are in use at most of the major lights on the Great Lakes.   U.S. Coast Guard, Ninth District, Cleveland

West Pierhead Light, known as "Cleveland Main Light," is located on the outer pierhead at the main entrance to Cleveland harbor, in Lake Erie. The light was established in 1911 and consists of an alternating flashing white light of 400,000 candlepower and a red light of 90,000 candlepower. The light is located 55 feet above the ground and can be seen for sixteen miles.   U.S. Coast Guard, Ninth District, Cleveland

Green Island Light, on the west end of Green Island in western Lake Erie, is of a type called "skeleton tower." It was built in 1939, is 67 feet high and has a flashing white 700-candlepower light that can be seen for fourteen miles.　　　　U.S. Coast Guard, Ninth District, Cleveland

The first lighthouse at Buffalo, New York.　　　*Phelp-Stokes Collection, New York Public Library*

Lighthouses take the most interesting variety of shapes, often highly distinctive and effective as architectural design. Four of these are (upper left) the Main Lighthouse at Port Arthur harbor, Ontario; (upper right) the Tibbits Point Lighthouse at Cape Vincent in the Thousand Islands region; (lower left) the lighthouse at Lorain, Ohio, harbor; and (lower right) White Island Lighthouse in the St. Lawrence.

**LIGHTHOUSES
BEACONS
AND BUOYS**

Old Mackinac Point Lighthouse, constructed in 1892, was disestablished late in 1957 when the value of its service depreciated because of the completion of the Straits of Mackinac Bridge. At that time the lighthouse was replaced by a series of lighted sound buoys and private aids to navigation. The lighthouse and station property were turned over to the State of Michigan for use as an historical museum and recreational area in 1960.   U.S. Coast Guard, Ninth District, Cleveland

Light and fog signal at Buffalo, New York.
   U.S. Coast Guard, Ninth District, Cleveland

This is a typical U.S. Coast Guard buoy tender. A lighted bell buoy and several spar buoys may be seen on her deck. A fleet of twelve of these vessels, as well as several buoy boats of various sizes, are strategically located around the Great Lakes. Each year they have a race with nature to remove the buoys before the heavy ice sets in, and replace them each spring with equal rapidity to get them into position before the shipping season gets under way. Several of the buoy tenders are equipped with ice-breaking bows and fight the channel-clogging ice to free ships that are unable to proceed under their own power during the winter months.   U.S. Coast Guard, Ninth District, Cleveland

Buoy on Lake Erie with a racing yacht in the background.
    Michigan Tourist Council

**LIGHTHOUSES
BEACONS
AND BUOYS**

After sandblasting, this buoy is being given a coat of rust-resisting red lead. After the first coat of red lead, the buoy will be painted with one of the newer types of plastic paints in a color to desig-nate its position in the shipping lanes.

U.S. Coast Guard

Hauling in a buoy at the end of a long season.

U.S. Coast Guard

Coastguardsman repairing the flasher on a buoy.

U.S. Coast Guard

Hopper Dredge Hains

One of the most useful and distinguished boats on the Great Lakes is the U.S. Army Engineer Hopper Dredge *Hains*.

The *Hains* was named in honor of Major General Peter Conover Hains, who had a long career as an officer of the Corps of Engineers. He graduated from the United States Military Academy in 1861, and it has been stated that he was the only officer to see active service in the Civil War, Spanish-American War, and World War I.

The *Hains* is called a hopper dredge because it has four hoppers, each with a capacity of approximately 221 cubic yards. When a channel is to be dredged, two dragheads, one on each side of the ship, suction up silt from the bottom of the channel and pour it into the hoppers. When the hoppers are filled to capacity, the dredge moves to a specially designated dump area where the material is released through doors at the bottom of the hoppers, which are then flushed with water.

The dredge operates wherever needed along the channels, harbors, and rivers of the Great Lakes. Normally it functions twenty-four hours a day, six days a week, from early March through late December. In the winter, it is berthed at the Engineers' Boatyard in Grand Haven, Michigan.

The Hains *with dragheads lowered.*   *U.S. Army Corps of Engineers, Detroit*

During World War II, the *Hains* went to the Philippine Islands and worked under such hazardous conditions as heavy ground swells, shallow reefs, sunken ships loaded with explosives, tangled cables, floating mines, and action by enemy aircraft. Once an enemy dive bomber narrowly missed making a direct hit. The ship traveled a total of 14,385 miles on its tour of duty and dredged and removed 1,204,590 cubic yards of material from North Manila Harbor, South Manila Harbor, and the Pasig River.

In 1959 the *Hains* was modified to enable it to pump out dredged material over the side. This modification adapts it to dredging shallow river channels. It is the only dredge in its class with this equipment.

The work of the *Hains* and its sister ships is particularly important now that the opening of the St. Lawrence Seaway calls for a general deepening and improving of lake harbor facilities.

Lengthwise and crosswise sections of the **Hains.**

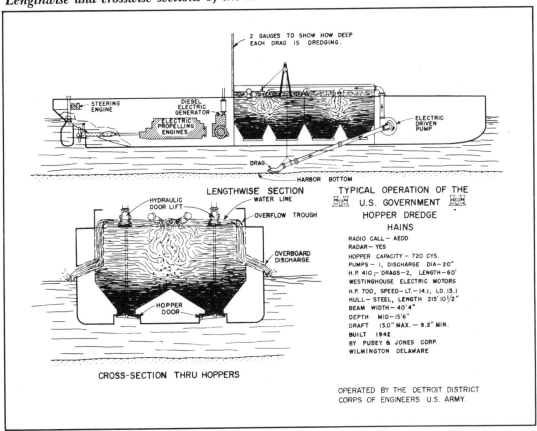

Army·U.S.Lake Survey Detroit·Litho.1956 - 1000

Great Lakes Bridges and Their Builders

MOST of the bridges that span the St. Lawrence or the rivers, canals, locks, and straits connecting the Great Lakes with one another are international bridges between the United States and Canada. Several are among the great engineering triumphs of the world.

The St. Lawrence River itself is crossed by three international bridges. The latest to be completed is the Seaway Skyway Bridge from Ogdensburg, New York, to Johnston, Ontario, on the most direct route between Ottawa and New York. Built at a cost of $20,000,000, the bridge is 13,510 feet long including approaches. It was completed in 1960.

The Roosevelt Bridge, built in 1899 and joining Cornwall, Ontario, and Roosevelt-town, New York, is a cantilever bridge. It has a channel span of 840 feet and carries both vehicular and railroad traffic.

The Thousand Islands Bridge, using islands as stepping-stones, extends seven and a half miles from Collins Landing, near Alexandria Bay, New York, to Ivy Lea, below Gananoque, Ontario. Those who cross this bridge by car or walkway can see over two hundred of the archipelago's islands, a particularly beautiful view at sunset when the river is tinged with the colors of the sky.

An engineer would find an interesting object lesson in the way natural topography is used to advantage at each point in the long structure. For example, a small rock island at mid-channel was the basis for the bridge's two-span continuous truss. And except for one main pier set in only seventeen feet of water, all the main piers are founded on exposed bedrock.

Looking upstream on the St. Lawrence River at the Roosevelt Bridge. On the left side is Roosetown, New York, and on the right side is Cornwall Island, Canada. The bridge was named for President Franklin Delano Roosevelt. Just below the bridge is the beginning of the land border between the United States and Canada, with the St. Lawrence flowing northeast to Montreal entirely within Canada.
U.S. Army Corps of Engineers

The Thousand Island Bridge seen from upstream on the St. Lawrence River. On the left side is Wellesley Island, on the right side, the New York shore. The total distance covered by the bridge, counting its two suspension spans and several smaller bridges and roadways, is six and a half miles.
U.S. Army Corps of Engineers

The bridge has five spans in all, with an underclearance of 120 feet above the river. It was opened to use in August 1938, with dedication ceremonies by President Roosevelt and Prime Minister Mackenzie King of Canada.

There are a number of bridges across the Niagara River. The Peace Bridge built in 1927 was the first highway crossing of the river south of Niagara Falls. It joins Buffalo, New York, and Fort Erie, Ontario. Because of the heavy ship traffic during the navigation season and because of a rapid swirling current, an ingenious scheme of "removable steel spud cribs" known as "falsework supports" was employed in building the structure. This bridge, the main span of which is 360 feet long, was completed in nine months.

The Peace Bridge viewed from the Buffalo side, looking toward Fort Erie, Ontario. This bridge was opened in 1927 by the Prince of Wales.
Chamber of Commerce, Buffalo

Other notable bridges across the Niagara River are the suspension bridge connecting Lewiston, New York, and Queenston, Ontario, and the steel arch Rainbow Bridge, or "Honeymoon Bridge," so named because of the thousands of newlyweds who have viewed Niagara Falls from that vantage point. The present Rainbow Bridge is the fifth bridge to be built at the location. The fourth was destroyed by a high ice jam on January 27, 1938. An early suspension bridge was built there in 1855 by John A. Roebling, who designed the Brooklyn Bridge. The present bridge was completed in 1941.

The Ambassador Bridge, completed November 15, 1929, spans the Detroit River between Detroit, Michigan, and Windsor, Ontario. The length of its main span is 1,850 feet. Its main towers are 363 feet high. The bridge has a vertical clearance of 152 feet. The distance from entrance to entrance is 9,200 feet. A souvenir plaque at the center of the bridge reads, "The Visible Expression of Friendship in the Heart of Two Peoples With Like Ideas and Ideals."

GREAT LAKES
BRIDGES AND
THEIR BUILDERS

View of the Lewiston-Queenston Bridge, looking down the Niagara River. On the left side is Queenston, Ontario, and on the right Lewiston, New York. On the New York side, a main road goes to Rochester and on the Canadian side a main road goes to Hamilton.

U.S. Army Corps of Engineers

Rainbow Bridge over the Niagara River, looking downstream. On the left side is Niagara Falls, Ontario, and on the right Niagara Falls, New York. At the left end of the bridge may be seen the famous Carillon Tower which has fifty-five bells, the largest weighing ten tons. Bell concerts and recitals are given from time to time. Rainbow Bridge was built in 1941 and has a central elevated catwalk four feet wide with a clear view of the falls to the south. The bridge is 1450 feet long.

U.S. Army Corps of Engineers

The first Niagara Falls suspension bridge, opened in August, 1848, occupied approximately the position of the present Rainbow Bridge. Here the view is upstream to the falls; the United States is on the left and Canada on the right. A carriage is being driven across the bridge, which had a total length of 759 feet. The weight of wire in the bridge was 35 tons and the weight of the flooring 40 tons, a total of 75 tons. This may be compared with the tens of thousands of tons of material in Great Lakes bridges today.   *Library of Congress*

A dramatic aerial view of the Ambassador Bridge linking Detroit on the left with Windsor, Ontario, on the right. Belle Isle is visible in the background. This stretch of river is the scene of the famed Gold Medal and Harmsworth Trophy speedboat racing.   *U.S. Army Photograph*

Beautiful Blue Water Bridge not only links Port Huron, Michigan, and Sarnia, Ontario, but connects with main highways through central Michigan and Ontario. It is a toll bridge. Bridge clearance may be judged from the large freighter passing under it. Chamber of Commerce, Sarnia

The Blue Water Bridge across the St. Clair River, between Port Huron, Michigan, and Sarnia, Ontario, is a cantilever design. Its main span is 871 feet long. Deck-girder approaches on the American side measure 2,283 feet; on the Canadian side, 2,657 feet. The total length is 1.25 miles. The bridge has a vertical clearance of 150 feet.

The bascule bridge over the locks in Sault Ste. Marie, Michigan, is mentioned because it is an outstanding example of the bascule, or quadrant, bridge that is used for short spans. It is a rigid trussed-type structure, a counterpoised or balanced drawbridge which is opened by sinking the counterpoise, thus lifting the bridge into the air and allowing ships to pass in the canal. This bridge forms a part of the International Railway Bridge linking Sault Ste. Marie, Michigan, and Sault Ste. Marie, Ontario.

The bascule bridge at Sault Ste. Marie open to let through a vessel. This photograph was taken before the new International Bridge was built. Michigan Tourist Council, Lansing

On this and following pages is a sequence of photographs which H. D. Ellis and H. J. Bell made of the building of the Mackinac Straits Bridge, one of the most remarkable series of construction pictures ever taken. The photographs are released by the Mackinac Bridge Authority.

Foundations

GREAT LAKES
BRIDGES AND
THEIR BUILDERS

Here the north cable anchorage pier is being built. On the barge beyond the pier is a floating grout-mixing plant (grout is "everything that makes concrete except the crushed rock"— sand, cement, etc., and water). Grout is being pumped through pipes to the bottom of the crushed rock layer in the pier. It diffuses outward and upward from the bottoms of the grout pipes, filling the spaces between the crushed rock. The surface area of this foundation is one-third the area of a football field.   Photo by H. D. Ellis

Here crushed rock and grout are being poured simultaneously for the north tower foundation caisson. The caisson is 116 feet in diameter and rests on bedrock 200 feet below water level. The freighter on the right is unloading crushed rock directly around the grout pipes in one part of the caisson, while the floating grout plant on the left pumps grout into a rock layer placed previously in another section.
Photo by H. D. Ellis

Superstructures

The superstructure of the north cable anchorage pier is here less than half its eventual 10-story-building height. The anchor bars can be seen to the rear (a similiar set is on the other side). These bars, partially imbedded in concrete, will transmit the 30,000-ton pull of the two cables to the pier.
Photo by H. D. Ellis

A "creeper derrick" moves part of the fourth tier of steel into place on the south tower. Fifteen tiers of steel eventually brought the tower to 552 feet, the equivalent of a 46-story building. The derrick moved up the tower as the height increased, always being high enough to erect the next piece of steel.
Photo by H. D. Ellis

Cable-spinning

At the top of the north tower, cat-walks used by cable-spinning crews are in place and cable spinning is in progress.
                                    Photo by H. D. Ellis

This view inside the anchorage shows workmen placing new loops of wire around the spinning wheel. Loops previously pulled across from the far anchorage have been placed around the strand shoes—linked to the anchor bars, which are imbedded in the concrete. The spinning wheel started back across the span a few seconds after this photograph was taken.
                                    Photo by H. D. Ellis

Here two spinning wheels are meeting in mid-span, each pulling two loops (four wires) across the span from cable anchorage to cable anchorage. For each double trip, eight wires are placed parallel to each other. Workmen stationed along the catwalk 220 feet above the Straits of Mackinac place the wires and adjust their positions and tension as the wheels pass.

Photo by H. D. Ellis

Workmen are placing temporary bands on strands of west cable near the top of the north tower in this view. Each strand contains 340 wires. Thirty-seven strands make up each cable, totaling 12,580 wires. Later, the strands lost their identities as the wires were compacted into one cylindrical mass.

Photo by H. J. Bell

Here the diameter of the east cable is being checked during the compacting operation, near the top of the south tower. The powerful compacting machine uses hydraulic (oil) pressure to "squeeze" the cable into a single mass 24.5 inches in diameter. The cables contain 41,000 miles of wire, enough to reach around the earth at the equator one and two-thirds times.
Photo by H. D. Ellis

The final operation is wrapping the cable. Here the west cable, center span, is being wrapped near the top of the south tower. Workmen are coating the cable with a heavy red-lead paste, followed by wrapping with #9 galvanized wire. The wrapping wire was then primed and painted, forming an effective seal for the cables.
Photo by H. J. Bell

Erecting Spans

The south approach spans reach out from the shore. In the background, crews are paving sections nearest the lower peninsula shore as other crews erect spans from pier to pier. Sixteen approach spans connect the suspension bridge to the lower peninsula.

Photo by H. D. Ellis

The approach spans here are reaching out toward the suspension-span portion of the bridge in the distance at the left. Temporary "falsework" helps support an approach span until it is completed, piece by piece, to the next pier. The falsework is then removed and placed between the next two piers, and the steel spans are erected out over it to the next pier.

Photo by H. J. Bell

Here the suspension span itself is being put into place. A stiffening truss section is being lifted from a barge to the north-side span. As made evident in this view, final positions of these truss sections were not achieved until virtually all of the sections had been lifted and made to bear on the main cables, thus properly distributing their load on the cables and causing the suspended spans to conform to their designed arc.　　*Photo by H. D. Ellis*

Road Building

Stringers are installed for the suspended-span roadway, seen here to the north from the main span. Following this stringer placement operation, cross beams and open steel grillwork completed the steel work for the suspended span roadway. While the inner-lane gridworkings were left open to help with the aerodynamic stability (an original design feature of the Mackinac Bridge), the two outer lanes were filled with lightweight concrete and surfaced with asphalt.

Photo by H. J. Bell

GREAT LAKES BRIDGES AND THEIR BUILDERS

Here are the suspended spans, completed, seen from the southeast.

Photo by H. J. Bell

The Final Bridge

Traffic flows over the completed roadways under the main tower in this view to the north from the south side span. The Mackinac Bridge is done!

Photo by H. J. Bell

In 1957 perhaps the greatest triumph in Great Lakes bridge-building was completed. This bridge, called the "Mackinac Bridge," the "Straits Bridge," and the "Mighty Mac," joins Mackinaw City and St. Ignace, spanning the Straits of Mackinac and joining the lower and upper peninsulas of Michigan. The total length, including approaches, is 26,444 feet, just over five miles.

The bridge, opened in November, 1957, in time to carry thousands of deer hunters to the northern peninsula of Michigan, was a dream of bridge builders for a hundred years, but people generally considered it impossible to build. The cost seemed prohibitive, and financing and issuing of bonds not feasible. Since an underwater glacial gorge in the Straits needed to be spanned, this in itself presented a terrible hazard. And such a bridge, it was argued, could never withstand the force of the gales that sweep across the Straits, or the thick ice that forms in the winter and crushes the strongest piles and wharves.

Prentice Marsh Brown, chairman of the Mackinac Bridge Authority ("Mr. Bridge," as he is known in his state), did more than any other one person to overcome the many obstacles, including those of financing the project. (The total cost, including the bond interest during the construction, was $99,800,000.) The engineer, David B. Steinman, famous for the bridges he has built in all parts of the world and whose firm also built the Thousand Islands Bridge and later the International Bridge connecting Sault Ste. Marie, Michigan, and Sault Ste. Marie, Ontario, surmounted the physical and technical difficulties, including those of wind and ice.

The Straits Bridge replaced the state-operated highway ferries that since 1923 provided year-round connection between the peninsulas of Michigan. The five-mile ferry crossing was made in approximately one hour. In busy vacation and hunting seasons, motorists often waited for hours before they could drive their cars aboard the ferry. The crossing time on the bridge is ten minutes. The capacity is 6,000 cars per hour. (The ferry carried 462 cars per hour.)

Some of the "vital statistics" of this great bridge between Lake Michigan and Lake Huron are as follows:

It is the longest suspension bridge in the world—8,614 feet between anchorages.

The central span of the suspension bridge, from tower to tower, is 3,800 feet, 300 feet longer than the span of the George Washington Bridge. Only the 4,200-foot span of the Golden Gate Bridge in San Francisco exceeds it.

Foundations for each of the two main towers of the suspension bridge rest on the rim of the submerged glacial gorge. Three foundations were carried down 200 feet below the surface of the water.

The steel towers that carry the cables are 552 feet high. Each contains 6,250 tons of structural steel.

The Mackinac Bridge is the world's safest bridge in a location of great danger. It was built, as Mr. Steinman said, "to withstand a hypothetical impossible ice pressure of 115,000 pounds per lineal foot, and against a hypothetical improbable wind pressure of 50 pounds per square foot." The greatest wind velocity ever recorded at the bridge site is 78 miles per hour, representing a wind force of 20 pounds per square foot.

New methods of scientific design gave the bridge absolute aerodynamic stability against all forms of oscillation "in all modes, *at all wind velocities and all angles of attack.*" This was important because of the startling destruction of the Tacoma Narrows Bridge in 1940 by cumulative catastrophic oscillations in a mild gale.

The new bridge has a vertical clearance of 155 feet. The height of the roadway above water, at midspan, is 199 feet.

As always, the work of building a large bridge created legends. A 220-pound Indian workman was walking a steel-mesh catwalk when it broke loose from its moorings. He caught the catwalk with his fingers and clung to it while it dropped 200 feet and came to a jerking stop. Then he removed his shoes and climbed back up to safety.

On October 31, 1962, the new International Bridge at Sault Ste. Marie was officially opened to traffic by Governor John B. Swainson of Michigan and Prime Minister John P. Robarts of Ontario. This most recent addition to the bridges joining Canada and the United States links Interstate 75 Freeway, which runs from Tampa, Florida, to Sault Ste.

David B. Steinman

Dr. David B. Steinman, designer and engineer of the Mackinac Brdge who later designed the International Bridge at Sault Ste. Marie, is a master builder of more than four hundred bridges on five continents. One of seven sons of a factory worker, he grew up in poverty on New York's East Side. Living in the shadow of Brooklyn Bridge, he dreamed of becoming an engineer of such a structure himself. His dream literally materialized when, in 1948, he was engaged to change the Brooklyn Bridge from a two-lane auto roadway into a six-lane concrete aerial highway. It seemed quite right that he should, in 1957, have been the man to undertake the "impossible" task of building the Mackinac Bridge. His great achievements were based upon a faith he himself expressed in the following poem:

HELP ME, LORD, TO BUILD MY SPAN

Anchored firm in solid rock,
  On Thy foundation let me build—
Strong to bear each strain and shock,
  An arch of dreams and faith fulfilled.

Help me, Lord, to build my span
  Across the chasm of the years;

Firm in purpose, true in plan,
  Above the drag of doubt and fears.

Help me to build on Thy high road
  A bridge to serve the common good;
To smooth the way and lift the load,
  A link of human brotherhood.

Marie, Michigan, with the recently completed Trans-Canada highway, which extends from the east to the west coast of Canada.

The bridge, begun in 1960, was completed at a cost of $20,000,000. It was designed by David Steinman's firm, Steinman, Boynton, Gronquist, and London. It spans the St. Marys River and the canals of the Soo Locks and offers the travelers who cross it splendid views of the locks and of lake shipping. The vertical clearance is 124 feet. This height conforms to the St. Lawrence Seaway bridge specifications. The roadway at its highest point is 145 feet above ground level. The length from plaza to plaza is two miles. The substructure consists of 62 piers supporting a total length of structure of 9,280 feet.

A condition of the sale of bonds to finance the International Bridge was that there be no other river crossing service within ten miles of the span, so the 74-year-old ferry service between Sault Ste. Marie, Michigan, and Ontario was discontinued.

It is noteworthy that the various bridges which connect the United States and Canada emphasize the peaceful conditions that have existed between these neighbors for a century and a half. These bridges, useful as they are and marvelous examples of the designer's art and the engineer's skill, stand in their beauty as monuments to the agreement of two great nations to live together in friendship and peace.

Dr. David B. Steinman on a boat at the Mackinac Bridge during the bridge's construction. He wears the workman's protection hat.

The International Bridge at Sault Ste. Marie seen from the Canadian side, with the American double span in the distance and the Canadian span in the foreground. In the center runs the St. Marys River.   International Bridge Authority, State of Michigan

A close view of the International Bridge's American span at the Soo. The two canals go under it, leading to the locks, and behind the span may be seen the old bascule bridge, raised.
International Bridge Authority, State of Michigan

Chapter 10

The St. Lawrence Seaway

UP UNTIL 1958, the Great Lakes constituted in themselves, with their connecting canal and lock systems, a seaway that potentially could handle most of the earth's vessels. The one obstacle was the upper St. Lawrence River which, with its old-style shallow-draft canals, blocked the way for larger ships.

On May 13, 1954, the United States Congress authorized the government to join Canada in the construction of the St. Lawrence Seaway, which would replace 22 small locks with 7 big ones, 5 of which Canada would build. So culminated much planning and striving by many individuals in both Canada and the United States over a period going back at least a hundred years. On April 25, 1959, the Seaway opened. It was dedicated on June 26 by President Eisenhower and Queen Elizabeth II.

The new venture accomplished two goals: it provided deep-water ship channels through which the larger part of the world's ocean-going vessels could reach the ports of the Great Lakes, and it provided dams and power-making facilities to furnish electricity for New York, Vermont, and Ontario.

Among the Seaway's navigational benefits: it cut the transit time from the head of the Great Lakes to Montreal by an average of twenty hours. It cut shipping costs from the Midwest to Europe by an average of $22.50 a ton. But the main benefit was the nonstop trip now possible for ocean-going freighters that previously had had to unload at Montreal. The new through trip made the Great Lakes truly the "Mediterranean of North America."

This new wonder of the world is the fourth greatest engineering project ever completed.

The Seaway is jointly financed by the United States and Canada. Apart from the power bill, it has cost the U.S. $130,000,000 and Canada $280,000,000, these figures including interest charges to 1963. Joseph H. McCann, U.S. Seaway Administrator, has noted that this is the only water-navigation project on the continent that is paying back money to the government. By the end of 1963, it will have paid back about $11,000,000.

THE ST. LAWRENCE SEAWAY

Both countries now have a continuous navigational channel at least 27 feet deep. Since there must be a safety margin, the actual maximum draft permitted is 25.5 feet. The Seaway's canals, dams, locks, and power plants divide into five sections according to the nature of the terrain:

1. The Lachine section, extending thirty-one miles upriver from Montreal, including two locks and ten bridges.

2. The Soulanges section, adding sixteen miles, to Lake St. Francis, including two locks and the Beauharnois Canal.

Three-way map of the St. Lawrence Seaway, with increasing detail.   *New York Times*

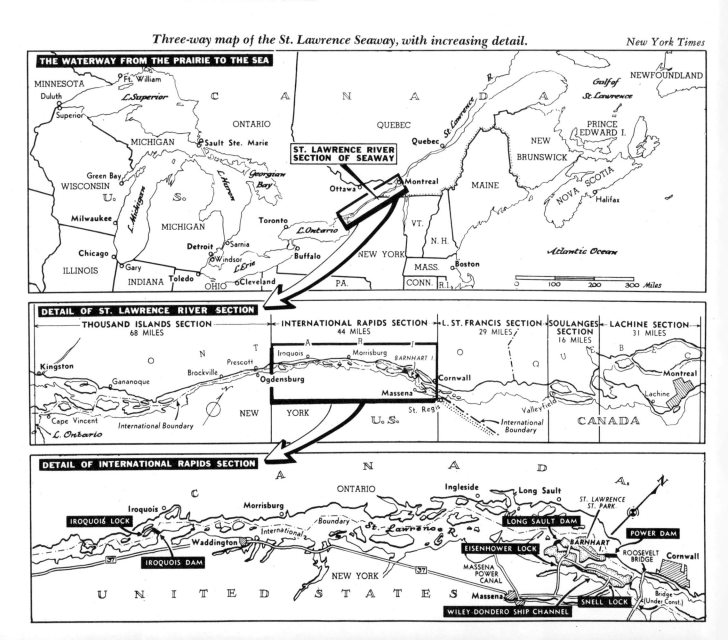

3. The Lake St. Francis section, adding thirty-one miles, to Cornwall.

4. The International Rapids section, adding thirty-six miles from Cornwall to Chimney Point, including the big power dam built jointly by the Canadians and Americans, as well as three more locks and three dams.

5. The Thousand Islands section, adding sixty-eight miles, to Lake Ontario.

A vessel coming up the St. Lawrence from the Atlantic will be 20 feet above sea level at Montreal. It will be lifted 48 feet by the St. Lambert and Cote Ste. Catherine Locks, bypassing the Lachine Rapids. The vessel will proceed along Lake St. Louis to the Beauharnois Locks and will be lifted the 81 feet to Lake St. Francis.

The Snell Lock and the Eisenhower Lock will lift the vessel 83 feet past the Long Sault Spillway Dam. This dam together with the Robert Moses—Robert H. Saunders Power Dam not only provides a new source of electric power, but also creates Lake St. Lawrence, 26 miles long.

Construction

Every great engineering work is done a little at a time. The St. Lawrence Seaway Authority dug eighteen miles of channel "in the dry" in the Laprairie Basin west of Montreal at the start of construction. Along this stretch, a dike was built to flank one side.

St. Lawrence Seaway Authority, Photo by Hans van der Aa

Several miles of channel were also dug from Côte Ste. Catherine Lock on Laprairie Basin upstream to Lake St. Louis. In the upper left of this photo may be seen a completed portion of 4,200 feet.

St. Lawrence Seaway Authority, Photo by Hans van der Aa

The St. Lambert Lock nearing completion. Also in the picture is the southern portion of the Victoria Bridge being modified to provide a minimum overhead clearance of 120 feet for shipping, and also to provide uninterrupted vehicular and rail traffic.

St. Lawrence Seaway Authority, Photo by Hans van der Aa

*The wall of the future Seaway Channel towered over forty feet
in a part of the overland channel being excavated to bypass the
Lachine Rapids, on the south shore of the St. Lawrence River.
In this area the ground was solid limestone. But along the Beauharnois Canal sandstone was encountered so hard it wore out
drill bits in eight hours, and the stone had to be softened by firing
it with kerosene torches at 4,000 degrees Fahrenheit. Workmen
burned, drilled, and blasted through two miles of solid rock.*
St. Lawrence Seaway Authority, Photo by Hans van der Aa

*Looking downstream over the excavation and construction of the Upper and Lower Beauharnois
Locks.*
St. Lawrence Seaway Authority, Photo by Hans van der Aa

The Iroquois Lock at the head of Lake St. Lawrence lifts the vessel 3 feet to the level of Lake Ontario.

The Welland Canal extends from Port Weller on Lake Ontario to Port Colborne on Lake Erie and has seven lift locks and one guard lock. The lifts vary from 43.7 feet to 47.9 feet, aggregating 327 feet total lift. Lock 1 at Port Weller is 865 feet long by 80 feet wide; Locks 2 through 7 are 859 feet long by 80 feet wide; Lock 8 at Port Colborne, the guard lock, is 1,380 feet long and 80 feet wide. At this point the vessel will have ascended a giant staircase of 550 feet between Montreal on the St. Lawrence and Port Colborne on Lake Erie, including 8 feet of natural slope. At this point, some 368 miles from Montreal, the St. Lawrence Seaway ends.

Before the vessel has continued through Lake Erie, the Detroit River, Lake St. Clair, the St. Clair River, Lake Huron, and St. Marys River, it will have been raised 10 feet by the gradual rise in the water course. At Sault Ste. Marie, the locks will lift the vessel 20 feet to Lake Superior. Between Montreal and Whitefish Bay in Lake Superior the vessel will have risen 580 feet, of which all but 18 feet are man-made and controlled.

Snell Lock constructors looking downstream across the upper sill, July, 1957.   *Perini Corp., Framingham, Mass.*

The Eisenhower Lock under construction, December, 1957.   *Morrison-Knudsen Co., Inc.*

The Long Sault Dam under construction.   *Power Authority of the State of New York*

If the French priests who, around 1700, built a ditchlike canal to help canoes and small boats around the Lachine Rapids could see the present Seaway, one may imagine how astounded they would be.

Today's visitors find it astonishing enough and they come in increasing numbers. Last year 750,000 people visited the Eisenhower Lock and an estimated 1,000,000 people visited the Seaway project generally. Upper Canada Village near Cornwall preserves many of the historic buildings of the early 1800's that were moved out of the Seaway area, and has become a kind of Canadian Williamsburg, preserving intact both old houses and an older way of life. Early trades, like a bakery complete with its equipment, are on display, and old hand-operated locks with old bateaux going through them.

The Seaway is designed to handle between 50 and 60 million tons of cargo annually, figured on an eight-month season. It is closed from approximately November 30 to April 15th, these dates being stretched when the weather permits. In 1962, almost 26 million tons were handled, approximately half capacity, but this figure was up 10 per cent over the year before and each year may be expected to show an increase.

Power

The Seaway's $600 million power project, built jointly by Canada and the United States, is one of mankind's greatest engineering feats. Power is generated in the International Rapids Section by harnessing the 92-foot drop in the water level between the eastern end of Lake Ontario and the powerhouse site. Previously this drop could not be used for power purposes because it was spread over a 125-mile stretch of river. It had to be concentrated at one point.

The job of doing that was begun August 10, 1954, and completed in 1958. The result is a main dam and powerhouses forming a continuous structure 3,300 feet long, with 16 generators in each powerhouse providing a maximum daily combined capacity of nearly 2,000,000 kilowatts.

Work on the Robert Moses–Robert H. Saunders Power Dam continued even at night under flood-lights. This night view was taken in August, 1956.　　　　*Perini Corp., Framingham, Mass.*

The materials required for completion of all structures on both sides of the river included: 3,200,000 cubic yards of concrete, 2,000,000 tons of sand, 3,200,000 tons of stone, 28,000 tons of structural steel, 20,200 tons of gates, hoists, and cranes, 59,300 tons of reinforcing steel, and 3,600,000 barrels of cement.

The Power Dam and Long Sault Dam formed a "head pond," Lake St. Lawrence, with an area of about 100 square miles.

Persons living in 20,000 acres on the Canadian and 18,000 acres on the American side had to be relocated. In the United States, 225 farm families and 500 cottage owners were displaced. On the Canadian side, seven communities and part of an eighth were moved, even cemeteries being carefully carried to a new location. One-third of the sizable town of Morrisburg was shifted—some 6,500 people.

View of the Power Dam, looking downstream, just after the breaching of the cofferdam, which can be seen behind the main dam. In this view, the United States is on the right, Canada on the left. Perini Corp., Framingham, Mass. Photo by Nick Podgurski

The new channel can handle ships of five to ten times the previous capacity. The main cargoes, ore and wheat, fill the holds of about nine-tenths of these ships. One of the major pressures behind the building of the Seaway was the discovery and development of high-grade Labrador iron ores. These have become a vital supplement to the ore fields in the Midwest that have been supplying the steel mills of Pennsylvania, Ohio, Indiana, New York, and Ontario. These new ores, in estimated shipments of 10 to 20 million tons a year, will flow from the "Labrador trough" west to balance the grain going east. Ore reserves in Labrador are believed to be in the billions of tons.

Dedication

Her Majesty Queen Elizabeth II and President Eisenhower at St. Lambert, Quebec, at the official opening of the St. Lawrence Seaway on June 26, 1959.   *St. Lawrence Seaway Authority*

The Royal Yacht Britannia's crossing through the ceremonial gates at the approach to the St. Lambert Lock marks the official opening of the St. Lawrence Seaway. *National Film Board of Canada*

Escorted by President Eisenhower, Queen Elizabeth leaves the Royal Yacht at the Lower Beauharnois Lock, following the ceremonies marking the official opening of the St. Lawrence Seaway, which took place earlier in the day. St. Lawrence Seaway Authority

**THE
ST. LAWRENCE
SEAWAY**

Well over 6 million tons of U.S. Great Lakes trade was with other countries in 1962. This is only about 2 per cent of the total waterborne trade in the Lakes area, but it is growing rapidly (up from 750,000 tons in 1956). And the tonnage figure is deceptive since the overseas trade tends to be finished products with a far higher dollar value than bulk domestic trade. Sixty-five per cent of American export trade originates from the area tapped by the great cities of the lakes. For Canada, this figure is modified by the trade of Montreal and Quebec, but it is still large and increasing.

The new Seaway will give all this trade a challenging stimulus. Already cities are remodeling port facilities, dredging entrances, and making other changes to adapt to the new possibilities. The five major connecting channels on the Great Lakes will have to be deepened to the 27 feet required for the Seaway (at the cost of an estimated $141 million). This work is already in progress.

Ports on the Great Lakes may now legitimately call themselves seaports. Toledo, for example, which had only 55 overseas vessels enter its port in 1952, had 215 in 1959, and 355 in 1961, and the increase will continue. Milwaukee notes in one day the arrival of European cars, Spanish olives, and Malayan rubber. Toronto has built a $10,000,000 sugar refinery to process raw sugar from the Caribbean. Europe and other parts of the world now have access to a new seacoast of 8,300 miles, more than the entire United States Atlantic seaboard. On this new inland seacoast, Cleveland is closer to Europe than Baltimore. Duluth and Fort William are as close as New Orleans.

The Finished Seaway

THE
ST. LAWRENCE
SEAWAY

The St. Lambert Lock, at the eastern Seaway entrance. In the background may be glimpsed the two-mile channel that brings vessels into the Seaway from the St. Lawrence River at Montreal. At the start of the lock is the Victoria Aerial Lift Bridge.
National Film Board of Canada

The Cote Ste. Catherine Lock, the second of the new locks of the St. Lawrence Seaway going up-stream, is a companion to the St. Lambert Lock in the canal going around the Lachine Rapids.
National Film Board of Canada

These are two of four bridges in the Montreal area that were modified to provide an overhead clearance of 120 feet for shipping. At right is the Honoré Mercier Bridge whose south shore approach was completely rebuilt so that the span above the channel would have a permanently fixed clearance. At the left is the double track Canadian Pacific Railway's Caughnawaga Bridge. Here vertical lift spans provide the required clearance over the channel. National Film Board of Canada

This is the Lower Beauharnois Lock which, with its companion, the Upper Beauharnois Lock, provides access from Lake St. Louis to the Beauharnois Canal. Here the lock is seen being filled for the first time as water rushes from side culverts into the lock chamber through ports at the base of the lock walls. In the background are the downstream miter gates of the lock. St. Lawrence Seaway Authority

The lower and upper locks at Beauharnois, looking upstream. Beyond lies the 16-mile Beauharnois Canal.

St. Lawrence Seaway Authority

And it is a stunning fact that for a ship entering the Seaway account has to be taken of the change from salt water to fresh, in mid-course. A vessel settles one foot deeper in fresh water than in salt for every 36 feet of draft.

The Great Lakes are now navigable by 80 per cent of salt-water ships. At least in part because of the new Seaway, Sverre Petterssen, chairman of the University of Chicago Geophysical Sciences Department, says that the Great Lakes region as a whole will become the greatest industrial region on earth, with a city twenty miles deep, from Milwaukee to Buffalo. Canada, with endless resources and territory, can be expected to match this growth.

This is the vision our astronaut saw at the opening of this book when he looked down at the file of ships going from Duluth and Fort William out across the five lakes to the ocean, and from the ocean another file of ships coming in. In this great expanse of blue water glistens a future that is only beginning to be seen.

A dispatcher controls traffic in the eastern section of the St. Lawrence Seaway from his position at the Beauharnois Locks.

National Film Board of Canada

View of a ship coming up the Beauharnois Canal. The canal was
dug in 1932 with the eventual complete Seaway in mind, to the
standard present depth of 27 feet.   *National Film Board of Canada*

*An unusual aerial view of the Robert Moses–Robert H. Saunders Power Dam unit. The Power
Dam is the large dam at the center of the picture. To the right of the cloud can be seen the Long
Sault Dam. On the left side in the foreground is the Snell Lock and at the other end of the Wiley-
Dondero Ship Channel (and under the shadow of the smaller cloud) can be seen the Eisenhower
Lock. This picture was taken in June of 1963.*   Power Authority of the State of New York

A close view of the Snell Lock in operation. In the background is the great series of power lines that lead from the Power Dam.

National Film Board of Canada

The Lock Lookers

Last year more than a million persons visited the Eisenhower Lock on the American side. From a special viewing platform they could see the great man-made spectacle of ships being lifted or lowered through the lock and could even chat and joke with passing sailors. The admission is ten cents.

Visitors not only talk to sailors. They offer encouragement and advice to the lock masters and ship captains, convinced that the vessels could never make it on their own. Residents of nearby Massena even become lock addicts. When a ship is going through, fans leave their homes and rush to the viewing platform.

Big as the lock is—800 feet long—the giant ships often seem barely able to squeeze into the chamber. No wonder the dock-side superintendents feel needed.

Even driving up to the lock is a drama. Suddenly, in the midst of fields and farmlands, a giant ship comes into view right on the road like a mirage in a desert. Even more amazing is that the automobiles can be driven right under the ships in the locks, by continuing on the road through the Eisenhower Tunnel which is at the far side of the viewing area on the left side of the lock, in the photograph.

The large parking space is usually well filled with cars.

The Eisenhower Lock.

Power Authority of the State of New York

THE ST. LAWRENCE SEAWAY

A large bulk carrier, the Sir Thomas Shaughnessy, is about to be lowered at the Eisenhower Lock while in the background can be seen another vessel tied up at the approach wall, waiting its turn.

St. Lawrence Seaway Development Corp.

Highway tunnel goes under the lock.

St. Lawrence Seaway Development Corp.

An old coach drives through the historic buildings of Upper Canada Village.

St. Lawrence Seaway Development Corp.

The Long Sault Dam built in the vicinity of the Long Sault Rapids closed the south channel of the St. Lawrence River. The Power Dam itself closed the north channel and these two mighty structures created the man-made Lake St. Lawrence, visible here behind the Long Sault Dam. Lake St. Lawrence is used both for power and navigation.   Power Authority of the State of New York

The long sweep of the completed Power Dam.   Power Authority of the State of New York

In the United States half of the
Power Dam, the turbine gallery
extends for nearly 1300 feet.
Power Authority of the State of New York

A large bulk carrier passes Car-
dinal, Ontario, on its way to the
Iroquois Lock.
National Film Board of Canada

**The Iroquois Lock and Dam. The Iroquois is the seventh and last lock on the St. Lawrence River
Section of the Seaway, taking vessels up to the level of Lake Ontario. The Seaway is completed by
the great locks of the Welland Canal described in Chapter 7.**   *Power Authority of the State of New York*

334

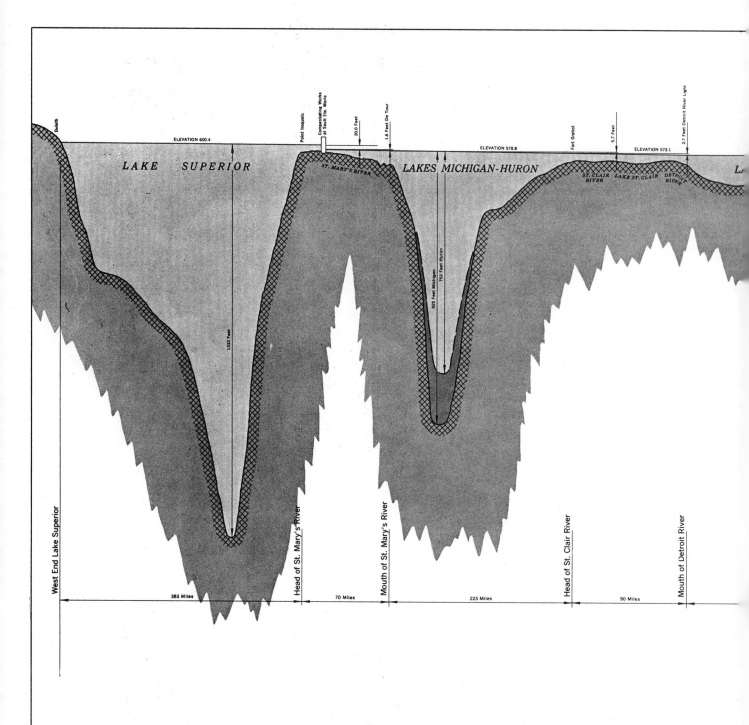

The water levels shown hereon represent average conditions.
Low Water Datum elevations for the lakes are as follows:

Lake Superior 600.0
Lakes Michigan—Huron 576.8
Lake St. Clair 571.7
Lake Erie 568.6
Lake Ontario 242.8

*Average Lake Ontario Level under present Regulation Plan
1958-C.

Army-U.S.Lake Survey, Detroit-Litho.1963-2,000

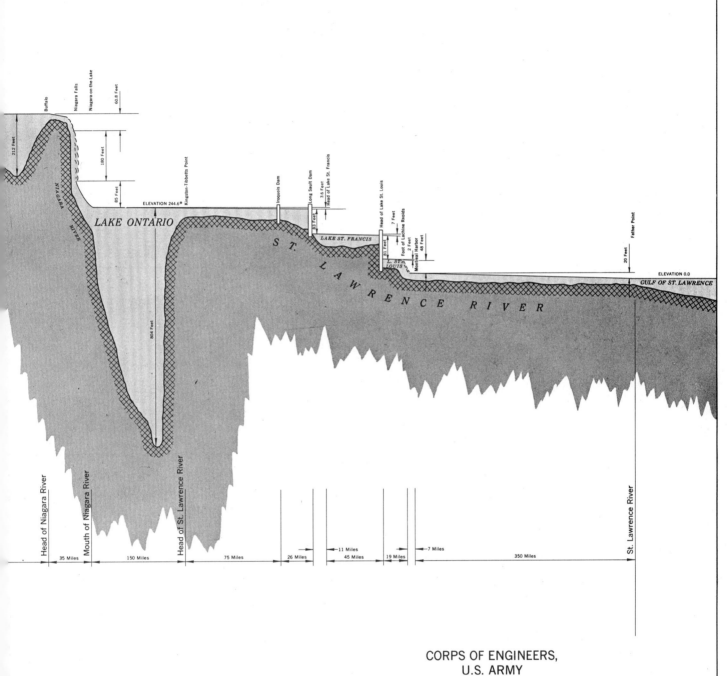

CORPS OF ENGINEERS,
U.S. ARMY
U.S. LAKE SURVEY

GREAT LAKES – ST. LAWRENCE RIVER
PROFILE

ELEVATIONS ON THE LAKE SURFACES ARE THE LONG TERM AVER-
AGES EXPRESSED ON INTERNATIONAL GREAT LAKES DATUM (1955).
SCALES HAVE BEEN DISTORTED TO CONVEY VISUAL IMPRESSION OF
DIFFERENCES IN ELEVATION WHICH ARE GIVEN TO THE NEAREST
FOOT EXCEPT WHERE DECIMALS ARE SHOWN.

The Great Lakes Timetable

c. 1000 and other dates—Viking exploration.

1535—Jacques Cartier, navigator and seaman from St. Malo, sails his three frail craft across the Atlantic and up the St. Lawrence, and lays claim to the new land in the name of His Most Christian Majesty, Francis I of France.

1608—Quebec is founded by Samuel de Champlain.

1615—Champlain reaches the Great Lakes via the French River into Georgian Bay and Lake Huron.

1622—Etienne Brulé becomes the first French explorer to reach Lake Superior.

1634—The gifted and youthful Jean Nicolet is sent by Champlain to the West to find the Emperor of Cathay. Instead Nicolet discovers Lake Michigan.

1641—Two intrepid Jesuit priests, Fathers Jogues and Rambault, establish a mission at Sault Ste. Marie, another at the tip of St. Ignace, a third near where Ashland, Wisconsin, stands today, and a fourth at the mouth of the Fox River at the head of Green Bay.

1669—Explorers discover Lake Erie which, until this time, had been closely guarded by the Iroquois.

1673—Father Marquette and Louis Jolliet make their historic trip by birchbark canoe down the Mississippi as far as the mouth of the Arkansas.

1678—Father Hennepin becomes the first white man to see the grandeur that is Niagara Falls.

1679—The year of one of the great unsolved mysteries of the Great Lakes. Robert Cavalier, Sieur de la Salle, builds the *Griffin,* 60 feet long, of from 45 to 60 tons, the first sailing vessel ever launched upon the Great Lakes. La Salle sails the *Griffin* across the lakes to Green Bay. There he loads it with furs and orders it sailed back to Montreal. On the way it disappears. No trace has ever been found of either ship or crew.

1701—A fort is built by the French at the site of Detroit. Antoine de la Mothe Cadillac selects the site and supervises the fort's construction.

1754—Hostility between the French and English finally breaks out in the French and Indian War, which is fought far from the main European arena of the Seven Years' War, 1756-63.

1759—General James Wolfe's daring strategy results in the capture of Quebec by the British. Both generals in this brilliant clash, Wolfe and French commander Louis Joseph de Montcalm, fall mortally wounded.

1763—Canada is ceded to England at the conclusion of the Seven Years' War.

1764—War between the Indian coalition, led by Pontiac, and the British concludes with the British in firm control of the Great Lakes.

1783—The Treaty of Paris concludes the American Revolution, fought almost completely away from the Great Lakes area. The boundary between the fledgling nation and Canada is established.

1787—The Northwest Territory is created by Constitutional Ordinance. From this far-sighted action eventually come the states of Ohio, Michigan, Indiana, Illinois, Wisconsin, and a part of Minnesota.

1797—The first crude lock to bypass the falls at Sault Ste. Marie is built by the North-West Fur Company.

1808—The American Fur Company is founded by John Jacob Astor.

1812—The War of 1812, generally considered a "senseless war," breaks out between the United States and England.

1813—Commodore Oliver Hazard Perry becomes one of the nation's first naval heroes by his victory over the British fleet, commanded by Commodore Barclay, in the Battle of Lake Erie (September 10) near Put-in-Bay.

1814—The Treaty of Ghent ends the War of 1812 with statesmanlike compromises on both sides.

1816—The digging of the Erie Canal (generally scoffed at as Clinton's Folly) begins.

1816—The Canadians launch the first steamship on the Great Lakes, christened the *Frontenac* after one of the great governors of early French Canada.

1817—The Americans launch the 220-ton steamer *Ontario* at Sackets Harbor, New York.

1818—The first lighthouse on the American side of the Great Lakes is built at Buffalo.

1818—*Walk-in-the-Water* is launched, the first steamship on Lake Erie.

1820—Michigan's Governor Lewis Cass presides at ceremonies at Sault Ste. Marie at which the British flag is lowered and the U. S. flag is raised in its place. Two years later the United States builds Fort Brady at the Sault.

1825—Work begins on the Welland Canal in Ontario to link Lakes Erie and Ontario and to bypass Niagara Falls.

1825—Erie Canal opens. Barges start to ply 363-mile route between Buffalo and Albany. Freight fares from Lake Erie to New York City plummet from $120 to $4 per ton.

1827—The steamer *Frontenac* burns in the Niagara River. (Five years later its American counterpart, the *Ontario,* is dismantled.)

1829—The Welland Canal opens for traffic. Forty locks make possible the 326-foot lift between Lake Ontario and Lake Erie and take navigation around Niagara Falls.

1841—The *Vandalia,* the first screw wheel vessel built on Great Lakes, is launched at Oswego, New York.

1844—Iron and copper are discovered in Michigan's upper peninsula.

1853—Work begins on the construction of a canal and locks at Sault Ste. Marie.

1855—The upper and lower lakes are linked with the opening of the canal and locks at Sault Ste. Marie.

1860—A total of 287 lives are lost when the excursion steamer *Lady Elgin* is rammed by the schooner *Augusta* and sinks in heavy winds between Chicago and Milwaukee.

1865-70—The peak of sailing activity on the Great Lakes, with nearly 2,000 vessels listed.

1871—Chicago is leveled by the great fire.

1881—To keep pace with increasing traffic, another lock, the Weitzel, is opened at the Sault.

1882—The first iron freighter on the Great Lakes, the *Onoko,* is launched at Cleveland.

1889—Inventor Alexander McDougall launches the first "whaleback" steamer, especially designed for use on the Great Lakes. Whalebacks never gain general acceptance, but during a nine-year period, 43 bulk cargo whalebacks, some barges and steamers, and one passenger boat of this design are launched.

1895—Canada opens a lock at the Canadian Sault.

1896—The Poe Lock is opened on the American side of the Sault.

1913—Fourteen freighters are lost or wrecked in what is generally known on the Great Lakes as "The Big Storm."

1914—Another lock, the Davis, is opened at the Sault.

1915—The Great Lakes' greatest catastrophe—overturning of the excursion steamer *Eastland* at Chicago—results in loss of 815 lives.

1916—Lake Erie is struck by the "Black Friday" storm. Four freighters are lost or wrecked.

1919—The Sabin Lock is opened at the Sault.

1927—The Prince of Wales dedicates the Peace Bridge over the Niagara River between Buffalo, New York, and Fort Erie, Ontario.

1929—The Ambassador Bridge linking Detroit and Windsor is opened.

1930—First traffic moves between Detroit and Windsor through tunnel beneath Detroit River.

1939—Blue Water Bridge between Port Huron and Sarnia is dedicated.

1943—The MacArthur Lock is opened at the Sault. New lock replaces the old Weitzel Lock and enables the Sault to handle more than 120 million tons of shipping in a single year.

1957—Mackinac Bridge, linking Michigan's upper and lower peninsulas, is opened.

1959—The St. Lawrence Seaway is opened (April 25). A joint Canadian-American project, the Seaway enables most ocean-going vessels to sail up the St. Lawrence and into the Great Lakes. Final construction costs for the Seaway between Montreal and Lake Ontario are $410 million, of which Canada spent $280 million while the United States contributed $130 million. A project to deepen the channels of the Detroit River, Lake St. Clair, the St. Clair River, the St. Marys River and Locks, and the Straits of Mackinac is also undertaken by the U. S. Army Corps of Engineers. This will involve expenditures of an estimated $146 million.

Bibliography

ALSBERG, HENRY G. *The American Guide, The Lake States and Middle Atlantic States.* New York: Hastings House, 1949.

AMBLER, CHARLES H. *A History of Transportation in the Ohio Valley.* Glendale, California: A. H. Clark, 1932.

BALD, F. CLEVER. *Michigan in Four Centuries.* New York: Harper, 1954.

_____. *The Sault Canal Through 100 Years.* Ann Arbor: University of Michigan Press, 1954.

BARCUS, FRANK. *Freshwater Fury.* Detroit: Wayne State University Press, 1960.

BEASLEY, NORMAN. *Freighters of Fortune—The Story of the Great Lakes.* New York: Harper, 1930.

BREBNER, J. BARTLET. *Canada, A Modern History.* Ann Arbor: The University of Michigan Press, 1960.

BROWN, PRENTISS M. *The Mackinac Bridge Story.* Detroit: Wayne State University Press, 1956.

CHANNING, EDWARD. *Story of the Great Lakes.* New York: 1909.

CUTHBERTSON, GEORGE A. *Freshwater.* New York: 1931.

DISTURNELL, JOHN. *The Great Lakes or Inland Seas of America.* New York: 1863.

_____. *Sailing on the Great Lakes.* Philadelphia: 1874.

_____. *Upper Lakes of North America.* New York: 1857.

GREAT LAKES—ST. LAWRENCE ASSOCIATION. *The Connecting Channels, New Horizons for Great Lakes Transportation.* Washington: 1957.

HATCHER, HARLAN H. *The Great Lakes.* New York: Oxford University Press, 1944.

_____. *Lake Erie.* Indianapolis: Bobbs-Merrill, 1945.

_____. *The Western Reserve.* Indianapolis: Bobbs-Merrill, 1949.

HAVINGHURST, WALTER. *The Long Ships Passing, The Story of the Great Lakes.* New York: Macmillan, 1953.

HENNEPIN, FATHER LOUIS. *A New Discovery of a Vast Country in America.* Chicago: 1903.

HEPBURN, ANDREW. *Complete Guide to the Great Lakes.* Garden City, N. Y.: Doubleday, 1962.

HOLBROOK, STEWART H. *Holy Old Mackinaw.* New York: Macmillan, 1938.

HOUGH, JACK L. *Geology of the Great Lakes.* Champaign: University of Illinois Press, 1958.

Illinois, A Descriptive and Historical Guide. Chicago: McClurg, 1939.

INCHES, H. C. *The Great Lakes Wooden Shipbuilding Era.* Vermilion, Ohio: Great Lakes Historical Society, 1962.

Inland Seas. Quarterly Journal of the Great Lakes Historical Society, Cleveland.

The Interlake Steamship Log (Cleveland), June, 1955.

IRELAND, TOM. *The Great Lakes—St. Lawrence Deep Waterway to the Sea.* New York: Putnam, 1934.

LAKE CARRIERS ASSOCIATION. *Annual Reports.*

LANDON, FRED. *Lake Huron.* Indianapolis: Bobbs-Merrill, 1944.

Lloyds Steamboat Directory. Cincinnati: 1856.

LOWE, KENNETH S. "Loneliest Place in America," *Motor News* (Detroit), August, 1959.

MALKUS, ALIDA. *Blue-Water Boundary.* New York: Hastings House, 1960.

Marine Review (Cleveland), 1913.

McDANIEL, RICHARD G. *Great Lakes—St. Lawrence Seaway Maritime Directory,* 1958. (First edition. St. Clair: 1957.)

Michigan: A Guide to the Wolverine State. New York: 1956.

Minnesota, A State Guide. New York: Viking, 1938.

The Ohio Guide. New York: Oxford University Press, 1940.

PARKMAN, FRANCIS. *The Pioneers of France in the New World.* Boston: 1903.

_____. *La Salle and the Discovery of the Great West.* Boston: 1903.

_____. *A Half Century of Conflict.* Boston: 1903.

Port of Detroit Log.

RATIGAN, WILLIAM. *Straits of Mackinac: Crossroads of the Great Lakes.* Grand Rapids: Eerdmans, 1957.

SMITH, EMERSON R. *Before the Bridge, A History and a Directory of St. Ignace and Nearby Localities.* St. Ignace: 1957.

SMITH, J. RUSSELL. *North America.* New York: 1925.

STEINMAN, DAVID B. and NEVILL, J. T. *Miracle Bridge at Mackinac.* New York: Harcourt, 1957.

STEINMAN, DAVID B., *et al. Bridges.* New York: 1960.

UNITED STATES COAST GUARD. *Historically Famous Lighthouses.* Washington: 1957.

WINSOR, JUSTIN. *Narrative and Critical History of America.* New York: 1889.

Wisconsin, A Guide to the Badger State. New York: Duell, Sloan and Pearce, 1941.

Acknowledgments

The authors gratefully acknowledge the helpful cooperation of the following individuals and organizations in securing pictures for this book:

Chamber of Commerce
Alexandria, Minn.

American Philosophical Society
Philadelphia, Pa.

Canadian Consulate General
New York, N. Y.

The Honorable Bryan Cathcart
Ontario Department of Travel and Publicity
Toronto, Ont.

Miss Judith A. Paha
Mr. Norbert G. Hudoba
Chicago Association of Commerce and Industry
Chicago, Ill.

Mr. Lyman F. Bergbom
Chicago Yacht Club
Chicago, Ill.

The Detroit News
Detroit, Mich.

Mr. Jack Grenard
Detroit Yacht Club
Detroit, Mich.

Mrs. Josiah E. Greene
The St. Louis County Historical Society
Duluth, Minn.

Mr. Jerry Sullivan
Ford Motor Company
Dearborn, Mich.

Mr. Marc Hardy
Mr. Kenneth Stewart
Department of Tourism, Fish and Game
Quebec, Que.

Mr. J. Russell Harper
The National Gallery of Canada
Ottawa, Ont.

Miss Eve Riley and Mrs. I. M. B. Dobell
McGill University
Montreal, Que.

Mr. Andrew H. Hepburn
New York, N. Y.

Capt. H. Chesley Inches
The Great Lakes Historical Society Marine Museum
Vermilion, Ohio

Mr. Gordon Wendt
Sandusky, Ohio

Mrs. Frances B. Macdonald
Indiana State Library
Indianapolis, Ind.

Mr. E. O. Jones, Jr.
S. C. Johnson & Son, Inc.
Racine, Wis.

Messrs. Kaplan, Ristow, and others
The Library of Congress
Washington, D. C.

Miss Geneva Kebler
Michigan Historical Commission
Lansing, Mich.

Members of the Michigan Historical Commission
in Lansing, Michigan, for making the Munson and
Albertype collections of photographs available

Mr. Eugene D. Becker
Minnesota Historical Society
St. Paul, Minn.

National Archives
Washington, D. C.

The New York Times
New York, N. Y.

Mr. John Bruel
Power Authority of the State of New York
New York, N. Y.

Mrs. Elizabeth R. Martin
The Ohio Historical Society
Columbus, Ohio

Mr. Paul Sherlock
Department of Development
Columbus, Ohio

Mr. G. W. Spragge
Mr. A. W. Murdoch
Mr. D. F. McOuat
Department of Public Records and Archives
Toronto, Ont.

Mr. C. Clyde Batten
The Royal Ontario Museum
Toronto, Ont.

Mr. John A. Lynch
Perini Corporation
Framingham, Mass.

Mr. Joseph H. McCann, Administrator
St. Lawrence Seaway Development Corporation
Detroit, Mich.

Mr. John Akin
St. Lawrence Seaway Authority of Canada
Ottawa, Ont.

Miss Elizabeth Payne
Mr. Willis H. Crosswhite
St. Lawrence Seaway Development Corporation
Massena, N. Y.

Mr. Richard E. Stoner, Photographer
Ashtabula, Ohio

Mr. F. Wells Robison
U. S. Army Engineers Lake Survey
Detroit, Mich.

Gen. Lester S. Bork
Fort Wayne Military Reservation
Detroit, Mich.

Mr. Paul H. Kangas
U. S. Coast Guard
Cleveland, Ohio

Lt. Col. R. Winkenwerder, Chief
Intelligence Division
Fifth U. S. Army
Chicago, Ill.

Mrs. Virginia S. Ellis
U. S. Army Corps of Engineers
Chicago, Ill.

Mr. J. L. Avesian
Col. Peter C. Hyzer
U. S. Army Corps of Engineers
Detroit, Mich.

Mr. R. E. Allgire
Mr. A. A. Tremer
United States Steel Corporation
Cleveland, Ohio

Mr. John H. Daley
U. S. Steel Corporation
Gary, Ind.

Miss Anne M. Sexton
The University of Western Ontario
London, Ont.

Mr. Eugene M. Roark
State of Wisconsin Conservation Department
Madison, Wis.

Mr. Paul Vanderbilt
The State Historical Society of Wisconsin
Madison, Wis.

Chambers of Commerce of Benton Harbor, Mich.; Ashland, Wis.; Brantford, Ont.; Burlington, Ont.; Cobourg, Ont.; Conneaut, Ohio; Duluth, Minn.; Dunkirk, N. Y.; Erie, Pa. (and Mitchell Advertising Agency); Fort Erie, Ont.; Grand Haven, Mich.; Grand Rapids, Mich.; Holland, Mich.; Kincardine, Ont.; London, Ont.; Lorain, Ohio; Mackinaw City, Mich.; Manistee, Mich.; Menominee, Mich.; Marquette, Mich.; Michigan City, Mich.; Monroe, Mich.; Mt. Clemons, Mich. (and The Macomb Publishing Company); Niagara Falls, Ont.; Niagara

Falls, N. Y.; Oakville, Ont.; Oconto, Wis.; Oshawa, Ont.; Oswego, N. Y.; Painesville, Ohio; Parry Sound, Ont.; Petoskey, Mich.; Port Colborne, Ont.; Port Hope, Ont.; Put-in-Bay, Ohio; Rochester, N. Y.; Sackets Harbor, N. Y.; St. Catherines, Ont.; St. Thomas, Ont.; Sandusky, Ohio; Sarnia, Ont.; Sault Ste. Marie, Mich.; Sault Ste. Marie, Ont.; Sheboygan, Wis.; Simcoe, Ont.; South Haven, Mich.; Sudbury, Ont. (and *The Sudbury Star*); Thorold, Ont.; Two Harbors, Minn.; Two Rivers, Wis.; Watertown, N. Y.; Waukegan-North Chicago, Ill.; Welland, Ont.; and Whitby, Ont.

Miss Ethel J. MacDowell
Ashtabula County District Library
Ashtabula, Ohio

Mr. G. L. Long
Bell Telephone Company of Canada
Montreal, Que.

Miss Janet Coe Sanborn, Editor of *Inland Seas*
Cleveland Public Library
Cleveland, Ohio

Miss Constance Sheehan
Carnegie Public Library
Conneaut, Ohio

Mrs. Bernice C. Sprenger
Mr. James M. Babcock
Burton Historical Collection
Detroit Public Library
Detroit, Mich.

Mr. James J. Bradley, Automotive History Collection
Detroit Public Library
Detroit, Mich.

Mr. Orville E. Lomoe, Executive Editor
Duluth News-Tribune
Duluth, Minn.

Miss Ida B. Reed
Dunkirk Free Library
Dunkirk, N. Y.

Mr. Gordon E. Copeland
Evanston Historical Society
Evanston, Ill.

Mr. Keith Denis, President
The Thunder Bay Historical Society
Fort William and Port Arthur, Ont.

Mr. Watt P. Marchman
The Rutherford B. Hayes Library
Fremont, Ohio

Mr. James L. Quinn
Mr. Donn P. Quigley
Neville Public Museum
Green Bay, Wis.

Miss Rosemary Brinkman
McGregor Public Library
Highland Park 3, Mich.

Doris L. Knott
Huron Public Library
Huron, Ohio

Miss Carrie Cropley
Kenosha County Historical Society
Kenosha, Wis.

Mr. H. P. Gundy
Kingston Historical Society
Kingston, Ont.

Mr. David Mitchell
Lewiston Historical Society
Lewiston, N.Y.

Miss Eleanor Short
Manistee City Public Library
Manistee, Mich.

Mrs. Loretta Madson
Public Library
Manitowoc, Wis.

Mr. Dawson M. Leigh
Midland Public Library
Midland, Ont.

Miss E. Albrich
Port Colborne Public Library
Port Colborne, Ont.

Miss Dorothy M. Mitts
Port Huron Public Library
Port Huron, Mich.

Mr. T. T. Ferris
A. B. Lucas Secondary School
London, Ont.

Mr. Richard A. Sampson
Racine County Historical Museum, Inc.
Racine, Wis.

Mr. Jack Hooley
Department of Public Information
Rochester, N.Y.

Mr. W. Stephen Thomas
Rochester Museum of Arts and Sciences
Rochester, N.Y.

Mr. Harry Whitely, Publisher
The Presque Isle County Advance
Rochers City, Mich.

Mr. Dudley A. White, Publisher
The Sandusky Register
Sandusky, Ohio

Miss Eileen Green
Carnegie Public Library
Sault Ste. Marie, Mich.

Mrs. Helen Irwin
International Bridge Authority, State of Michigan
Sault Ste. Marie, Mich.

Miss Katherine Wales
University of Toronto Library
Toronto, Ont.

Mr. Lee H. Gregory
Joseph Mann Library
Two Rivers, Wis.

Ruth W. Gregory
Waukegan Public Library
Waukegan, Ill.

Mr. John A. Tyler
Conneaut, Ohio

Robert J. Kelly
Henry J. Sullivan
Messrs D. Collins, C. W. Dreier, and J. G. Mudie
Detroit Edison Company
Detroit, Mich.

The Great Lakes Commission

Mr. Herman D. Ellis
Mr. J. J. Bell
Mackinac Bridge Authority

Mr. George N. Scroggie, Department Engineer
Harbours and Rivers, Engineering Branch
Department of Public Works, London, Ont.

Mr. Edward Schmid
Reserve Mining Company
Silver Bay, Minn.

Mr. R. L. Guthman
Cleveland-Cliffs Iron Company
Cleveland, Ohio

F. Clever Bald, Director
Michigan Historical Collections
University of Michigan
Ann Arbor, Mich.

Miss Virginia Tibbals
Mrs. Helen R. McIntyre
University of Michigan Transportation Library
Ann Arbor, Mich.

Mr. Howard H. Peckham, Director
Mr. William S. Ewing, Manuscript Librarian
The Clements Library
University of Michigan
Ann Arbor, Mich.

We are also indebted to the Oglebay, Norton Company for the use of the map "100 Years in the Region of the Great Lakes" for the cover of our book, and to Sherwin Williams for permission to reproduce on the inside covers the smokestack insignia of the lake carriers.